Milton and the Natural World overturns prevailing critical assumptions by offering a fresh view of *Paradise Lost*, in which the representation of Eden's plants and animals is shown to be fully cognizant of the century's new, scientific natural history. The fabulous lore of the old science is wittily debunked, and the poem embraces new imaginative and symbolic possibilities for depicting the natural world, suggested by the speculations of Milton's scientific contemporaries including Robert Boyle, Thomas Browne, and John Evelyn. Karen Edwards argues that Milton has represented the natural world in *Paradise Lost*, with its flowers and trees, insects and beasts, as a text alive with meaning and worthy of experimental reading.

Karen L. Edwards is Lecturer in the School of English at the University of Exeter, and has previously taught at Kenyon College in the USA.

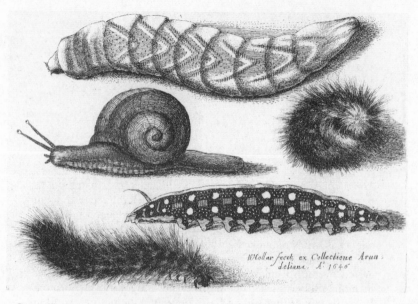

Caterpillars and snail, by Wenceslaus Hollar, from *Muscarum scarabeorum* (Antwerp, 1646), a series of eleven etchings drawn from insects in the curiosity cabinet of Thomas Howard, Earl of Arundel.

MILTON AND THE NATURAL WORLD

Science and Poetry in *Paradise Lost*

KAREN L. EDWARDS

CAMBRIDGE
UNIVERSITY PRESS

#4067SO10

PUBLISHED BY THE PRESS SYNDICATE OF THE UNIVERSITY OF CAMBRIDGE
The Pitt Building, Trumpington Street, Cambridge, United Kingdom

CAMBRIDGE UNIVERSITY PRESS
The Edinburgh Building, Cambridge CB2 2RU, UK http://www.cup.cam.ac.uk
40 West 20th Street, New York, NY 10011-4211, USA http://www.cup.org
10 Stamford Road, Oakleigh, Melbourne 3166, Australia

© Karen L. Edwards 1999

First published 1999

Printed in the United Kingdom at the University Press, Cambridge

Typeset in Monotype Baskerville 11/12½ pt. [SE]

A catalogue record for this book is available from the British Library

Library of Congress cataloguing in publication data

Edwards, Karen L.
    Milton and the Natural World: Science and Poetry in *Paradise Lost* / Karen L.
Edwards.
        p.   cm.
    Includes bibliographical references and index.
    ISBN 0 521 64359 7 (hb)
        1. Milton, John, 1608–1674.   Paradise Lost.   2. Literature and
science – England – History – 17th century.   3. Milton, John,
1608–1674 – Knowledge – Natural History.   4. Milton, John, 1608–1674 –
Knowledge – Science.   5. Science in literature.   6. Nature in
literature.   I. Title.
    PR3562.E39 1999
    821'.4–dc21   99-11230 CIP

ISBN 0 521 64359 7 hardback

For Santina Siena

Contents

Illustrations

ix

Acknowledgments

I have learned that writing a book creates and is sustained by community. The community that has made it possible for me to write this book stretches between two continents and across a lifetime. Without Denis Pereira Gray, Bettine Fitzgerald Costa, and Cloriene S. Barrett (who contradicted me at a crucial moment), I wouldn't have begun to begin the writing.

My former colleagues at Kenyon College, especially Don and Sally Rogan, Royal Rhodes, Linda Metzler, and Terry Schupbach, have taught me that community nourishes body as well as spirit. Generations of my students at Kenyon College and the University of Exeter, especially those intrepid Kenyon–Exeter Program students who traveled between the two, have shown me that community doesn't ever stop growing.

My heartfelt thanks to Anthony Fothergill, Michael Wood, and Gordon Campbell for generously reading and commenting on early drafts of this book, and for encouraging me to continue the project. Thanks, too, to members of the British Milton Seminar, who listened to work-in-progress and shared the wealth of their expertise with me. My colleagues at the University of Exeter have contributed in richly individual ways to this undertaking. I am especially grateful to Mark Davie, Diane Davies, Charles Page, and Robert Lawson-Peebles. The Research Committee of the University funded travel for research and conferences related to this book, as did the School of English.

I owe many thanks to the librarians and staff of the British Library, the Rockerfeller, Sciences, and John Hay Libraries of Brown University, and the libraries of Exeter University. A National Endowment for the Humanities Fellowship made it possible for me to do research at the John Carter Brown Library in Providence, Rhode Island, an experience both highly productive and highly pleasurable, thanks to Norman Fiering and his staff. An Audrey Lumsden-Kouvel Fellowship in Renaissance Studies supported three months at the Newberry Library in Chicago, where I had the good fortune to meet and work with Julie Mulroy; my thanks to Fred Hoxie and to a fine reference staff headed by Hjordis Halvorson. I owe special thanks to Andrew Baster and the Wills Library of Guy's Hospital. Josie Dixon at Cambridge University Press has been a most patient and supportive editor, and my book has benefited from the comments of two anonymous readers at the Press.

It may be that the demands made upon community are most strenuous as a project enters the last stage, or perhaps it is just that community shows its strength when the need is greatest. It is with love and pleasure that I acknowledge the community that has sustained me in this last year: Adele Davidson, Brian Edgar, David and Carol Edwards, George and Winnie Edwards, Avril Henry, Nancy Leopold, Peter and Inna New and Lia Matyushina, Brigid Pailthorpe, Edwyna Prior and David Beaumont, Esther Rashkin, and Jo Whitmore. My deepest gratitude to them – and, finally, to Santina Siena, who magnificently expresses community in ways practical and spiritual, with unfailing generosity, intelligence, and humor, and who has done so for as long as I have known her.

Abbreviations

BJHS	*British Journal for the History of Science*
CPW	*Complete Prose Works*
ELH	*English Literary History*
JEGP	*Journal of English and Germanic Philology*
JHI	*Journal of the History of Ideas*
MLN	*Modern Language Notes*
MP	*Modern Philology*
NQ	*Notes and Queries*
OED	*Oxford English Dictionary*
PE	*Pseudodoxia Epidemica*
PL	*Paradise Lost*
PMLA	*Publications of the Modern Language Association*
PP	*Past and Present*
RES	*Review of English Studies*
SA	*Samson Agonistes*
UTQ	*University of Toronto Quarterly*

Introduction

John Milton gives his Adam and Eve what he no longer had when he created them – sight. Unlike their author, Adam and Eve *can* read the "book of knowledge fair"; for them, "wisdom at one entrance" is *not* "shut out." For him, the pain of the loss perhaps never fully abated. The near-sonnet embedded in the invocation to light in book III of *Paradise Lost* does not permit the easy consolation that sight is well lost for insight.

> Thus with the year
> Seasons return, but not to me returns
> Day, or the sweet approach of even or morn,
> Or sight of vernal bloom, or summer's rose,
> Or flocks, or herds, or human face divine;
> But cloud in stead, and ever-during dark
> Surrounds me, from the cheerful ways of men
> Cut off, and for the book of knowledge fair
> Presented with a universal blank
> Of nature's works to me expunged and razed,
> And wisdom at one entrance quite shut out.
> So much the rather thou celestial Light
> Shine inward, and the mind through all her powers
> Irradiate, there plant eyes, all mist from thence
> Purge and disperse, that I may see and tell
> Of things invisible to mortal sight.   (*PL*, III.40–55)[1]

The passage turns, as the poem turns, upon God's ability to bring light out of darkness. But the anguish of having to endure the interval of darkness is given full expression; the turn to consolation is almost unbearably delayed until line 51, and the full stop after "shut out" which precedes it is grim in its finality. In this passage as elsewhere in Milton's works, grief for the loss of sight is unmistakable. If the grief were not profound, the consolation would be superficial. *Expunged* and *razed* are violent words; faith that wisdom will find another entrance coexists with the grievous pain of having lost *this* entrance.

But Adam and Eve, blessed in the "open sight / Of day-spring," sing their morning hymn as the sun's light declares (makes both bright and knowable) the landscape of Eden (*PL*, v.138–39). They articulate what the created world declares, God's "goodness beyond thought, and power divine" (*PL*, v.159). As Milton represents it in *Paradise Lost*, the newly created world is indeed a book to be read for pleasure and instruction. The book is fair, but it is also demanding, its sense sometimes plain but more often obscure. It could not be otherwise and be of its historical moment. Knowing how to know and represent the natural world was a highly complex undertaking in the middle decades of the seventeenth century. In terms of scientific knowledge, the world was turning upside down; the old philosophy was beginning to give way to the new, though raggedly and reluctantly. The central argument of this book is that in its representation of the creatures of the natural world, *Paradise Lost* precisely registers the complex historical moment of its making. By the time Milton began to write his epic, the stock of plant and animal lore derived from classical and biblical antiquity, the Middle Ages, and the earlier Renaissance (lore that was familiar, densely elaborated, and symbolically rich) had begun to be measured against the experiential knowledge that his contemporaries were rapidly gaining and which more often than not confuted the old lore. Yet the critical literature has been largely silent about the ways in which Milton's representation of a concretely imagined garden of Eden might have been affected by the experiences and experiments of the new philosophers. That is the question my book explores. *How* to read the book of knowledge had become the subject for passionate debate in Milton's day; I will argue that it is a debate which *Paradise Lost* fully and knowledgeably joins.

When fit readers open the book of the world that Milton has represented in the poem, they find a text in which the discourses of the old and new philosophies mingle and cohabit. Michel Foucault designates the waning of the old and the waxing of the new as a shift of episteme. His *The Order of Things* is perhaps the most suggestive and the most problematic of the many attempts to describe the change from a pre-scientific to a scientific mentality in the seventeenth century.[2] Foucault's approach is avowedly synchronic: he sets the two epistemes next to each other, as it were, and how they manage at their historical intersection does not interest him. His concern is with discontinuity (a reaction, Roger Chartier argues, against those who would produce a universalizing philosophy of history), and so he exaggerates rupture. *Paradise Lost* is located just at that juncture of epistemes which Foucault's "archaeological" approach disregards. More useful than rupture and discontinuity for understanding the poem is what Pierre Bourdieu calls "lag" and Chartier explains as the "time to understand."[3] They are referring to the time taken by a population to recognize and respond to a changed material condition, but the term may usefully be applied to the time taken by a population to recognize and respond to a changed epistemological condition. Lag points to that period when old and new ways of knowing promiscuously mingle. It furnishes a corrective to overdependence on a notion often attributed to Foucault: the notion of "competing" discourses, oppositional discourses whose collision produces fissures in the text. Locating discursive oppositions and fissures is a valuable antidote to construing a text as smoothly homogeneous, but an exclusive interest in rupture allows the poet's strategies for assimilating, reconciling, and re-ordering heterogeneous material to escape attention. Those strategies in *Paradise Lost* are remarkably sophisticated and fully developed, as we will see in parts two and three. This may be because Renaissance poetics possessed a powerful model for reconciling heterogeneity in its fusing of classical and biblical material – though the extent to which such material was *perceived* as being heterogeneous is itself open to question. The merging of classical and Christian elements was not, in any case, a merger of equals; Christianity was the controlling discourse, and classical material was molded to fit the shape of the biblical material. So, too, there is a controlling discourse in Milton's fusing of the old and new philosophies, and it is the *latter*, I will argue. Milton is on *this* side of modernity.

My project is thus in vigorous disagreement with the method and conclusions of Kester Svendsen's *Milton and Science*, which established the critical tradition relegating Milton to scientific backwardness:[4]

it is the old science, rather than the new, which bulks large in Milton, despite his spectacular allusions to Galileo and his interest in some elements of the new cosmology. Donne made much of the "new philosophy" but Milton very little. Most of his science is traditional and conventional, a literary as well as scientific commonplace.[5]

If the Yale edition of Milton's prose and the biography by William Parker may be taken as signs, Svendsen's has become the orthodox view. In his introduction to the first volume of the *Complete Prose Works*, Don Wolfe asserts that Milton was "essentially unaware of the endless potentialities of the scientific method."[6] William Parker, summing up the significance of Milton's life and work, states that "he exhibited but slight awareness of the world-shaking scientific discoveries of his time."[7] It is an astonishing claim, that Milton was innocent of the knowledge of a fundamental feature of his historical time and place. Yet Svendsen's view has prevailed for forty years.

Two main points need to be made about Svendsen's conclusions. Even lag cannot explain how a man writing in 1650 could hold purely Elizabethan attitudes toward the natural world. Such an assertion requires a theory of historical anachronism to justify itself. Second, by assuming that Milton's allusions to the lore of the old philosophy indicate a bland endorsement of it, Svendsen promulgates a thin reading of *Paradise Lost*. So, he reasons, because fallen angels are turned into amphisbaenas in book x of *Paradise Lost*, Milton must therefore believe in the existence of two-headed snakes. But science does not lie on the surface of *Paradise Lost* in the form of facts (or myths); it must be sought in a close reading of the poem.[8] My book argues, contrary to Svendsen, that Milton's depiction of Edenic plants and animals is cognizant of the century's new experience of the natural world, experience which derived from Europeans' travel in Asia, Africa, and the Americas, from the observations of natural historians, from the accessibility of creatures alive or dried, and from the circulation of illustrated books. This experience subtly shapes the poem's representations and directs the way they function in the poetry. Yes, there *are* amphisbaenas in Milton's poem, but (as we will see in chapter 4) they are signs of the *mis*construing of the created world. In Svendsen's essentially ahistorical treatment of it, the poem becomes a monument to scientific backwardness.

Several recent studies have begun to contest Svendsen's claims, studies placing Milton in the context of contemporary philosophical debates. Stephen Fallon has looked at Milton's conception of the nature of matter in *Milton among the Philosophers*.[9] He concludes that Milton's monistic version of animist materialism is "a response to an urgent philosophical debate" being waged, on the one hand, by mechanistic contemporaries such as Hobbes and Descartes, and on the other, by the Cambridge Platonists.[10] In *The Matter of Revolution*, John Rogers argues that the philosophy of monistic vitalism emerging at the mid-century, with its emphasis upon "agency" and "organization," supported the development of social and political liberalism in writers such as Milton, Marvell, and Cavendish.[11] Harinder Marjara's *Contemplation of Created Things: Science in "Paradise Lost,"* which answers Svendsen by way of Thomas Kuhn, construes the scientific perspective of the poem as being inconsistently rather than consistently old-fashioned.[12] Milton, argues

Marjara, chooses in a given instance what is most useful from among the many paradigms for understanding the natural world that were available to him in the middle of the century. Fallon, Rogers, and Marjara provide a welcome opposition to Svendsen's picture of a scientifically outmoded Milton. They are concerned with Milton's natural *philosophy*, however, and the study of plants and animals in the seventeenth century belongs to natural *history*.

The distinction has its roots in classical antiquity and corresponds roughly to the difference in approach between Aristotle and Pliny. "The Plinian ideal of natural history," remarks Phillip Sloan,

intended it to be a collection of reports on all topics, particularly those of detail about natural objects . . . Natural history, conceived in these terms, has less the character of organised scientific inquiry than that of an empirical data base for such inquiry. The theory and method of science, pursued primarily in antiquity by Aristotle and Galen, which sought a causal understanding through philosophical principles, was not properly a concern of the early natural histories.[13]

The natural histories of the late Renaissance took as their model Pliny's expansive, practical, summarizing mode. Precisely because they developed initially as natural history rather than as natural philosophy – as encyclopedic collections of heterogeneous "facts" rather than as the systematic study of causality – botany and zoology took their modern forms relatively late.[14] Fallon, Rogers, and Marjara are not concerned with the new natural history of the period and its impact on Milton's depiction of paradise. Fallon's interest in the contemporary context of Milton's ontology leads him to concentrate not on the representation of Edenic materiality but on the "philosophical" War in Heaven. Marjara is chiefly concerned with Milton's imagining of a universal system, which entails a concentration on cosmology. Neither Fallon nor Marjara analyzes the specific *poetic* effects which embody Milton's science. Rogers does so, though he is interested not in Adam and Eve's paradisal environment, but rather in the poem's rendering of images of social and political organization.

When we take seriously the proposition that the natural world in *Paradise Lost* has been represented as a book of knowledge, then we will regard its depictions of insects and cedar trees, roses and leviathans, as worthy of close study and alive with meaning. These are *not* the meanings that the old emblematic tradition offers; they cannot be epitomized; they are not exhausted with one reading, or even several. In the middle decades of the seventeenth century, the astounding complexity of living organisms was becoming ever more apparent to experimental

philosophers. Milton has so written the book of the world that its creatures, too, ask for and respond to continual re-reading and re-thinking.
They disclose new beauty and new intricacy each time they are revisited.
As Milton represents it in *Paradise Lost*, God's "other book" offers, as the
poet believed the Bible did, a source of never-ending pleasure for the
reader who meditates on it day and night. That the mysterious heavens
should offer such interpretive pleasure is not surprising; that lemon balm
or crocodiles might do so *is* surprising. There is, indeed, a longstanding
critical fascination with the astronomy of *Paradise Lost*. An earlier generation of critics declared it to be advanced (the only part of Milton's
science to be so praised).[15] There was perhaps a kind of analogy oper-
ating between the lofty status of astronomy among the sciences and the
high cultural status of Milton among English poets. As Carlo Ginzburg
has observed, traditional beliefs about the heavens were sustained by
symbolic, theological, and political assumptions about the "high" and
the forbidden.[16] Milton's avowed poetic aim, "[t]hat with no middle
flight intends to soar / Above the *Aonian* mount" (*PL*, 1.14–15), and his
position in English literature make very attractive the wish to claim him
for the new astronomy. The crown of revolutionary heroism, moreover,
belongs to those who defy the forbidders; pairing Milton and Galileo
compliments both. It may be time now to redress the imbalance in favor
of the "high" – as the seventeenth century itself was doing. The telescope was revealing new worlds to the eye, but so was the microscope.
The microscope not only validated anew the worth of the humblest
creeping thing; more generally, it reinforced the value of observing the
ordinary flora and fauna with which humanity shares the earth.

   Criticism has assigned a negligible role to seeing the physical world in
Milton's representation of Eden.[17] It has assigned only slightly more
significance to seeing images of the physical world. It is possible that
critics have unconsciously attributed proleptic effects to Milton's blindness; surely few would agree with T. S. Eliot's assumption of its symbolic
or aesthetic appropriateness. ("Milton may be said never to have seen
anything."[18]) It is more likely, as Christopher Hill has argued, that
Milton's status as artist and scholar has led critics "to look exclusively to
literary sources for his ideas."[19] Due in large part to Hill's influence, this
critical situation has now changed; scholarship has become increasingly
interested in the turbulent political and religious debates carried on by
radical groups in Milton's day. But interest in the visual as another opposition to the literary has still not received much attention. R. M. Frye's
Milton's Imagery and the Visual Arts was until recently the major exception

to this rule.[20] His approach, however, remains firmly within the tradition of scholarly high culture that Hill criticizes: Frye compares the allusions in *Paradise Lost* to "an extensive vocabulary of visual imagery relating to sacred subjects" developed over centuries.[21] Diane McColley's *A Gust for Paradise: Milton's Eden and the Visual Arts* serves as a corrective to what she describes as Frye's failure to treat the Fall "as a violation of a good creation whose repair is part of the process of regeneration."[22] Accordingly, McColley's study investigates the relationship between Milton and those other artists who have depicted "an energetic 'state of innocence'" and elaborated the "topos of original righteousness."[23] By thus defining their approach as the investigation of sacred or high art and its relationship to Milton, both Frye and McColley exclude from consideration what is arguably the most important feature of representing the natural world in Milton's day: its *separation* from a tradition of representing sacred subjects.

We must not underestimate the hunger of the seventeenth century *to know what things looked like*. Some of the representations and descriptions circulating in Milton's day, like those in Robert Hooke's *Micrographia*, were what we would now call "scientific."[24] Others were not, like those which Thomas Browne considers in book v of *Pseudodoxia Epidemica*, "*Of many things questionable as they are commonly described in Pictures*."[25] A distinction between the "scientific" and the "popular" is one that the seventeenth century did not yet make, although Browne regards traditional renditions of the creatures with some amusement and the occasional flash of exasperation. But he and his contemporaries regard with unalloyed excitement the wonders being discovered by macro- and microscopical observers. The illustrations in *Micrographia* demonstrated to seventeenth-century readers an astounding beauty in even the humble mite (fig. 1). Moreover, it was beauty fresh and unexpected, beauty never seen before on earth. Viewers of the book's engravings were able to share in the sense of astonishment and exhilaration that Hooke expresses in his preface:

By the means of Telescopes, *there is nothing so* far distant *but may be represented to our view; and by the help of* Microscopes, *there is nothing so* small, *as to escape our inquiry; hence there is a new visible World discovered to the understanding. By this means the Heavens are open'd, and a vast number of new Stars, and new Motions, and new Productions appear in them, to which all the antient Astronomers were utterly Strangers. By this the Earth it self, which lyes so neer us, under our feet, shews quite a new thing to us, and in every* little *particle of its matter, we now behold almost as great a variety of Creatures, as we were able before to reckon up in the whole* Universe *it self*.[26]*

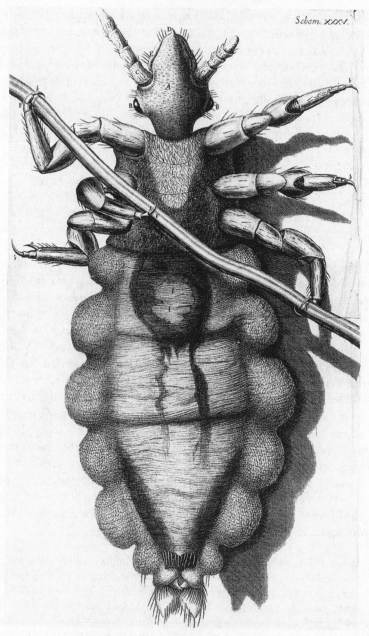

1 Mite, from *Micrographia* (1665) by Robert Hooke; "*by the help of* Microscopes . . . *a new visible World discovered to the understanding.*"

At the conclusion of the preface, Hooke affects modesty in presenting his "little Objects" to the world:

hoping also, that I should thereby discover something New to the World, I have at length cast in my Mite, into the vast Treasury of A Philosophical History. *And it is my* hope, *as well as* belief, *that these my* Labours *will be no more comparable to the* Productions *of many other* Natural Philosophers, *who are now every where busie about* greater *things; then my* little Objects *are to be compar'd to the greater and more beautiful* Works of Nature, *A Flea, a Mite, a Gnat, to an Horse, an Elephant, or a Lyon.*[27]

But the pun on "mite" with its allusion to the biblical story of the widow's offering (Mark 12.42–44) indicates that Hooke knows very well the surpassing value of what he offers to his readers. *Micrographia* is a feast for the sense of sight and a celebration of its power. Hooke expresses the hope in his preface that "*there may be found many* Mechanical Inventions *to improve our other Senses, of* hearing, smelling, tasting, touching," but the need for hope suggests how far sight was already outstripping the other senses as the surest way to discover the world.[28] Milton did not need to have looked through the lenses of a microscope to be aware of the age's intense desire to see and know, and to feel again the anguish of being presented with a universal blank.

It is entirely characteristic of the mid-seventeenth century that Hooke should assert the value of his undertaking by linking his new observations of creatures to the Bible by way of a play on words. Excitement at the prospect of a natural world infinitely richer and more complex than had before been imagined, abiding engagement with modes of reading the sacred text, and delight in the way words play with each other – these features are constantly in evidence when we consider not only Milton's treatment of the natural world but that of his experimentalist contemporaries. My project allies itself with those studies which embrace the implications of what has always been maintained about the early modern period: that it is artificial and misleading to separate poetry from other disciplines. Exploring the implications of this intellectual seamlessness for Milton's poetry means looking at *Paradise Lost* in its relationship to seventeenth-century natural history and the work of such contemporaries as Thomas Browne, Robert Boyle, John Evelyn, and Robert Hooke. My book offers a counter version to the critical tradition that compares Milton's "encyclopedic" epic solely to literary and theological encyclopedias (i.e., hexameral poems and patristic and Renaissance commentaries on Genesis). New *kinds* of encyclopedias were reflecting the new interests of the experimental philosophers – among them, illustrated natural histories, herbals, atlases, curiosity cabinets and their catalogs, botanical gardens, and menageries. I will argue that *Paradise Lost*, while not ignoring the learning of the traditional encyclopedias, nonetheless fully acknowledges the new encyclopedias in its depiction of plants and animals. Milton would have considered it the duty of a writer of epic to embrace *all* the learning of his day, even if some of it was in the process of being discredited and some of it was still highly speculative.

The old emblematic natural history is indeed present in *Paradise Lost*; Svendsen is not mistaken to point to it. But it is not given the poem's representational endorsement. The old science is invariably invoked for the less interesting, and less demanding, interpretive option. Its presence in the poem is often marked by sly humor, its inclusion carried out in such a way as to incorporate an acknowledgment of its unreliability. At the same time, the poem consistently makes available new representational possibilities suggested by the experimental philosophy, and it does so with excitement, wit, and creative relish. What I see as the mark of experimentalism upon the poem's depiction of a creature is this: the necessity for a reader's imaginative engagement in the process of making meaning. This is, in part, because experimentalism in the mid-seventeenth century tends to open areas of uncertainty rather than to establish certainties; more precisely, it opens up areas of *scientific* uncertainty which are *poetically* liberating. Again and again in the poem, Milton's representation of creatures allows a reader to find meaning in that space between old certainties partially eroded and new uncertainties beginning to emerge. When Adam and Eve – and the fit reader – turn to the book of the world that Milton has represented in *Paradise Lost*, they find a text of glorious and meaningful "verses" which can be formed into a pattern, and then recombined to form another. To think in terms of a kaleidoscope rather than of two sharply delimited paradigms helps one avoid the danger of construing a Milton untouched by the constraints of his historical moment, whether manifested in a free choice between paradigms or in complete ignorance of one of them.

To find "science" in *Paradise Lost*, it is necessary to look very closely at the way the poetry works. Such a thing as a survey of the poem's entire natural history is therefore not possible, and I have chosen a number of crucial representations to focus on in part one, which deals with animals, and part two, which deals with plants. Before we turn to specific representations, however, we need to think in more detail about how fit readers of the seventeenth century set about reading the book of the

world. Chapter 2 looks at the methods of some of Milton's experimentalist contemporaries. Chapter 3 considers what Milton understood by
reading the world – and explores what "the world" may have meant as
far as animals and plants are concerned in the seventeenth century.
Chapters 2 and 3, then, are about how to read the book of the world.
Chapter 1 is about how *not* to read it.

PART I

Re-reading the book of the world

Corrupting experience: Satan and Eve

> Experience, next to thee I owe,
> Best guide; not following thee, I had remained
> In ignorance, thou open'st wisdom's way,
> And giv'st access, though secret she retire.
>
> (*PL*, ix.807–10)

That Eve praises experience almost immediately after she eats the forbidden fruit has suggested to many readers that Milton intended to criticize experience as a route to wisdom. Stanley Fish argues that the form of Satan's temptation is to invite Eve to "taste of his experience."[1] She accepts and subsequently makes the same offer to Adam: "On my experience, Adam, freely taste" (*PL*, ix.988). Fish comments: "The value Eve finds in experience (things seen) is the value she assigns to it, and that will be whatever she wants it to be. Experience is only a word for what happens to reality when it is filtered through the medium of time and space – Man's medium not God's."[2] Georgia Christopher reads the whole of Eve's temptation scene as "a contest between the words of God and almost everything that goes under the rubric of 'experience.'"[3] For Linda Gregerson, more recently, "'experience' is by this point in Milton's poem another name for the devil"; it is an "idol [Eve] erects as an instrument for and testament to self-creation."[4]

Yet even these round condemnations are tempered by an awareness that Eve has been persuaded to accept from Satan a debased and straitened version of experience, and this is what she praises. Georgia Christopher explains that Eve ought to have discounted her "new experience" (being flattered by a beautiful serpent) in the face of her "previous experience with God's word."[5] Indeed, the premise of Christopher's book is that experience is the proving ground for Milton's Reformed hermeneutics: "faith becomes a 'poetic' activity – a passionate reading of a divine text . . . followed by a reading of experience through this text."[6] Linda Gregerson's thesis, that "*The Faerie Queene* and *Paradise Lost* are devices for the formation, and reformation, of subjects," is also dependent upon a notion of experience as leading to growth in understanding.[7] The subjects to be reformed are readers in and readers of the poem. It is the experience of reading, Gregerson maintains, that effects their reformation.

Experience is in fact a concept indispensable to most critical studies of Milton's work. Historical and biographical studies assume that Milton's intellectual, political, and spiritual development occurs in response to his lived experience. Thematic and reader-response approaches assume that the experience of reading his poems instructs and enlightens the reader. Generic and formalistic studies assume that Milton becomes more experienced and hence more skillful in his handling and adaptation of poetic and rhetorical modes.[8] Virtually any study of Milton's work, that is, which considers the manifestation of change over time (whether articulated as growth, development, rupture, revision, or response, on the part of author, character, or reader) assumes that experiencing leads to knowing. Yet scholars have dismissed Eve's praise of experience at the Tree of Knowledge as necessarily culpable. It may be that this contradictory critical stance results from post-Victorian discomfort with the term itself, tainted with suggestions of illicit sexuality when used of a woman. It is more likely that critics who condemn Eve's reliance upon experience have simply assumed that the term denotes that which is limited, ephemeral, and hence trivial, when Eve clearly ought to be concerned with that which is infinite, eternal, and essential. Such an implicit condemnation is unwarranted: historically, experience has played a complex and powerful role in theories about the gaining of knowledge. It is true that Eve is misguided in praising her experience at the Tree of Knowledge, but it is not true that praising experience is always, necessarily, misguided.

We need to begin with a basic question: what is it that Satan persuades Eve to call "experience"? The question has historical implications. At a moment in the seventeenth century when the very concept of "the natural" was being turned upside down, Milton represents Eve's experience as being fully involved in the natural world. She plucks fruit from a tree and consumes it, at the behest of a serpent, in a paradisal garden. In the context of this depiction of the natural world, the term *experience* unmistakably gestures toward the new, or experimental, philosophy. This philosophy, notes Robert Boyle in an observation which is repeated *ad infinitum* in his own and his contemporaries' writings, "is built upon two foundations, reason and experience."[9]

Experience in its modern guise, experiment, has become virtually synonymous with the scientific revolution. Eve's postlapsarian paean to "experience," in short, is not *historically* innocent.

> Experience, next to thee I owe,
> Best guide; not following thee, I had remained
> In ignorance, thou open'st wisdom's way,
> And giv'st access, though secret she retire.   (*PL*, ix.807–10)

If the experience Eve praises were identical to the experience endorsed by the new philosophers, then Kester Svendsen would be right about Milton's scientific backwardness. Implicating the new experimental methodology in the fall of humankind would certainly be a clear mark of Miltonic disapproval. But Eve's experience is *not* that sort of experience.

Stanley Fish is one of a very few critics to connect Eve's experience at the Tree with the "experience" of the new philosophy. He makes the connection with characteristic élan but fails to develop its rich implications. As Christopher and Gregerson do, Fish holds that the experience of reading *Paradise Lost* is intended to reform the reader. He, too, acknowledges that the experience which Eve accepts from Satan is a diminished thing. However, unlike Christopher and Gregerson, Fish is willing to name the experience Satan offers: it is, he says, "empirical science."[10] He thus paraphrases Satan's proposition: "Do not believe what science does not affirm."[11]

> O sacred, wise, and wisdom-giving plant,
> Mother of science, now I feel thy power
> Within me clear, not only to discern
> Things in their causes, but to trace the ways
> Of highest agents, deemed however wise.
> Queen of this universe, do not believe
> Those rigid threats of death; ye shall not die:
> (*PL*, ix.679–85)

"The true objection to Satan's method," declares Fish, "is the presumption, which the word 'science' is meant to conceal, of assuming that God cannot work effects contrary to those his creatures are able to discern in nature."[12] But the true objection to Satan's method is its fraudulence. Satan is guilty of falsifying experimental data, for he has not of course eaten any fruit. When, in effect, he invites Eve to "make experiment" of the fruit, his experiment is not the sort advocated by the new philosophers.[13] There is a cunning resemblance, but it is only a resemblance.

The anachronistic term *empirical science* blunts Fish's analysis of Satan's method. The term posits as a finished product something that was still coming into existence in the mid-seventeenth century. By using the twentieth-century term, Fish effaces the history inscribed in Milton's representation, the history of the evolving of the discourse of the new philosophy. When he asserts that Eve should have realized that God is not limited to doing things according to *her* experience of the law of nature, Fish implies that she ought to set aside what she has learned of the regularity and order of the natural world. Yet holding fast to her own reading of nature's ordered ways would have enabled Eve to see the talking snake, with his tale of a sudden, fruit-induced transformation, for the monstrosity it is. By representing Satan as lying about the fruit, which amounts to obscuring the true nature of the created world, Milton shows that Satan has abused the potential of the new experimental philosophy for instilling wisdom – *not that it has no such potential*. *Paradise Lost* shows that the new philosophy is as liable to abuse as theology or history. It *also* shows the new philosophy to be as capable as they are of providing a clearer understanding of God's providential design. How the poem does so – how it demonstrates the ways in which the "book of knowledge fair" can open an entrance to wisdom – is the subject of the following chapters. First, however, it is necessary to look in more detail at Satan's perverting of that possibility.

To apprehend the enormity and cleverness of his perverting requires us to untangle the complicated semantic knot formed by *experience* and *experiment* in the middle of the seventeenth century. Not only are the two terms inscribed in confusingly intertwined discursive fields; the concepts they signify are in dramatic flux. Let us begin the untangling by looking at what might be thought of as the two ends of the string: the role of experience in the old deductive logic of the Aristotelian scholastics, and its role in the new inductive logic of the Baconian philosophers. Peter Dear observes that for the scholastics, "experience designated a universal statement of fact, supposedly constructed from the memory of many singular instances, and its universality expressed its intended status as an evident truth which might form a premise in a scientific demonstration."[14] A singular experience, in other words, had to be converted into a universal truth before it could be used in deductive logic. The conversion was accomplished by means of a prior induction, as Dear implies: a singular experience was observed always to fulfill certain conditions and hence could be said to represent a universal truth. Thus universalized, experience could serve as a premise in deductive argument. The

Baconian new philosophers, however, dispensed with the last step, declaring that inductive logic by itself was a sufficient basis for suggesting the truth. They claimed, Dear states, the legitimacy of experiential matter "in historical reports of events, often citing witnesses. The singular experience could not be *evident*, but it could provide *evidence*."[15] Deductive arguments can be deceptive, the Baconians held; it is better to rely solely upon matters of fact.

In his tempting of Eve, Satan offers what looks like an inductive argument. He adduces experience (eating the fruit) as evidence for a general conclusion ("whoso eats thereof, forthwith attains / Wisdom"), specifically citing the presence of witnesses: "round the tree / All other beasts that saw, with like desire / Longing and envying stood" (*PL*, IX.591–93). Induction, however, does not draw principles from a single experience – witnessed here, in any case, only by inarticulate beasts, unable to say what they have seen. In a rhetorical ploy of great cleverness, the speechlessness that ought to invalidate their witness serves instead to bolster Satan's claim about the efficacy of the fruit: "I was at first as other beasts" (*PL*, IX.571), he says, and in the *act* of so saying, he demonstrates his difference. But of course his difference from other beasts has nothing to do with the power of the fruit, and the experience he reports never took place. It is, simply, a lie, a piece of deception designed to push Eve into superstitious apprehension of what the fruit can do.

The word *occult* is nowhere mentioned but everywhere implied at Eve's temptation. Indeed, its manifold senses underlie Satan's representation of the experience at the Tree. Historians of science have long noted that the scent of the occult clung to notions of experience until at least the late sixteenth century. This is a legacy, Charles Schmitt explains, from the medieval opposition between magic and its association with the contingent (available only through experience), and those disciplines "considered to be determined by a structured and logical order, knowable through reason."[16] Schmitt points to the Renaissance magus Cornelius Agrippa of Nettesheim, who constantly cites "experience" to confirm his authority.[17] We will see that the figure of the magus is doubly relevant to Satan's temptation strategy. It is, however, the politics of possessing occult knowledge which is the most immediately apparent thrust of the strategy.

When he invites Eve to taste of the fruit, Satan invites her to join a group, "the gods," whose control is based on the shared possession of occult or privy knowledge.[18] In the serpent's promise, knowing and belonging coalesce: "ye shall be as gods, / Knowing both good and evil as they know" (*PL*, ix.708–09). Eve assumes, as Satan intends her to assume, that to become one of this elite she need only eat the fruit, as if eating it were a kind of initiation. Indeed it is, though not of course in the way Satan implies. He ends his temptation by inviting her to taste, proleptically conferring upon her the title that depends on the tasting: "Goddess humane, reach then, and freely taste" (*PL*, ix.732). Having eaten, Eve imitates the behavior of the serpent, initiated before her. He addresses her as "sovereign mistress" (*PL*, ix.532) and licks the ground she treads on; she in turn calls the Tree "sovereign" (*PL*, ix.795) and makes "low reverence" (*PL*, ix.835) to it.

More precisely, she makes "low reverence"

> as to the *power*
> That dwelt within, whose presence had infused
> Into the plant sciential sap, derived
> From nectar, drink of gods.
>
> (*PL*, ix.835–38; emphasis added)

Eve does not try to understand how "the power" works. The occult or hidden nature of its efficacy causes her no alarm and raises no questions; she is content simply to perceive its effect (as she thinks), its "operation blest / To sapience" (*PL*, ix.796–97).[19] Earlier the serpent had claimed that the fruit's power enabled him "to discern / Things in their causes" (*PL*, ix.681–82), that is, to discern the true connection between cause and effect. The power of the fruit is not sufficient, it appears, to disclose the cause of its *own* effect. But of course mystification is Satan's aim. When the serpent declares that the alteration within him is "Strange" (*PL*, ix.599), Milton uses the pre-eminent seventeenth-century term for signaling something alien to be marveled at.[20] Do not try to understand how and why the fruit produces its effect, *strange* implies; there is a wonderful power in the fruit, and access to it is by way of ingestion, not intellection. In the word *taste*, reiterated throughout the temptation scene, the notion of testing or trying merges with the notion of eating.[21] The implication is clear: Eve can find out the virtue of the fruit only by making experiment of it, that is, by experience.

Turning to the complex semantic histories of *experiment* and *experience*, we can discern two strands of meaning in the seventeenth-century usage of each word. One strand involves an informal, pragmatically observational mode ("let's try it and see what happens");[22] the other, a more formal observational mode involving, at its most extreme, artificially constructed testing whose purpose is to discover something unknown.[23] By the eighteenth century, the first strand of meaning, in which knowledge or "proof" was seen to derive largely from informal observation, had come to be signaled primarily by the word *experience*. The second strand of meaning, in which the notion of testing is dominant, had attached itself by the end of the seventeenth and the beginning of the eighteenth century to the word *experiment*. During the decades in which Milton was writing, the strands of meaning had just begun to separate. As terms and as concepts, *experience* and *experiment* were almost, but not entirely, interchangeable.

What a repentant Eve calls in book x her "sad experiment" would today be called her "sad experience":

> Adam, by sad experiment I know
> How little weight my words with thee can find,
> Found so erroneous, thence by just event
> Found so unfortunate;   (*PL*, x.967–70)

This is the sole occurrence of *experiment* in *Paradise Lost*; *experience* is Milton's usual choice.[24] Insofar as the two terms *are* interchangeable, Eve's words indicate how thoroughly repentance has altered her view of her actions. The experience she had earlier announced with some complacency – "On my experience, Adam, freely taste, / And fear of death deliver to the winds" (*PL*, ix.988–89) – she now regards as "sad," that is, as lamentable or calamitous.[25] Assigning *experiment* rather than *experience* to Eve allows Milton to suggest a further refinement of her repentance: she realizes in book x not only that she has misunderstood her experience but also that she has failed to use its potential for discovery. Rather than to "make experiment" of the serpent's claims, she chooses to accept the experience he offers.

Yet Eve's initial response to the serpent is a scientific one, entirely worthy of a new philosopher. Upon hearing the serpent's words, she asks, "What may this mean? Language of man pronounced / By tongue of brute, and human sense expressed?" (*PL*, ix.553–54). She perceives at once, correctly, that she needs to test the truth of the serpent's speech, in the double sense of *how* and *what* he speaks. Had she persisted in this line of inquiry, she might have arrived at the truth: the serpent's "speaking" is but a feat of natural magic. But she does not persist. Instead, Eve the budding natural philosopher lets herself be dazzled and deceived by Satan the natural magician.

The success of Satan's seduction of her hinges upon Eve's initial willingness to believe that the serpent is actually speaking. To accomplish this effect, Satan draws upon the resources of natural magic. Against these, a shrewd application of the principles of the new philosophy might have prevailed. This does not imply that natural magic and the new philosophy are inherently antithetical. On the contrary, as Stuart Clark states, natural magic in the early modern period ought to be seen as "a branch of natural philosophy which specialized in occult causation."[26] We will return to the way in which Satan produces the effect of speaking in the serpent, but first we need to consider more carefully the relationship between natural magic and the new natural philosophy. Allies in their shared interest in occult causes, they become antagonists whenever natural magic seeks to mystify rather than to elucidate the marvels of Creation.

Francis Bacon, vehement in his condemnation of a "degenerate" natural magic, calls a "pure" or "reformed" natural magic "the science which applies the knowledge of hidden forms to the production of wonderful operations; and by uniting (as they say) actives with passives, displays the wonderful works of nature."[27] As Bacon's definition suggests, natural magic and the new philosophy have in common an interest in "hidden forms" or occult qualities. The old Aristotelian orthodoxy had declared that occult (as opposed to manifest) causes could not be explained or studied because they were imperceptible to the senses. The new philosophers disagreed. With their more expanded notion of "the natural" and a greater readiness to admit ignorance, they placed occult causes within the bounds of legitimate inquiry.[28] True miracles were the only exception to this rule, for they involved the abrogation of natural law. All other occult events, no matter how remarkable, were properly regarded as "the result of developing natural powers . . . miracles only in the etymological sense: things worthy of wonder," that is, "*mira* not *miracula*."[29]

Daniel Sennert passionately defends the study of the new "scientific" occult:

all more learned Philosophers and Physitians . . . have constantly taught, that the Causes of many things in natural Philosophy and Physick do depend upon hidden Qualities . . . if the true Original of these qualities be sought into, (whereof few have taken care) the knowledg thereof wil produce as certain science as that of the first Qualities . . . it is a ridiculous thing to deny that which is manifest by Experience, because we cannot tel the reason thereof. As if it were impossible any thing might happen in Nature of whose cause we are ignorant. We are ignorant of most things.[30]

The operation of antipathies and sympathies, stellar and planetary influences, the activities of spiritual and angelic beings – all were considered occult in the seventeenth century.[31] So were magnetism, gravitation, and purgation. So, too, were the baleful effect of the basilisk's gaze and the power of the remora to halt a moving ship. All of these, Clark notes, "were 'occult' simply because their causes were hidden beyond the reach of human intellect, and because their remarkable effects were merely manifested to experience, not rationally explained."[32] When natural magic concerned itself with the investigation of these hidden causes and the mimetic production of their remarkable effects, its ends were compatible with those of the new philosophy.[33]

Bacon thus welcomes the contributions of a natural magic "restored to its ancient and honourable meaning" and condemns a corrupt version of it that lends itself to the glorification of the magus and depresses an energetic inquiry into occult causes.

But this popular and degenerate natural magic has the same kind of effect on men as some soporific drugs, which not only lull to sleep, but also during sleep instil gentle and pleasing dreams. For first it lays the understanding asleep by singing of specific properties and hidden virtues, sent as from heaven and only to be learned from the whispers of tradition; which makes men no longer alive and awake for the pursuit and inquiry of real causes, but to rest content with these slothful and credulous opinions; and then it insinuates innumerable fictions, pleasant to the mind, and such as one would most desire, – like so many dreams.[34]

A degenerate natural magic, in other words, tempts humanity to assume that patience, labor, co-operative endeavor, and the passage of time are not necessary to the advancement of learning. Clark observes that Bacon's praise of a "restored" natural magic is related not only to his hopes for natural philosophy but to his assertion that even the marvels attributed to sorcery and witchcraft should not be dismissed without investigation. "For it is not yet known," Bacon asserts,

in what cases, and how far, effects attributed to superstition participate of natural causes; and therefore howsoever the use and practice of such arts is to be condemned, yet from the speculation and consideration of them (if they be diligently unravelled) a useful light may be gained, not only for the true judgment of the offences of persons charged with such practices, but likewise for the further disclosing of the secrets of nature.[35]

Bacon's assertion rests on the belief that no matter how marvelous they appear, the effects produced by or attributed to demons and witches are natural. Only God is capable of supernatural effects – Satan is but

"Gods Ape," notes King James – and anything natural can be profitably investigated. It is hardly surprising to find new philosophers borrowing techniques of investigation from the skeptical tradition of demonology.[36]

Older than humanity, incorporeal, "Not tied or manacled with joint or limb . . . in what shape they choose / Dilated or condensed" (*PL*, 1.426, 428–29), demons were held to have the advantage over human beings in understanding occult causes. Satan, said King James, voicing a commonplace of the age, was "farre cunningner then man in the knowledge of all the occult proprieties of nature" and hence a better natural magician.[37] Thomas Browne in *Pseudodoxia Epidemica* acknowledges Satan's superior ability to exploit the natural world:

Beside being a naturall Magician he may performe many acts in wayes above our knowledge, though not transcending our naturall power, when our knowledge shall direct it; part hereof hath been discovered by himselfe, and some by humane indagation which though magnified as fresh inventions unto us, are stale unto his cognition: I hardly beleeve, he hath from elder times unknowne the verticity of the loadstone; surely his perspicacity discerned it to respect the North, when ours beheld it indeterminately. Many secrets there are in nature of difficult discovery unto man, of easie knowledge unto Satan, whereof some his vain-glory cannot conceale, others his envy will not discover. (*PE*, 63)

Small wonder that a natural magician might resort to demons' aid when the attempt to understand and manipulate the occult virtues of nature became too frustrating. Such "aid," needless to say, invariably led to the confusion of the magician: though gifted in the understanding of occult causes, Satan and his minions were known to provide only false enlightenment to their human disciples. Natural law limited what Satan could effect, but "there was nothing that he might not *appear* to effect."[38] He has thereby "inveigled no small part of the world into a credulity of artificiall Magick" (*PE*, 63), observes Thomas Browne.

Ascertaining the cause of marvelous effects was a project to which seventeenth-century natural philosophers and demonologists alike devoted themselves. It was a project requiring great acuity. Clark notes that there were in effect four explanatory categories for natural marvels: "real demonic effects, illusory demonic effects, real nondemonic effects, and illusory nondemonic effects."[39] Among the benefits of natural philosophy, argues Robert Boyle, is the protection it affords against being ensnared by illusory effects, demonic or real. Someone who genuinely understands the workings of nature, Boyle claims in *The Christian Virtuoso*, will not mistake the effects of natural magic, for those of a divine power. And by this well-instructed wariness, he will be able to discover the subtil cheats and collusions of imposters; by which, not only multitudes of all religions, especially heathen, but even learned men of most religions, for want of an insight into real philosophy, have formerly been, or are at this day, deluded, and drawn into idolatrous, superstitious, or otherwise erroneous tenets or practices.[40]

Milton's Eve is drawn into precisely the idolatrous and superstitious practices that Boyle warns against. To use Clark's terms, she mistakes an illusory demonic effect for a real nondemonic one. Two undeluded explanations for the serpent's speaking appear at the outset of the temptation at the Tree.[41] The narrator proposes that Satan, having caught Eve's attention,

> with serpent tongue
> Organic, or impulse of vocal air,
> His fraudulent temptation thus began.   (*PL*, IX.529–31)

At the word *Organic* in line 530, the apparently figurative "serpent tongue" (roughly equivalent to "forked tongue") reveals itself to be material, though not organic in the physiological sense.[42] Satan does not, for he cannot, turn the serpent's tongue into an organ of speech. Rather, he uses the tongue as a mechanical means (*organum*) of producing sounds, as if it were a musical instrument (specifically, an organ).[43] "[O]r impulse of vocal air" expresses both an alternative to and an elaboration of the use of the instrumental tongue. The phrase suggests that Satan harnesses the speech-like sounds made naturally by the inanimate air; it equally suggests that he manipulates pulses of air to produce sounds from the serpent's tongue, as air produces sounds from an organ.[44] These explanations would have occasioned no surprise to Milton's contemporaries. Thomas Browne points out that the "naturall effects" Satan achieves typically derive from "his owne principality the ayre" (*PE*, 67). As King James observes, the "stile of *the Prince of the aire* is given unto him," for he has "affinitie with the aire as being a spirite," and hence "the power of the forming and mooving thereof."[45]

Upon hearing herself addressed by the serpent, Eve's first reaction is to marvel at his voice (*PL*, IX.551) and then to question whether his tongue can be an organ of speech – a possibility, she reflects, which was "denied / To beasts, whom God on their creation-day / Created mute to all articulate sound" (*PL*, IX.555–57). Eve initially displays, that is, what Robert Boyle would call a "well-instructed wariness." She also possesses the "insight into real philosophy" that Boyle posits as the

complement to wariness. She has, after all, some experience of the
effects produced by air. It is true that she does not know Satan's title,
"Prince of the Air." However, as part of the "fit audience" for
Raphael's tale, she might have noticed that the archangel repeatedly
associates Satan with the air. In addition, she has heard from Raphael
a description of the angelic symphony, which includes "all organs of
sweet stop" (*PL*, VII.596) and whose sounding harps make the earth and
air *re*sound (*PL*, VII.560–61). She herself has enjoined the winds to
"Breathe soft or loud" in praise of their maker (*PL*, V.193), implying a
recognition that in its movement, air imitates human sounds. Yet Eve
fails to apply her insight to the marvelous talking snake and misses the
opportunity to "make experiment." What she greets at first as a marvel,
and hence a candidate for further investigation, swiftly becomes in her
eyes a "miracle" (*PL*, IX.562), by definition beyond the reach of human
understanding. Her command to the serpent, "Redouble then this
miracle, and say, / How camest thou speakable of mute" (*PL*,
IX.562–63), hints that she is too willing to renounce the possibility of a
natural explanation.

After they arrive at the Tree, Eve asks no more questions about "the
tongue of brute." Satan is wholly successful in diverting her attention
from the puzzle of the serpent's speaking to the "miracle" of the fruit's
effects. He does so by speaking with the passion and inventiveness of
"some orator renowned / In Athens or free Rome" (*PL*, IX.670–71). But
the "great matter" he comes to praise is a great lie; as his subject matter
is base, so is his eloquence debased. He resembles a great orator of old
precisely as a mountebank does – and indeed, the "new part" Satan
"puts on" at the Tree is that of a mountebank. He gives a performance
of enormous inventiveness and energy, one which combines the arts of
political oratory, theatre, and preaching, as Fowler notes.[46] But every
element of the performance is directed towards enhancing the value of
the fruit in order to make it more desirable in Eve's eyes. Just so, the
bravura performances of the *ciarlatani* haunting the piazzas of seventeenth-century Italian cities functioned as advertisements for the
"secrets" they hawked, i.e., the secrets of nature. Eating the fruit is the
"secret" Satan sells to Eve. In this context, *secrets* refers to recipes or pre-
scriptions that lay claim to unlocking the occult powers of things and
making them available for use.[47] William Eamon traces the "secrets" tradition back through the Middle Ages, and notes that at its most learned
and respectable, it shared the philosophical assumptions of Bacon's
"restored" natural magic:

The professors of secrets affirmed the superiority of experience over reason in the search for scientific knowledge. They believed that nature was permeated with "secrets" and occult forces that lay hidden underneath the exterior appearances of things. Neither reason nor authority, nor any of the traditional instruments of inquiry, they insisted, were capable of gaining access to the occult interior of nature.[48]

By the late sixteenth century, inexpensive, popular collections of secrets had begun to appear in print, and the tradition gradually declined from respectable erudition.[49] The *ciarlatano* who, mounted on his bench, performed in the marketplace of Italian cities to draw a crowd and sell his secrets, represents the debased end of the tradition.

Ben Jonson draws the portrait of a mountebank in Act II of *Volpone*, when Volpone, dressed accordingly, enters and proclaims "the miraculous effects of this my oil . . . the admirable virtues of my medicaments, and mine own excellency in matter of rare and unknown secrets."[50] The art of the mountebank, suggests Jonson's portrait, lies in persuading an audience, first, that his nostrum has an inherent, secret virtue, and, second, that he has no art except that of knowing the secret. Jonson thus puts a claim to knowledge at the heart of mountebankery. Before Volpone enters, two characters disagree about that claim:

SIR POLITIC
    They [the mountebanks] are the only knowing men of Europe!
    Great general scholars, excellent physicians,
    Most admired statesmen, professed favourites,
    And cabinet counsellors to the greatest princes!
    The only languaged men of all the world!

PEREGRINE
    And I have heard they are most lewd imposters,
    Made all of terms and shreds; no less beliers
    Of great men's favours than their own vile medicines;
    Which they will utter upon monstrous oaths,
    Selling that drug for twopence, ere they part,
    Which they have valued at twelve crowns before.[51]

Sir Politic Would-Be is naive and gullible; Peregrine is worldly wise. The latter's condemnation of mountebanks is clearly endorsed by the play – as is Sir Politic's inadvertent equation between mountebanks, on the one hand, and scholars, physicians, statesmen, favorites, and cabinet counsellors, on the other.

Whereas Jonson assigns credulity and skepticism to separate

characters, historical accounts suggest a rather more mixed response to mountebanks on the part of individual spectators. Fascinated by the dramatic performances of Italian *ciarlatani,* several early modern English tourists recorded what they saw. Thomas Coryate's description of Venetian mountebanks in 1608 contains a mixture of admiration and distrust, the mixture that characterizes Eve's first response to the talking serpent in the garden of Eden. Coryate's description reveals quite clearly that his half-reluctant willingness to credit the mountebanks' claims for their "drugs and confections" comes from the power of their dramatic performances:

> while the musicke playes, the principall Mountebanke which is the Captaine and ring-leader of all the rest, opens his truncke, and sets abroach his wares; after the musicke hath ceased, he maketh an oration to the audience of halfe an houre long, or almost an houre. Wherein he doth most hyperbolically extoll the vertue of his drugs and confections:

> *Laudat venales qui vult extrudere merces.*

> Though many of them are very counterfeit and false. Truely I often wondred at many of these naturall Orators. For they would tell their tales with such admirable volubility and plausible grace, even *extempore,* and seasoned with that singular variety of elegant jests and witty conceits, that they did often strike great admiration into strangers that never heard them before: and by how much the more eloquent these Naturalists are, by so much the greater audience they draw unto them, and the more ware they sell . . . I have observed marveilous strange matters done by some of these Mountebankes . . . I have seen a Mountebanke hackle and gash his naked arme with a knife most pittifully to beholde, so that the blood hath streamed out in great abundance, and by and by after, he hath applied a certaine oyle unto it, wherewith he hath incontinent both stanched the blood, and so throughly healed the woundes and gashes, that when he hath afterward shewed us his arme againe, we could not possibly perceive the least token of a gash.[52]

The essential elements of the mountebanks' performance as detailed by Coryate – their elaborate preparations (designed to draw a crowd), their "admirable volubility and plausible grace," the "marveilous strange matters" they recount, and their ability "most hyperbolically [to] extoll the vertue" of their remedy – are present in Satan's performance at the Tree of Knowledge in *Paradise Lost.* There is no need for the serpent to "hackle and gash" himself, as Coryate's mountebank does: merely *saying* that he feels the power of the fruit appears to demonstrate that power.

In true mountebank fashion, Satan first elevates himself, then holds Eve's attention with an elaborate show of preparation:

>   now more bold
> The tempter, but with show of zeal and love
> To man, and indignation at his wrong,
> New part puts on, and as to passion moved,
> Fluctuates disturbed, yet comely and in act
> Raised, as of some great matter to begin.
> As when of old some orator renowned
> In Athens or free Rome, where eloquence
> Flourished, since mute, to some great cause addressed,
> Stood in himself collected, while each part,
> Motion, each act won audience ere the tongue,
> Sometimes in highth began, as no delay
> Of preface brooking through his zeal of right.
> So standing, moving, or to highth upgrown
> The tempter all impassioned thus began.   (*PL*, IX.664–78)

One is put in mind of Olivia's observation in *Twelfth Night*: "Sure you have some hideous matter to deliver, when the courtesy of it is so fearful."[53] The serpent's initial "courtesy," unlike Viola/Cesario's, captivates his audience rather than putting her on her guard (though even the canny Olivia eventually succumbs to the speaker's charms). As any mountebank knows, holding an audience's attention is equivalent to extorting from them an investment of time; having invested their time, they are more likely to invest their coins. For charlatans, the art of oratory is the art of salesmanship. Mountebanks, remarks Peregrine in *Volpone*, are they not "quacksalvers, / Fellows that live by venting oils and drugs?"[54] The gerund perfectly combines selling and windy oratory.

In the final speech of the temptation scene, Satan vents the fruit of the forbidden tree with as much fervor as any mountebank venting his oils and drugs.

>   O sacred, wise, and wisdom-giving plant,
>   Mother of science, now I feel thy power
>   Within me clear, not only to discern
>   Things in their causes, but to trace the ways
>   Of highest agents, deemed however wise.
>
>   (*PL*, IX.679–83)

Just as the nostrum-mongering *ciarlatani* of the late Renaissance claimed occult curative powers for their wares, so Satan claims those powers for his fruit. But we should not conclude that Milton has depicted an Eve gullible enough to be taken in by the equivalent of a snake-oil salesman or a fairground confidence trickster. Satan's promotion of his marvelous remedy, like the venting of other mountebanks, is not completely dissimilar to the mode of respectable medical practitioners of the period, for the periphery of medical respectability was not far from the center in the seventeenth century.[55] In particular, the rise of Paracelsian medicine encouraged an acceptance of remedies with occult powers by inserting elements of natural magic into "physic."[56] The humoral basis of traditional Galenic medicine was thoroughly understood by patients and physicians alike; the drugs it favored were intended to balance the humors, a familiar and hence explicable process. Paracelsians, in contrast, drew upon "literature and techniques wellnigh incomprehensible to the uninitiated."[57] They introduced "chemical" or "metallic," i.e., non-herbal, drugs into the medical marketplace. Such drugs were understood "to operate in an occult way on 'the total substance' of the body rather than on one of its humours."[58] The notion of medicine that affected the whole body, long accepted by practitioners of magic healing, gained favor among mainstream doctors as the influence of Paracelsianism spread in England after 1640.[59] Europe's increasing colonial trade, moreover, insured a constant supply of exotic new substances for medicinal use, substances whose marvelous efficacy was not infrequently proclaimed. It is not surprising that trained physicians and irregular practitioners alike found a public willing to try their secret remedies. If respectable physicians were not averse to admitting what looked like magical elements into their practice, who could be certain that untrained and irregular healers were necessarily wrong in their claims for occult cures?

Volpone exuberantly lists the complaints his medicine will cure – "the *mal caduco*, cramps, convulsions, paralyses, epilepsies, *tremor cordia*, retired nerves, ill vapours of the spleen, stoppings of the liver, the stone, the stranguary, *hernia ventosa, iliaca passio*."[60] Satan's "secret," too, is a panacea. His first task is therefore to represent Eve's condition to her as diseased. (That she calls the fruit "the cure of all" (*PL*, IX.776) before consuming it marks his success.) He begins by representing God as a magus powerful only in the possession of secrets – representing him, that is, as Thomas Browne and others represent Satan, as "a naturall Magician [who] may performe many acts in wayes above our knowledge, though not transcending our naturall power." Therefore God has to resort to intimidation, implies Satan:

> Queen of this universe, do not believe
> Those rigid threats of death; ye shall not die;
> How should ye? By the fruit? It gives you life
> To knowledge

* * *

> Why then was this forbid? Why but to awe,
> Why but to keep ye low and ignorant,
> His worshippers;　　　　　　　　(*PL*, ix.684–87,703–05)

The role of skeptical unmasker is the perfect mask for a charlatan. Even as he seems to de-mystify God's power, Satan continues to mystify the fruit, apparently offering experiential evidence for its virtue: "Look on me, / Me who have touched and tasted, yet both live, / And life more perfect have attained" (*PL*, ix.687–89). Of course the serpent has not "touched and tasted" the fruit, but on the basis of his fabricated evidence, he constructs a persuasive narrative: "I have tried this fruit; the divine impostor derives his power from it; it has remarkable powers; it will cure all your ills; try it." Eve does try it. What she later calls her experience – "On my experience, Adam, freely taste" – is in fact the experience of being gulled by a charlatan's tale.

We can now return to Fish's claim that the diminished experience Eve accepts from Satan is "empirical science," and that she should have known that God can set aside the law of nature when he pleases. This amounts to saying that Eve ought not to trust her own experience of the natural world. Fish cites in evidence of his claim *Samson Agonistes*, lines 300–25, "where the chorus explains that the operation of natural causes does not bind God."[61] But the opinions of the chorus are not necessarily those of Milton, and in any case the cited passage refers not to natural but to Jewish ceremonial or ritual law. The passage forms part of a specific theological argument. The lines at issue are the following:

> As if they would confine the interminable,
> And tie him to his own prescript,
> Who made our laws to bind us, not himself,
> And hath full right to exempt
> Whom so it pleases him by choice
> From national obstriction, without taint
> Of sin, or legal debt;
> For with his own laws he can best dispense. (*SA*, 307–14)

Puzzled that God had allowed Samson to marry the (Philistine) woman of Timna, the Chorus concludes that God can exempt anyone he chooses from obedience to the ceremonial law. It is futile to look for rational explanations; "Down Reason then" (*SA*, 322), they shrug. In fact, the Chorus has just excused itself from the responsibility of seeking the spirit behind the letter of the law.[62] They have made the mistake, as Joan

Bennett remarks, of seeing "God's right as based on his omnipotence rather than on the justice which defines his divine nature."[63] Instead of assuming God's consistency and trying to understand how it manifests itself in the matter of Samson's marriage, the Chorus falls back on superstitious fear of God's power. Even if the Chorus were speaking here of divine disruptions to nature's order, their thinking provides no model for Eve.

Nothing warrants, in fact, applying the passage from *Samson Agonistes* to the law of nature. When in *De Doctrina Christiana* Milton *does* speak of miracles (Fish's "effects contrary to those [God's] creatures are able to discern in nature"), it is to assert that God makes use of them under only two circumstances: either "to demonstrate divine power and strengthen our faith" or "to ensure a weightier condemnation for those who do not believe."[64] Neither of these conditions obtains at the scene of Eve's temptation in Eden. Milton does not in fact have a great deal to say about the "extraordinary providence of God." He is much fuller in his description of "God's ordinary providence,"

by which he maintains and preserves that constant and ordered system of causes which was established by him in the beginning.

This is commonly and indeed too frequently called Nature; for nature cannot mean anything except the wonderful power and efficacy of the divine voice which went forth in the beginning, and which all things have obeyed ever since as a perpetual command.[65]

Milton is insisting here upon the created character of nature. In an earlier chapter of *De Doctrina*, he notes that nature and fate have sometimes been treated "as if they were to be identified with this supreme being."[66] On the contrary, Milton states: just as "fate" means that which is "*fatum*, spoken, by some almighty power," so "nature or *natura* implies by its very name that it was *natam*, born."[67] Nature is not a self-sufficient, independently functioning system that operates apart from God's will. Nonetheless, except for the very restricted occasions when God's "extraordinary providence" is put into effect, nature can be depended upon to act in a consistent and regular fashion, according to the law established for it at the Creation.

Given Milton's presumption that nature is a "constant and ordered system of causes" (and as such, available for rational analysis), Eve should indeed have been more skeptical about an articulate snake. This is the charge usually laid against her. Fish inverts it, claiming that Eve ought not to have believed Satan's claim that God is bound by nature's laws. To make this claim, Fish confines himself to discussing Satan's arguments (about eating the fruit) and ignores Satan's physical manifestation (as a serpent). But separating what he says from how he appears is not possible in this instance. The extraordinary talking snake says to Eve, according to Fish, "Do not trust anything extraordinary." This is a paradox along the lines of " 'All Cretans are liars,' said the Cretan." The point is that Eve ought to have been more, not less, of an empiricist; she ought to have pitted her experiential knowledge more polemically against Satan's. Fish's accusation –

The value Eve finds in experience (things seen) is the value she assigns to it, and that will be whatever she wants it to be. Experience is only a word for what happens to reality when it is filtered through the medium of time and space – Man's medium not God's[68]

– needs to be turned inside out: Eve does not assign *enough* value to her experience. There *is* value in things seen, in a world created good by the Creator, in a reality filtered through time and space, if his creatures approach it in the proper frame of mind.

If Eve had adequately valued her previous experience of the natural world, how might she have responded to a mountebank with a magical nostrum? Our answer does not have to be entirely speculative. The most eminent of Milton's experimentalist contemporaries, Robert Boyle, carefully recorded his encounters with untutored and irregular practitioners of physic, encounters which it is instructive to compare with Eve's encounter at the Tree. Boyle maintained the need to take seriously the experiential knowledge claimed even by empirics and their ilk. Indeed, he warns his readers against allowing "the mistaken name of emperick" to cause them to dismiss the remedies such physicians have discovered, though the discoveries may be the result of accident or chance.[69] Boyle's seizing upon the term *empiric* is significant. Derived from the name of the ancient sect of Greek physicians, *empiric* came to denote one whose knowledge was based on experience rather than on theory or training; hence, one who was an untrained physician; hence, a quack.[70] The assumptions at work in this semantic history are ones which Boyle needed to combat. His worry about *empiric* is not a quibble; it encapsulates the turmoil attendant upon establishing a new basis for authority in knowledge. Thus he warns against assuming that those who lack formal training in physic and who claim to base their knowledge on experience are necessarily quacks. The knowledge that they have to offer must not be dismissed out of hand, he insists; nor must it be accepted without making experiment. In the second part of *The Usefulness of Natural Philosophy*, Boyle reflects:

but probably the knowledge of physicians might not be inconsiderably increased, if men were a little more curious to take notice of the observations and experiments, suggested partly by the practice of midwives, barbers, old women, empiricks, and the rest of that illiterate crew, that presume to meddle with physick among our selves.[71]

Wariness mingles here with grudging respect for a knowledge born of experience.[72] Rose-Mary Sargent argues that "[i]n Boyle's usage, *learned* and *illiterate* are clearly descriptive, not evaluative, terms."[73] It is hard to see, however, how "that illiterate crew" can be anything other than derogatory. In combination with the charge of presumptuous meddling, the phrase suggests that Boyle's attitude toward untrained practitioners is more mixed than Sargent allows.

Boyle is indeed remarkable in preserving a balance between open-mindedness and skepticism in his accounts of "the observations and experiments" of untrained practitioners. Let us look at one such account, the account of a chemical remedy peddled by an empiric of Amsterdam.[74] Boyle employs here all the methodological tools which Eve needed in order to guard against culpable credulity. The account is lengthy, but providing exhaustive detail is one of the central features of Boyle's method.

And now I am upon the discourse of the peculiar operations of mercury, and of unusual ways of evacuation, I am tempted to subjoin an odd story, which may afford notable hints to a speculative man, as it was related to me both in private, and before illustrious witnesses, by the formerly commended chymist of the French king: he told me then a while since, that there is yet living a person of quality, by name Monsieur *de Vatteville*, well known by the command he hath or had of a regiment of *Switzers* in *France*, who, many years ago following the wars in the Low Countries, fell into a violent distemper of his eyes, which, in spite of what physicians and surgeons could do, did in a few months so increase, that he lost the use of both his eyes, and languished long in a confirmed blindness; which continued till he heard of a certain empirick at *Amsterdam*, commonly known by the name of *Adrian Glasmaker* (for indeed he was a glazier) who being cried up for prodigious cures he had done with a certain powder, this colonel resorted to him, and the empirick having discoursed with him, undertook his recovery, if he would undergo the torment of the cure: which the colonel having undertaken to do, the surgeon made him snuff up into each nostril about a grain of a certain mercurial powder, which in a strangely violent manner quickly wrought with him almost all imaginable ways, as by vomit,

siege, sweat, urine, spitting, and tears, within ten or twelve hours that this operation lasted, making his head also to swell very much; but within three or four
days after this single taking of the drastick medicine had done working, he
began to recover some degree of sight, and within a fortnight attained to such
a one, that he himself assured the relater, he never was so sharp-sighted before
his blindness. And the relater assured me, that he had taken pleasure to observe,
that this gentleman, who is his familiar acquaintance, would discern objects
farther and clearer than most other men. He added, that Monsieur *de Vatteville*
told the relater, he had purchased the way of making this powder of the empirick, and had given it to an eminent surgeon, one *Benoest* (an acquaintance of
the relater's) by whom he had been cured of a musket shot, that had broken his
thigh-bone, when the other surgeons would have proceeded to amputation; and
that this *Benoest* had with this powder, administred as before is related, cured a
gentlewoman of a cancer in the breast. All which, and more, was confirmed to
the relater by the surgeon himself. But in what other stubborn and deplorable
cases they use this powder, I do not particularly remember. The preparation of
it, which a chymist did me the favour to tell me by word of mouth, as a thing
himself had also made, was in short this: that the remedy was made by precip-
itating quicksilver with good oil of vitriol, and so making a turbith, which is
afterwards to be dulcified by abstracting twenty or twenty five times from it pure
spirit of wine, of which fresh must be taken at every abstraction. But I would
not advise you to recommend so furious a powder to any, that is not a very skillful chymist and physician too, till you know the exact preparation, and particular uses of it.[75]

Beginning with the noncommittal "odd," Boyle is careful to refrain in
the first part of the narrative from passing judgment on the "furious
powder." (He had undoubtedly concluded against the powder by the
time he wrote, but the narrative conveys the evolution of his attitude.)
About two-thirds through the account, his tone changes. After reporting
the surgeon's assurance that the powder had cured breast cancer, Boyle's
account loses its particularity and becomes almost careless (e.g., "All
which, and more"; "I do not particularly remember"; "twenty or twenty
five times"). It is as if he has heard tell of one cure too many.

   Perhaps the most striking feature of the account is the number of witnesses it cites to the effectiveness of the "furious powder." Recent scholarship on Boyle has begun to concentrate on his philosophy of
experimentation, in which the role of corroboration is central.[76] Rose-
Mary Sargent, most prominently, takes issue with Steven Shapin and
Simon Schaffer's influential view of Boyle as a naive empiricist who
"regards experimentally produced matters of fact as self-evident and
self-explanatory."[77] She cites in particular Boyle's attitude toward witnesses as demonstrating his sophisticated understanding of the factual,

"a new category in the seventeenth century."[78] Boyle, she argues, regarded observation and experiment as essential for the gathering of facts, the two activities serving as the basis upon which to refute or confirm theoretical claims and, ultimately, upon which to suggest "causes."[79] To make certain of the facts of observation and experiment, especially when a witness reported an extraordinary or unexpected occurrence, Boyle commonly sought corroboration. This could take the form of a duplication of the event witnessed or of testimony from another witness.[80] Thus in the account of the experiment of mercury, he is careful to add Benoest's confirmation to Vatteville's account of the cure wrought by Glasmaker's powder. Sargent notes that Boyle spoke or corresponded directly with "his informants" whenever possible, usually seeking additional information about their observations.[81] Because he believed that "[t]he more background knowledge one has about the variety of phenomena in nature, the better one can judge the credibility of reports about new phenomena," Boyle as astute questioner constitutes himself as a kind of witness.[82] Indeed, he often serves as witness to the *unlikelihood* of the tale he recounts.

Eve's first response to Satan's claims about the fruit suggests that she has the instincts of a Boylian witness. Her attitude perfectly combines experimental skepticism and open-mindedness.

> Serpent, thy overpraising leaves in doubt
> The virtue of that fruit, in thee first proved:
> But say, where grows the tree, from hence how far? (*PL*, ix.615–17)

She does not abandon skepticism upon arriving at the tree; however, she *does* abandon open-mindedness.

> Serpent, we might have spared our coming hither,
> Fruitless to me, though fruit be here to excess,
> The credit of whose virtue rest with thee,
> Wondrous indeed, if cause of such effects.
> But of this tree we may not taste nor touch;
> God so commanded (*PL*, ix.647–52)

Line 649 signals an attempt to close the matter: *rests* rather than *rest* would have indicated that Eve sees the need for corroboration of the serpent's testimony. But for her, the fruit and the circumstances surrounding the serpent's eating of it are beyond the reach of observation or experiment. In this context, her otherwise logical extension of God's prohibition, "we may not taste *nor touch*," is mistaken, indicating that Eve has set the fruit apart from the rest of Creation, so that it becomes an object of superstitious fear.[83] Her fear quite shuts out wisdom at one

entrance. It is true that Eve does not need the new experimental methodology to prove to her that she ought not to eat the fruit. Yet, had she
sought corroboration of the serpent's claims, refusing to credit his claims
until she had such corroboration, she would have exposed Satan as a
charlatan. Experimentalism does not conflict with and indeed would
have complemented the theological injunction not to eat the fruit.

When she abandons her skeptical and open-minded spirit of inquiry,
Eve leaves herself vulnerable to manipulation. Satan, grossly exaggerat-
ing the fruit's virtue, is finally able to persuade her that it is the cure of
all, a panacea. In believing its power to be so immense, she approaches
idolatry. In contrast, Robert Boyle, asked to give an opinion on the question of "the universal medicine," characteristically and at length establishes a position between acceptance and denial of the possibility:[84]

till I be better satisfied about those particulars than yet I have been, I am unwill-
ing either to seem to believe what I am not yet convinced of, or to assert any
thing, that may tend to discourage human industry; and therefore I shall only
venture to adde on this occasion; that I fear we do somewhat too much confine
our hopes, when we think, that one generous remedy can scarce be effectual in
several diseases, if their causes be supposed to be a little differing. For the theory
of diseases is not, I fear, so accurate and certain, as to make it fit for us to neglect
the manifest or hopeful virtues of noble remedies, whereever we cannot recon-
cile them to that theory. He that considers what not unfrequently happens in
distempered bodies by the metastasis of the morbifick matter, (as for instance,
how that, which in the lungs caused a violent cough, removed up to the head
may produce, as we have observed, a quick decay of memory and ratiocination,
and a palsy in the hands and other limbs) may enough discern, that diseases,
that appear very differing, may easily be produced by a peccant matter of the
same nature, only variously determined in its operations by the constitution of
the parts of the body where it settleth: and consequently it may seem probable
to him, that the same searching medicine, being endowed with qualities destructive to the texture of the morbifick matter, where-ever it finds it, may be able to
cure either all, or the greatest part, of the disease, which the various translation
of such a matter hath been observed to beget. Moreover, it oftentimes happens,
that diseases, that seem of a contrary nature, may proceed from the same cause
variously circumstanced; or (if you please) that of divers diseases, that may both
seem primary, the one is but symptomatical, or at most secondary in relation to
the other; as a dropsy and a slow fever may, to unskillful men, seem diseases of
a quite contrary nature, (the one being reputed a hot and dry, the other a cold
and moist distemper) though expert physicians know they may both proceed
from the same cause, and be cured by the same remedy.[85]

His reference to "human industry" indicates Boyle's assumption that if
a widely effective medicine is shown to exist, it will have to be created or
discovered through diligent research. It will not be handed to humanity

by an empiric who chances upon it "on a day roving the field" (*PL*, IX.575). Nor, Boyle leaves unsaid, will it be the "cure of *all*" diseases. Instead, he qualifies *all* to mean "all diseases having the same cause." We are too skeptical, he argues, if we think that diseases having the same cause will *not* respond to "one generous remedy." Discriminating among causes is thus essential to healing. Satan, in contrast, gestures toward the multiple causes of Eve's imputed dis-ease – "These, these and many more / Causes import your need of this fair fruit" (*PL*, IX.730–31) – as if the very number of causes releases him from the obligation of specifying them. Needless to say, a detailed exposition of these fictional causes would be fatal to Satan's inflammatory rhetoric.

Like Robert Boyle, Thomas Browne muses on the "universall remedy." Unlike Boyle, Browne openly voices his skepticism, concluding that death is the only panacea humanity will ever find:

I can cure the gout or stone in some, sooner than Divinity, Pride, or Avarice in others. I can cure vices by Physicke, when they remaine incurable by Divinity, and shall obey my pils, when they contemne their precepts. I boast nothing, but plainely say, we all labour against our owne cure, for death is the cure of all diseases. There is no Catholicon or universall remedy I know but this, which thogh nauseous to queasie stomachs, yet to prepared appetites is Nectar and a pleasant potion of immortality.[86]

Browne imagines humanity quaffing death in pleasant anticipation of eternity. Milton represents Eve greedily engorging death without restraint. Yet Milton seems to agree with Browne. Eve is shown to be proleptically correct when she pronounces the fruit "the cure of all." In a postlapsarian world, experience has a new name; as "tribulation," it will test life itself.

> I at first with two fair gifts
> Created him endowed, with happiness
> And immortality: that fondly lost,
> This other served but to eternize woe;
> Till I provided death; so death becomes
> His final remedy, and after life
> Tried in sharp tribulation, and refined
> By faith and faithful works, to second life,
> Waked in the renovation of the just,
> Resigns him up with heaven and earth renewed.   (*PL*, XI.57–66)

God's care for fallen humanity ultimately makes good the arch-charlatan's lie. As Maureen Quilligan puts it, "In *Paradise Lost* Satan does not finally create even destruction."[87]

The Fall, for Milton, was historical, but it was not inevitable. To have avoided it, Eve need only have repeated God's injunction and turned away from the serpent. However, had she "made experiment" of the serpent's claims, she would not only have avoided the Fall; she would have discovered in the created world further evidence of the Creator's glory, power, and wisdom. Such, at least, is Boyle's argument:

For the Works of God are not like the Tricks of Juglers, or the Pageants that entertain Princes, where concealment is requisite to wonder; but the knowledg of the Works of God proportions our admiration of them, they participating and disclosing so much of the inexhausted Perfections of their Author, that the further we contemplate them, the more Foot-steps and Impressions we discover of the Pefections [sic] of their Creator; and our utmost Science can but give us a juster veneration of his Omniscience.[88]

Natural philosophy functions as sex education does: greater understanding is more effective than ignorance as a defense against the consequences of seduction. Yet Eve knows enough. Had she properly valued her own experience of the natural world, she would not have been led astray by the marvelous talking serpent. But she accepts his interpretation of God's other book for her own, a form of intellectual laziness with the most serious consequences. Speaking of our individual responsibility to work out the meaning of God's Word for ourselves, Milton declares in *De Doctrina Christiana*: "God offers all his rewards not to those who are thoughtless and credulous, but to those who labor constantly and seek tirelessly after truth."[89]

CHAPTER 2

Experimentalists and the book of the world

Subtle, treacherous, and plausible, the patter of Satan the charlatan demands close reading. So, too, does Satan's serpent body, which is a text belonging to the genus, or the genre, "creeping thing." Whether or not the serpent actually crept on its belly before the Fall was a matter of debate among Renaissance biblical commentators.[1] That it went erect is a theory that Thomas Browne relegates to the "strange relations made by Authors . . . which if we beleeve we must be apt to swallow any thing" (*PE*, 43). Milton has been accused of being "vague" on the question in his representation of the serpent in book IX of *Paradise Lost*. But how the serpent moved in the garden of Eden is a question too important in the seventeenth century to be answered vaguely. Creeping and its obverse, going erect, are of concern to those philosophers newly investigating the structure of human and animal bodies, and both modes of locomotion have implications for classification and hierarchy. "Going erect" touches on the issue of human dignity as endowed by the Creator. "Creeping" designates a category of animals derived from the first chapter of Genesis, a category in the seventeenth century including insects, worms, snakes and other reptiles, and tiny mammals. Whether the Edenic serpent *ought* to be represented as a creeping thing is a question which thus fuses theology and natural philosophy in a way disturbing to modern sensibilities.

It is, however, precisely the sort of question raised by an attempt in the mid-seventeenth century to imagine and represent the creatures inhabiting the garden of Eden. Alastair Fowler lays out three possibilities for the serpent: that he went on his belly before and after the Fall; that he went upright before the Fall and on his belly afterwards; and that he went upright only while Satan was making use of him (*PL*, IX.496–504n). Milton, states Fowler, does not decide between the second and third possibilities. There is a fourth possibility, however, and it goes some way to addressing Thomas Browne's fear that we have turned the prelapsarian world into a place of monstrosities. Milton's description of the serpent, a "head / Crested aloft" above a "circular base of rising folds, that towered / Fold above fold a surging maze" (*PL*, IX.498–500), *may* imply a prelapsarian way of moving. But if so, it is a way that has not entirely vanished from the earth. Milton and his contemporaries could have seen in natural histories of the day depictions of New World snakes rearing up above their coiled bases, or "tails."[2] Milton's description of the serpent in book IX perfectly conveys the raised and threatening postures of these actual serpents – and in so doing finds a way of reconciling the very different attitudes of the natural world dictated by the old and new learning. The project of reconciliation suggests that in its poetic mode, *Paradise Lost* resists the loss it chronicles. In the middle of the seventeenth century, the "loss of Eden" *also* entailed the loss of a way of understanding Eden. *Paradise Lost* does not try to salvage the old learning in which Adam, Eve, the serpent, and the garden had for centuries been inscribed. It attempts, more courageously, to *renovate* the old learning by accommodating it to the new.

Raphael's account of Creation in book VII of *Paradise Lost* provides a sustained lesson for Adam and Eve in how to read "creeping things," and for the fit reader in how to read the poem's representation of the natural world. The archangel's praise of creeping things occurs at the culmination of his description of non-human Creation. Magnifying the humblest of God's creatures is, at one level, utterly traditional; it traces its ancestry back to classical and biblical antiquity, most notably to the proverbial imperative, "Go to the ant, thou sluggard; consider her ways, and be wise" (Proverbs 6.6).[3] The tradition of what one historian has called "small-animal valorization," however, was reshaped and given fresh impetus by developments in natural history in the seventeenth century.[4] One might point specifically to the appearance of Thomas Mouffet's treatise on insects in 1654; the popularity of insects as items in curiosity collections (see frontispiece); the repeated investigations by Fellows of the Royal Society into the question of spontaneous generation; and the fact that insects were the first subjects to be represented as they appeared under the microscope.[5] The impact of specific developments such as these are scarcely detectable in Raphael's praise of creeping things. But if we think of the new philosophy as generating both new speculations and new admissions of ignorance, then we can that see Raphael's traditional encomium has indeed been touched by the new knowing. The fusing of the traditional and the modern is entirely characteristic of Milton's representation of the natural world.

> At once came forth whatever creeps the ground,
> Insect or worm; those waved their limber fans
> For wings, and smallest lineaments exact
> In all the liveries decked of summer's pride
> With spots of gold and purple, azure and green:
> These as a line their long dimension drew,
> Streaking the ground with sinuous trace; not all
> Minims of nature; some of serpent kind
> Wondrous in length and corpulence involved
> Their snaky folds, and added wings.   *(PL, VII.475–84)*

Milton's hexameralist predecessor, Du Bartas, enjoins his book not to blush at bearing "upon thy paper-Tables" the insects "Limn'd with the pencill of my various Verse."[6] Far from blushing at including them in a paean to Creation, *Paradise Lost* magnifies the role of insects. To these lowly creatures belongs the high honor of revising and animating the ancient trope that the world is God's other book.

As they trace linear patterns upon the ground with their sinuous, brilliantly colored bodies and intricate movements, the "minims" – both the tiniest of creatures and single down-strokes of a pen – transform the surface of the earth into an illuminated manuscript.[7] They transform it, more precisely, into a manuscript which is *being* inscribed and illuminated.[8] Hence Raphael does not tell Adam and Eve what the inscription says. He cannot. As the book of the world is always in the process of being written, so too it must always be in the process of being read. The necessary incompleteness of the task is the most striking – and historically the most crucial – feature of Raphael's lesson on how to read the book of the world. It implies that no final, nor even a single, interpretation of the densely rich text of Creation is available for readers, and that therefore interpretation must be ongoing and continual.

The implied necessity for ceaseless interpretive activity puts Milton's use of the trope of God's other book in resonant relation to contemporary theories about reading the Bible and about knowing the natural world. These two activities will be the focus of this chapter and the next. In chapter 3 we will turn to Bible-reading practices in the mid-seventeenth century and consider their relationship to the depiction of the natural world in *Paradise Lost*. For the remainder of this chapter, we need to examine the place of natural history in the new philosophy and to look at the way two of Milton's contemporaries, Thomas Browne and Robert Boyle, think about reading the book of the world. We will only *seem* to lose sight of Milton and *Paradise Lost*. In fact, we cannot properly understand the poem's representation of the natural world until we first reconsider and enlarge our notion of scientific activity at the dawn of the scientific revolution.

Attempts to capture the sensory richness of protoscience, its concreteness, its disorderliness, its distaste for abstraction and systemization, its agnosticism on questions of basic ontology, and its suspicion of great theoreticians, must depend to some extent on the record of what has not survived to become incorporated into modern science.[9]

So Catherine Wilson characterizes the task faced by those who would challenge the picture of early modern science presented by standard histories of the scientific revolution. Such histories, she argues, construe from a selection of the historical data an early science which is primarily mathematical and mechanistic.[10] Their construing is teleological, the result of valuing in the natural philosophy of the seventeenth century only that which most closely resembles modern science. Among other effects, Wilson notes, this approach means that the Baconian or non-mathematical activities of the early modern period – that is, natural history, medicine, chemistry, and what we now call biology – were typically described as "lagging behind" physics and astronomy and were omitted from accounts of the scientific revolution.[11] That is no longer the case. Wilson's is one of a growing number of studies arguing for the scientific character of the neglected fields, a development which has produced and is the product of a richer, more expansive notion of "the scientific" for the early modern period.[12] Of these fields, natural history is of central importance to Milton's representation of the garden of Eden in *Paradise Lost* and hence to this study, but it is also of central importance to the new philosophy itself. Given the current widespread interest in environmental issues, it is perhaps not surprising to find a historian of environmental sciences declaring bluntly, "If there was a 'scientific revolution', natural history participated as fully as the physical sciences."[13] Other historians have concentrated on the complexity of the relationship between natural philosophy and natural history in the seventeenth century, noting that the relationship has yet to be fully worked out. Harold Cook nevertheless insists that "much of the new philosophy can be characterized as a way of exploring nature that emphasized natural history as the key to a true natural philosophy."[14] Similarly, Joseph Levine has observed that the Fellows of the early Royal Society perceived, if not a revolution, at least "a drastic alteration of traditional knowledge in *all* the sciences and philosophy."[15] This, Levine argues, they attributed to a method which they associated with Bacon and called (too vaguely no doubt) "observation and experiment." They understood the potential importance of mathematics and of physics but accepted for most of the sciences the preliminary labor of discovery and classification in what they and we still call natural history.[16]

If we ignore those early modern experimentalists who were active in natural history, warns Levine, we banish a good portion of the early Royal Society "to a pre-scientific or un-scientific limbo."[17]

As this new generation of studies demonstrates, by designating as "science" only that which is mathematical, objective, and abstract, we have turned our backs on "contemporary appraisals of the limitations of the mechanical philosophy and the wide vistas opened by a nonrigorous, unsystematic empiricism."[18] Confusion and engagement, playfulness and reverie, delight in sensory perception and acceptance of contingency – to see these qualities as alien to early modern science is to misunderstand and reduce the very nature of the experiences and experiments it valued. "The descendants of Descartes comprise both theoreticians and fantasists," Wilson muses, "but Descartes himself is neither one nor the other, for there was no structure in 1640 that could prise and hold those categories apart."[19] One aim of this book is to demonstrate the "wide vistas" of the imagination opened to poetry by the new philosophy, and specifically by natural history, in its earliest decades, those middle decades of the seventeenth century when "a nonrigorous, unsystematic empiricism" flourished. For this project, it is necessary to give as much weight to experimentalism's confessions of ignorance, its excited utopian speculations, and its disorderly claims of discovery on every hand as to its sober investigations of the mathematics of motion and its painstaking accretion of "facts."[20] Scientific uncertainty proves to be liberating for poetry – and also for science. The sources of playfulness, imaginative vision, sensory richness, and concreteness are, after all, the same, whether such creativity manifests itself in the new philosophy or in epic poetry. Hence early experimentalism's bold way with a metaphor. It is hardly surprising that allusions to the world-as-book are ubiquitous in the writings of the new philosophers, especially when they engage with natural history. The trope gathers up at least three of the profoundest concerns of the seventeenth century: how to know the natural world, how to interpret God's word, and how to assess the authority of antiquity. Not only are allusions to the trope ubiquitous; they are richly various in emphasis and application.

The trope of the world as God's other book might be thought of as a conceptual hinge. When it was inherited by early modernity from antiquity and the Middle Ages, the trope had hardened into a cliché.[21] It is cited near the beginning of Du Bartas's *Divine Weeks and Works*, for instance, as if it were going to play a central role in the poet's representing of Creation. In fact, the citation is perfunctory, neither generating nor inspired by detailed "readings" of the created world.

> The World's a Booke in *Folio*, printed all
> With God's great Workes in Letters Capitall:
> Each Creature, is a Page, and each effect,
> A faire Caracter, void of all defect.   (*Divine Weeks*, i.i.173–76)

Reading *this* folio requires neither training nor expertise, neither effort nor good eyesight, Du Bartas explains:

> To read this Booke, we neede not understand
> Each Strangers gibbrish; neither take in hand
> *Turkes* Caracters, nor *Hebrue* Points to seeke,
> *Nyle's Hieroglyphikes*, nor the Notes of *Greeke*.
> The wandring *Tartars*, the *Antartikes* wilde,
> Th'*Alarbies* fierce, the *Scithians* fell, the Childe
> Scarce seav'n yeare old, the bleared aged eye,
> Though void of Arte, read heere indifferently.
> But he that weares the spectacles of *Faith*,
> Sees through the Spheares above their highest heigth:
> He comprehends th'Arch-moover of all Motions,
> And reades (though running) all these needfull Notions.
> (*Divine Weeks*, i.i.185–96)

Reading the book of the world does not even require a material text. The reader knows beforehand that hares *always* mean fearfulness; sparrows, lustfulness; turtle-doves, chastity. Michel Foucault has declared that the pre-Classical world is "covered with signs that must be deciphered."[22] But the signs had already been deciphered; the book of the world had long since been read and interpreted.

Inheriting this exhausted trope, the experimental philosophers awakened it to new life as a rationale for observation of and experiment upon the natural world. There are thus as many references to reading God's other book after 1640 as before, but beneath the apparent continuity is a shift in the metaphor's function. Peter Dear expresses understandable impatience with assuming that their invocation of the trope *explains* the new philosophers' notion of experiment (or "contrived experience," as he deftly terms it):

Historians routinely refer to Baconianism, the Royal Society, and the metaphor of reading the book of nature (with its Paracelsian as well as Galilean overtones) to argue that the seventeenth century saw a move towards discovering nature through the senses, using observation and experiment.[23]

If the trope did not *explain*, however, it certainly *justified*. The culturally acceptable and non-binding locution of "reading the book of the world" licensed a wide range of activities, many of them unconventional, for the experimentalists.[24] By invoking the trope, they signaled respect for traditional priorities without letting themselves be held back by them. The venerable analogy between the Bible and the natural world helped reassure experimentalists and their public that there was nothing atheistic about their pursuits.

Yet the trope is much more than a conventional cover for unorthodox pursuits. The variety of ways in which individual experimentalists explain *how* to read God's other book, and then proceed to do so, suggests that the trope is a site for articulating theories about observing and "making experiment of" the natural world. Moreover, the fact that the early experimentalists cherish what is in effect a literary, humanistic trope – a trope whose deepest impulse is hermeneutic – is further evidence that limiting early science to the realm of the mathematical and the mechanical is invalid. The more inclusive notion of early science propounded by Wilson and others makes room for the exegetical Thomas Browne as well as for the structuralist Robert Boyle. Let me explain why I think it essential to include Browne in a consideration of early experimentalism. He has famously been called "Janus-faced,"[25] but Charles Raven protests that "[t]he age, as Browne reflected it, is no longer facing both ways; it has made the turn; and in intention Browne is definitely modern."[26] It would be better to see Browne not as two-faced but as mediatory. Including Browne in our consideration of early "science" sensitizes us to the many ways in which an alertness to the new experimentalism can manifest itself *in writing* – for reading Browne must have been one of the primary means by which many seventeenth-century people got to know, or were persuaded that there was merit to, the new philosophy. Browne's works, which "defy all comparison,"[27] alert us to the richly various ways in which new philosophical thinking could be articulated or expressed. Thus we can detect the presence of that thinking in writing which is not obviously or directly concerned with the new philosophy. Browne's work, in short, helps us to see the "scientific" in Milton's writing. In Milton's representation of the natural world, one can see the qualities characteristic of Browne's contemplation of it, the same probing, cautious, humorous attempts to discriminate between what might be true and what is customarily taken to be true – and the same desire to salvage as much as possible from the past. Not only does *Paradise Lost* not contradict Browne's careful conclusions about, say, the existence of the griffin or the nature of the amphisbaena; more significantly, it imitates – but in modes appropriate to the decorum of epic poetry – the subtle reasoning behind Browne's conclusions.

Browne's work also helps us see the "poetic" in Robert Boyle's work, Boyle being the leading figure and most prolific exponent of the new philosophy. I will suggest that Browne's style – his way of articulating his doubts and his surmises about the way the natural world had been and was being construed – had an important influence on Robert Boyle's development of a style appropriate for experimentalism. This approach will also allow us to see surprising confluences in the work of Milton, on one hand, and Boyle and other experimentalists, on the other.[28] To maintain a strict division between science and poetry in the seventeenth century, that is, to exclude Browne and ignore Milton, perpetuates a conception of early experimentalism that is anachronistic and intellectually impoverished. Similarly, to exclude Boyle from and ignore Browne in a consideration of *Paradise Lost* is to diminish our conception of early modern poetry and its ability to represent the natural world.

The remainder of this chapter, then, will look at the ways in which Thomas Browne and Robert Boyle shape the ancient trope of the world-as-book to suit their own theoretical purposes. The following chapter will return to Milton, to the implications of what we saw briefly in looking at Raphael's praise of creeping things. I will argue that Milton's way of representing the natural world in *Paradise Lost* is experimental in a double sense. It is based on Milton's devotional practice, his "experimental" reading of the Bible; and this practice, applied to the natural world (God's "other scripture"), is parallel to and cognizant of the scientifically experimental rendering of the natural world evident in the style of Browne, Boyle, and other new philosophers. Milton's poetic style – his "infinite suggestiveness" – is exactly what we should expect of one who advocates an experimental reading of the natural world.[29] For the time being, however, we need to turn our attention to Thomas Browne and to one of *his* meditations on "creeping things."

This passage from *Religio Medici* might well serve as a parable about the interweaving of poetry and early science, imagination and measurement, in Milton's day:

what reason may not goe to Schoole to the wisedome of Bees, Aunts, and Spiders? what wise hand teacheth them to doe what reason cannot teach us? ruder heads stand amazed at those prodigious pieces of nature, Whales, Elephants, Dromidaries, and Camels; these I confesse, are the Colossus and Majestick pieces of her hand; but in these narrow Engines there is more curious Mathematicks, and the civilitie of these little Citizens, more neatly set forth the wisedome of their Maker; Who admires not *Regio-Montanus* his Fly beyond his Eagle, or wonders not more at the operation of two soules in those little bodies, than but one in the trunck of a Cedar?[30]

Browne's version of "small-animal valorization" is imported almost verbatim into the preface of Henry Power's book of microscopical observations, *Experimental Philosophy*.

Who therefore with the Learned Doctor, admires not Regiomontanus *his Fly beyond his Eagle, and wonders not more at the operation of two souls in those minute bodies, than but one in the trunk of a Cedar? Ruder heads stand amazed at those prodigious and Colossean pieces of Nature, as Whales, Elephants, and Dromedaries, but in these narrow Engines there is more curious Mathematicks, and the Architecture of these little Fabricks more neatly set forth the wisdom of their Maker.*[31]

Yet Browne himself derives the example of the wooden eagle and the iron fly of Regiomontanus from Du Bartas's *The Divine Weeks and Works*.[32] From a poem, that is, which has been described as a mine of scientific misinformation, by way of Browne's meditations on religion, Regiomontanus's fly ends up in one of the representative works of the new philosophy.

Among more traditional historians of science, the suspicion lingers that Browne's interest in verbal constructs of the natural world (his own and others') surpasses his interest in the natural world – even though a strict or simple division between *res* and *verba* has long been regarded as an inadequate theoretical frame for understanding the scientific revolution.[33] It is only when we give due weight to "both the 'otherness' of seventeenth-century science and its continued involvement with its past," as Catherine Wilson urges us to do, that we see how clearly Thomas Browne's concerns are precisely those of other early experimental philosophers.[34] Certainly *they* included him among themselves, as the history of Regiomontanus's fly suggests.[35] The way Browne sets out his understanding of how to read the metaphoric book of the world in *Religio Medici* amounts to a statement of his experimentalist principles. He alludes to the trope several times, the first allusion appearing as he reflects on Paul's injunction to the Colossians, "Beware lest any man spoil you through philosophy and vain deceit" (Colossians 2.8):

Beware of Philosophy, is a precept not to be received in too large a sense; for in this masse of nature there is a set of things that carry in their front, though not in capitall letters, yet in stenography, and short Characters, something of Divinitie, which to wiser reasons serve as Luminaries in the abysse of knowledge, and to judicious beliefes, as scales and roundles to mount the pinnacles and highest pieces of Divinity.[36]

Browne urges a careful delimiting of that "Philosophy" which is to be avoided; for *natural* philosophy, he implies, can lead us *to* rather than *away from* God, if we read the creatures wisely and judiciously. He glances at the doctrine of signatures when he speaks of the "set of things that carry in their front . . . something of Divinitie."[37] The phrases which interrupt the main clause – "though not in capitall letters, yet in stenography, and short Characters" – contradict Du Bartas's comfortable assurance that "[t]he World's a Booke in *Folio*, printed all / With God's great Workes in Letters Capitall." The marks of divinity that one finds in the creatures cannot be read with ease, Browne asserts; they are in shorthand and must be deciphered.

Browne supports his central argument, that Paul does not mean for us to shun natural philosophy, by setting the creatures next to the verse from Colossians. That is, he reads the biblical verse in light of these metaphorical verses, employing as his overarching principle of interpretation the conviction that God wishes to reveal himself to humanity. What he means by "wiser reasons" and "judicious beliefes" becomes apparent as Browne develops the trope. Declaring that "Contemplations Metaphysicall" cannot lead us to an apprehension of God, he recommends an alternative route:

my humble speculations have another Method, and are content to trace and discover those expressions hee hath left in his creatures, and the obvious effects of nature; there is no danger to profound these mysteries, no *Sanctum sanctorum* in Philosophy: The world was made to be inhabited by beasts, but studied and contemplated by man: 'tis the debt of our reason wee owe unto God, and the homage wee pay for not being beasts; without this the world is still as though it had not been, or as it was before the sixt day when as yet there was not a creature that could conceive, or say there was a world. The wisedome of God receives small honour from those vulgar heads, that rudely stare about, and with a grosse rusticity admire his workes; those highly magnifie him whose judicious enquiry into his acts, and deliberate research into his creatures, returne the duty of a devout and learned admiration.[38]

The thrust of the passage is announced by the punning *speculations*, which implies the necessity for both a physical and a metaphorical looking into. Browne contrasts here two ways of viewing and hence two

ways of admiring the created world. To gape and stare is to treat *mira* as
miracula; it is to look *at* without attempting to look *into* the natural world,
which constitutes improper admiration. Proper admiration requires on
the viewer's part an energetic attempt to understand. When we inquire
and search into the creatures and articulate what we see ("say there was
a world"), we complete God's act of creating and thus become part of
it. Our conceiving is a creation. The "*deliberate* research" that Browne
recommends suggests a weighing up (from Latin *lībrāre*, weigh). Such
judicious pondering underlies the construing of the natural world in
Pseudodoxia Epidemica and in *Paradise Lost*. We magnify God, Browne
explains, when we *speculate* the creatures, that is, when we collect and
organize our observations and seek to fit them into a pattern.[39]

Browne's abiding distrust of literal interpretation explains why he so
frequently applies the notion of the encoded or hieroglyphic script to the
book of the world.[40] Several versions of the hieroglyph appear in the
fullest exposition of the trope in *Religio Medici*.

Thus there are two bookes from whence I collect my Divinity; besides that
written one of God, another of his servant Nature, that universall and publik
Manuscript, that lies expans'd unto the eyes of all; those that never saw him in
the one, have discovered him in the other: This was the Scripture and Theology
of the Heathens; the naturall motion of the Sun made them more admire him,
than its supernaturall station did the Children of Israel; the ordinary effects of
nature wrought more admiration in them, than in the other all his miracles;
surely the Heathens knew better how to joyne and reade these mysticall letters,
than wee Christians, who cast a more carelesse eye on these common
Hieroglyphicks, and disdain to suck Divinity from the flowers of nature.[41]

Browne's statement that the book of nature is written in "Hieroglyphicks," "mysticall letters," and "flowers of nature" redeems the
trope from what seems at first glance a standard formulation.
Hieroglyphs advertise the necessity for interpretation; they frustrate a
literal reading. (Repeatedly in *Pseudodoxia Epidemica*, Browne finds a misguided literalism at the root of superstition.) But literalism is not the only
danger he discerns in careless reading. He implies a warning about the
semiotic treatment of the creatures that writers like Du Bartas help per-
petuate. For Du Bartas, the creatures are "Letters Capitall"; or, as
Malvolio might say, "there is no obstruction" in knowing what (or how)
they mean. Browne disagrees; the creatures ought to be seen as "*mysticall* letters," as writers of classical antiquity realized. We Christians, he
implies, forget that meaning results from acts of interpretation; when we
assume that meaning is transparent, we deprive ourselves of the true

spiritual nourishment that comes from the labor of re-interpreting. Even the common and ordinary effects of nature are extraordinary, requiring us to exercise deep ingenuity and careful attentiveness when we interpret and articulate them.

Let us summarize Browne's theories about knowing the natural world, as he expresses them tropically in *Religio Medici*, before considering their consequences for the development of an experimental style. Given his critical allusions to Du Bartas's poem, we can assume that Browne's thinking about the world as a book emerges in opposition to conventional notions. These held that the world must be read symbolically; that each creature, correctly understood, stands for a moral quality or points a lesson; that the correct understanding is easily available to everyone. Against the convention, Browne consistently speaks of the encoded or hieroglyphic script of Creation. Although he suggests that to read the script requires diligent research and inquiry, he avoids optimistic claims that we will soon be able to interpret it. He speaks nowhere of a key for decoding nature's cipher.

Browne's opposition to conventional symbolic treatment of the creatures, set out theoretically in *Religio Medici*, is put into practice in his immensely popular *Pseudodoxia Epidemica*, published first in 1646 and numerous times thereafter.[42] The target of Browne's wit and seriousness is the way in which human beings have misconstrued the natural world *because of errors in reading*. Repeatedly he finds that an erroneous notion about the natural world has arisen because a classical or biblical trope has been taken literally, a word has been mistranslated, or a verbal ambiguity has been improperly resolved. What is most apt to strike modern readers about *Pseudodoxia Epidemica* (apart from the sheer "unnaturalness" of the natural world it probes) is the thoroughness with which Browne authorizes his criticisms of vulgar errors. (Surely, we say to ourselves, it must have been *obvious* that an elephant can bend its knees?) What may well have been most striking to Browne's contemporaries, however, is the delicate suggestiveness with which he presents alternative explanations for phenomena that the "vulgar errors" have tried to explain. His style enacts the claim made in the address to the reader, that he is not "Magisteriall" in his opinions – a claim wholly consonant with imagining a book of nature inscribed in hieroglyphs. Since we cannot yet read the inscription, there is no justification for assuming an authoritative rhetorical posture. The fragmentary, piecemeal structure of *Pseudodoxia Epidemica* is in harmony with its anti-magisterial strategy. And because it refuses to pretend to a totalizing interpretation of the book of the world, it exerts an important influence on the development of what Robert Boyle calls a "diffident" style, appropriate for suggesting theories. In other words, Browne's "literary" style – regarded at best an irrelevance and at worst a distracting veneer by generations of historians of science – most clearly marks his contribution to the new philosophy.

We are fortunate, as Rosalie Colie puts it, that "Dean Wren [the father of the architect] had the habit of marking books."[43] Among other marked books is his copy of the first edition of *Pseudodoxia Epidemica*.[44] At the last sentence of Browne's address to the reader, Dean Wren makes a particularly tart comment. To understand what might have provoked the comment, it is useful to look at the concluding paragraph of "To the Reader."

Lastly, wee are not Magisteriall in opinions, nor have wee Dictator-like obtruded our conceptions, but in the humility of Enquiries or disquisitions, have only proposed them unto more ocular discerners. And therefore opinions are free, and open it is for any to thinke or declare the contrary. And wee shall so farre encourage contradiction, as to promise no disturbance, or reoppose any Penne, that shall Elenchically refute us, that shall onely lay hold of our lapses, single out digressions, Corollaries, or ornamentall conceptions, to evidence his own in as indifferent truths. And shall only take notice of such, whose experimentall and Iudicious knowledge shall solemnly looke upon it; nor onely to destroy of ours, but to establish of his owne, not to traduce or extenuate, but to explaine, and dilucidate, to adde and ampliate, according to the laudable custome of the Ancients in their sober promotions of Learning. Unto whom notwithstanding, wee shall not contentiously rejoyne, or onely to justifie our owne, but to applaud or confirme his maturer assertions; and shall conferre what is in us unto his name and honour. Ready to bee swallowed in any worthy enlarger: as having acquired our end, if any way, or under any name wee may obtaine a worke, so much desired, at least, desiderated of truth.[45]

Next to *desire* and *desiderated*, Dean Wren irritably writes, "Whats the Difference?" One suspects that the groundwork for his irritation was laid by the earlier sequence: "not to traduce or extenuate, but to explaine, and dilucidate, to adde and ampliate." Dean Wren could easily have asked his question there.

Simon Wilkin, Browne's nineteenth-century editor, answers the Dean: "By collectors, every thing which they do not possess is classed among *desiderata*, whether *desirable* for its rarity or not: Browne evidently meant to say, that his work was *at least* among the *desiderata* of literature, if not *desired* or *desirable*."[46] It is a good answer – unless the question asked by Dean Wren is actually, "Why use words which are so alike?" That is, "Why use words whose similarity calls the reader's attention to the writer's style, to the very texture of the writing?" Why indeed, especially when the similarity of form almost disguises the difference in meaning? The *OED* attributes to the verb *desiderate* a greater sense of lacking or wanting than *desire* has.[47] By moving from *desired* to *desiderated*, Browne clearly implies that the work of enlarging inquiry (the work that truth desiderates) is still ongoing; it remains largely unfinished. The end of his inquiry, therefore, is achieved *not* if he persuades his readers to accept the opinions expressed in *Pseudodoxia Epidemica*, but if he persuades his readers to prod, try, and question them. Dean Wren's response is thus exemplary. He is provoked into testing Browne's assertion and ends by asking one of the crucial questions for philosophy (natural or otherwise): what is the difference?

Pseudodoxia Epidemica is usually described as an encyclopedia, a Baconian "*Calendar* of *Falshoods*," as if its most important task is to list and label discrete entities, the "vulgar and common errors" of the running title. Browne acknowledges in "To the Reader" that he is "proposing not onely a large and copious List" of "encroachments" on knowledge, but that he is also, "from experience and reason, attempting their decisions."[48] It is important to allow *attempting* its full implication of uncertain success, its emphasis on process rather than result. If we pass it off too quickly as simple rhetorical modesty, we lose an important perspective on Browne's style. (It *is* rhetorical modesty, but it is not simple.) The full running title of *Pseudodoxia Epidemica* is not "Vulgar and Common Errors," after all, but "*Enquiries* into Vulgar and Common Errors." A careful balance is suggested between willingness to designate a tenet as erroneous and wariness in stating why it is erroneous. The persuasive force of the work aims simultaneously at dissuasion and suggestion, that is, it attempts to persuade readers to relinquish one idea and to consider something in its place. Browne's task, like Penelope's, consists of *un*-weaving the philosophical tapestry of the past, picking apart the tissue of false assumptions and deluded commonplaces that covers the natural world and weaving a new *but only provisional* tapestry.

When, therefore, Browne declares in his address to the reader that his style is not "Magisteriall," he invites readers to test or try his opinions. His style supports that implicit invitation. Dean Wren may have been provoked by Browne's distinctive diction – but he may equally well have been amused by it. It is perfectly possible to imagine "Whats the Difference?" being jotted down in a sudden spurt of interest, in a spirit of serious inquiry. The point is that Browne's style is not transparent (that desideratum of Thomas Sprat). It calls attention to itself and by so doing makes it impossible for readers to disregard the constructed nature of Browne's opinions. Moreover, by adopting a style that does not assert but which rather involves his readers in the process of speculating, Browne makes it more likely that they will carry on speculating rather than turning to dogged assertion. (This might be regarded as a particularly innovative version of the cooperative endeavor so favored by Baconian philosophers.)

There is yet another possibility for the tone of Dean Wren's marginal remark: lighthearted jest, a response in kind to the verbal playfulness evident on every page of *Pseudodoxia Epidemica*. Arguably the most distinctive feature of Browne's writing is the discursively sophisticated pun. In *Pseudodoxia Epidemica*, he characteristically exposes worn commonplaces or venerable truths to the judgment of ancient authority, to new information received (not uncritically) from experimenters, observers, travelers, and collectors, and, finally, to his own experience. Then he issues the result of his thinking in a highly concentrated, sometimes oracular, pronouncement: a play on words which simultaneously crystallizes his conclusions and permits an ironic distance from them.

For a brief example, let us return to the question of "going erect" with which the chapter began. Browne's discussion of human erectness in *Pseudodoxia Epidemica* proceeds from the commonplace that "onely Man hath an erect figure, and for to behold and looke up toward heaven" (*PE*, 291). Defining erectness as being "largely opposed unto proneness," he remarks that "in Serpents and Lizards we may *truly* allow a proneness" (*PE*, 292; emphasis added) – all other animals having "some part of erectnesse." Browne then considers two animals new to Europeans, the penguin and the praying mantis.

> And if that be true which is delivered of the Penguin or *Anser Magellanicus*, often described in Maps about those Straits, that they goe erect like men, and with their breast and belly do make one line perpendicular unto the axis of the earth; it will almost make up the exact erectnesse of man. Nor will that insect come very short which we have often beheld, that is, one kinde of Locust which stands not prone, or a little inclining upward, but in a large erectnesse, elevating alwayes the two fore legs, and susteining it selfe in the middle of the other foure: by Zoographers called *mantis*, and by the Common people of Province, *Prega Dio*, the Prophet and praying Locust, as being generally found in the posture of supplication, or such as resembleth ours, when we lift up our hands to heaven. (*PE*, 292)

Browne's point is that if a bird and an insect may also be described as "erect," then we need to reconsider the nature of humanity's erectness.

He promptly does so, arguing that the old commonplace fails to distinguish between standing erect and the ability to raise one's eyes. More dangerously, he implies, it links a literal and a figurative looking upward, but in a facile and hence misleading way. He delicately suggests that to understand humanity's *unique* erectness, the physical action and the intellectual action must first be distinguished. Only then – and only in the case of human beings – can they be merged again.

What is at stake here is a questioning of the ancient and venerable system of correspondences.[49] Given that fact, we can understand why Browne prudently makes his suggestion by means of elegant and serious wordplay:

and therefore men of this opinion understood not Plato when he said that man doth *Sursum aspicere*, for thereby was not meant to gape or looke upward with the eye, but to have his thoughts sublime, and not onely to behold, but speculate their nature with the eye of the understanding. (*PE*, 293)

The pressure of the entire passage focuses on *speculate* (a favorite site of wordplay for Browne), whose full significance – the fusion of physical gazing and intellectual consideration – can be appreciated only after it is understood that the literal and figurative do not *have* to be fused. Other creatures go erect, but they cannot apply reason to what they see. The pun on *speculate* illuminates the doubleness that explains the unique erectness of human beings, a doubleness which consists both of posture and attitude, erectness and rectitude. The pun epitomizes both Browne's point and his mode of proceeding: it constitutes a tolerant, open-minded invitation to the reader to participate in the speculation (about human beings' ability to speculate). For human beings, those great and true amphibians, a pun is the perfect linguistic equivalent.

To dismiss Browne as a lowly herald who prepares the way, or clears the intellectual ground, for one greater (say, Robert Boyle) is to underestimate his importance.[50] In calling attention to the qualities of early experimentalism that have been ignored by grand narratives which highlight the development of objectivity, Catherine Wilson singles out fancy, or even fantasy, an imaginative playfulness that delights in the sensory richness of the world, an almost haphazard bringing together of the *res* of the physical world. "The charm of what Hooke calls the 'real, the mechanical, the experimental philosophy,'" she asserts, "lies in its similarity to child's play."[51] She finds that works like Francis Glisson's *Tractatus de natura substantiae energetica* (1672) and Giovanni Borelli's *De motu animalium* (1681), works of serious biology, are also "reveries," and the

latter, "a fantastic work of the analogical imagination."[52] "Such fancies
. . . can exert an influence," she maintains.[53] Wilson's alternative history
suggests why Browne's experimentalist contemporaries so admired and
imitated him, a fact which has not hitherto been explained by historians
of science. Browne's writing epitomized for his experimentalist contemporaries the union of intellectual seriousness and imaginative playfulness that generated rather than closed off inquiry. That union is one of
the hallmarks of early experimentalist writing, its presence characteristically signaled by passages expressing wonder and delight. From this perspective, Browne's contributions to the development of early science lie
in his distinctive style rather than in spite of it. What *Pseudodoxia Epidemica*
did was to provide a model for a suggestive, non-magisterial style that
could promote debate and ongoing inquiry. The problem – probably the
chief problem – for the new philosophers of the middle decades of the
seventeenth century was that they could not explain all, or indeed most,
of the natural effects they could perceive and describe. How to find a
rhetorical mode that could admit its inability to explain such occult
causes and yet persuade readers to accept its approach to the natural
world was a thorny problem for the experimentalists.

No one any longer maintains that a plain style sprang full-grown from
the head of the new philosophy in the middle of the seventeenth century.
Barbara Shapiro, looking at the changing meaning of *probability* in the
period (from "plausibility" to "likelihood based on evidence"), has analyzed the new demands made thereby on rhetoric. She locates a "linguistic crisis" at the mid-century. "Those who sought knowledge in
experience, matter of fact, and experiment," she notes, "had no agreed
mode by which to communicate their findings."[54] More recently, Steven
Shapin has called attention to the new philosophy's search not for a
single, appropriate style, but for *styles* appropriate to different levels of
experimental certainty. In the 1650s, he notes, Robert Boyle began to
address the problem, eventually suggesting that different styles were
needed for narratives of experiments and matters of fact, on the one
hand, and for hypotheses and theories, on the other.[55] In both cases,
Boyle aims for what he calls "nakedness," that is, transparency, a style of
writing which attempts to represent the mind *in the process of* discovery
and reflection. There are, however, important differences in Boyle's conception of the two styles. The recording of matters of fact requires, he
states, a modest though confident style, "philosophical" rather than
"rhetorical," one which attempts to convey the immediacy of experience
by means of lengthy periods.[56] Putting forward hypotheses, on the other

hand, requires a style much more diffident. He acknowledges, in the "Proëmial Essay" of *Certain Physiological Essays*, that his reader may well wonder

> that in almost every one of the following essays I should speak so doubtingly, and use so often, *perhaps, it seems, it is not improbable*, and such other expressions, as argue a diffidence of the truth of the opinions I incline to, and that I should be so shy of laying down principles, and sometimes of so much as venturing at explications. But . . . having met with many things, of which I could give myself no one probable cause, and some things, of which several causes may be assigned so differing, as not to agree in any thing, unless in their being all of them probable enough; I have often found such difficulties in searching into the cause and manner of things, and I am so sensible of my own disability to surmount those difficulties, that I dare speak confidently and positively of very few things, except of matters of fact. And when I venture to deliver any thing, by way of opinion, I should, if it were not for mere shame, speak yet more diffidently than I have been wont to do.[57]

He revealingly adds that all too often, "what pleased me for a while, as fairly comporting with the observations . . . was soon disgraced by some further or new experiment, which at the time of the framing of those notions was unknown to me, or not consulted with."[58] By 1665, the desire for transparency had become subsumed under the demand for a "plain" style, and the difference between the style appropriate for fact and that appropriate for speculation began to disappear. Even so, Thomas Sprat's translation of "plainness" to mean mathematical precision devoid of metaphor is crudely reductive.[59]

Boyle does not say where he derived his idea for the wary and diffident style appropriate for suggesting hypotheses. Steven Shapin acknowledges, with some reluctance, that Boyle's distinction between a style appropriate for facts and a style appropriate for hypothesis may be Baconian in origin: Bacon had distinguished between a "magistral style," which enforces acceptance, and an "initiatory style," which invites discussion: the former "requires that what is told should be believed"; the latter, "that it should be examined."[60] Browne himself is alluding to the Baconian distinction when he declares to the reader of *Pseudodoxia Epidemica*, "Wee are not Magisteriall in opinions." Bacon's own concise, chiseled, epigrammatic style hardly conveys speculative uncertainty, however, and speaking of *Sylva Sylvarum*, Boyle states that he has "declined that succinct way of writing."[61] It is in *Pseudodoxia Epidemica* that Boyle would have seen a diffident but expansive style in operation. Browne's Baconianism, that is, would have been more usable to Boyle than Bacon's Baconianism. Admiring Browne's learnedness but lacking his rhetorical and linguistic confidence, Boyle "translates" Browne's playful, punning avoidance of assertion into explicit expressions of uncertainty, into "*perhaps, it seems, it is not improbable*" – the last of which has a distinctly Browneian flavor.[62] That Boyle may have found in Browne's writing a model for or at least a respected version of the "wary and diffident" style helps explain why younger experimentalists imitated Browne's style as late as the 1660s, as did Joseph Glanvill in *The Vanity of Dogmatizing* (1661) and Henry Power in *Experimental Philosophy* (1664).[63] Glanvill and Power evidently saw *Pseudodoxia Epidemica* as a work written in a style compatible with Boyle's recommendations.

According to John Harwood, the world as a book is "the most important metaphor in Boyle's writings."[64] Rose-Mary Sargent more cautiously observes that Boyle uses this "common and somewhat paradoxical metaphor" as a "device for justifying his pursuit of science to the theologians."[65] Although her term "device" may query Boyle's commitment to the trope, Sargent goes on to state that it played "an important role in the development of his ontology." His repeated use of the trope, she explains, allows us access to some of his fundamental assumptions about the natural world:

Considered as a text, the world is a coherent, albeit extremely complex whole, written all at once, where all of the parts are perfectly suited to the purposes for which the completed object was designed.[66]

Sargent's view, however, attributes to Boyle something of the physico-theologians' untroubled conviction that it is perfectly possible to see and understand. My reading of Boyle suggests that he is less secure both about the human ability to discern and about the coherence of the world. Perhaps because he had separated himself more decisively than Browne from the tradition of Renaissance humanism, he shows less interest in pushing the metaphoric entailments of "book" and "reading." His use of the trope tends to be bolder, more opportunistic, and less consistent than Browne's. The assumptions about the natural world to which it gives us access are offered with a mixture of excitement and hesitancy, a mixture which is a far cry from the smooth complacency of the physico-theologians.

One of Boyle's fullest expositions of the trope appears in *The Usefulness of Experimental Natural Philosophy*, first published in 1663. He sets it out early in the essay, as if to reassure readers that he is going to propose nothing disturbingly unconventional. That impression is quickly dispelled. Having appropriated Browne's term *hieroglyphicks*, he offers a distinctive and characteristically unconventional version of the trope:

for the book of nature is to an ordinary gazer, and a naturalist, like a rare book of hieroglyphicks to a child, and a philosopher: the one is sufficiently pleased with the oddness and variety of the curious pictures that adorn it; whereas the other, is not only delighted with those outward objects, that gratify his sense, but receives a much higher satisfaction, in admiring the knowledge of the author, and in finding out and inriching himself with those abstruse and veiled truths dexterously hinted in them.[67]

Du Bartas's trope had contrasted the reader "void of Arte" and the reader who "weares the spectacles of *Faith*." Boyle's trope contrasts the artless and the artful reader, or the ordinary reader and the reader trained in natural philosophy. For Browne, the hieroglyphic book of the world is difficult for all readers; for Boyle, who is perhaps responding to the root of *hieroglyphic* (from Greek *hiero*, "sacred"), the meaning of the book is at least partially open to a priesthood of exegetes. This special class of readers is able to find out the truths "hinted" by the text, though they remain "abstruse and veiled."[68]

From this introduction, Boyle moves immediately into a praise of dissection. This is a baffling jump of logic, until one arrives, several pages later, at a further paragraph on the trope, which helps explain why he connects dissection with reading the book of the world. Let us look at the later paragraph before returning to the issue of dissection. Here, Boyle's reflections on the trope are even more tinged with Browne than they had been earlier:

for as (such is God's condescension to human weakness) most of the texts, to whose exposition physiology is necessary, may be explicated by the knowledge of the external, or at least more easily observed qualities of the creatures; so, that there are divers not to be fully understood without the assistance of more penetrating indagations of the abstrusities of nature, and the more unobvious properties of things, an intelligent and philosophical peruser will readily discern.[69]

Boyle wields the phrase *penetrating indagations* as Browne wields the term *speculation*: it works at both a literal and a figurative level.[70] It is as if Boyle has learned from Browne to make his own text embody what he perceives about God's text, that is, that some words cannot be fully understood without a recognition that two layers of meaning are at work. The exegetical method for all God's texts is physiology, or natural philosophy, Boyle declares. But some of them, to be "fully understood," require

"more penetrating indagations." *Fully*, however, is almost immediately
undercut by *abstrusities* and *unobvious properties*. Boyle seems to wish to say
that the difference between the obvious and unobvious, the external and
internal, qualities of creatures is like the difference that exists between
the hieroglyph and its translation (in Browne's formulation), or between
the literal and the symbolic (in Du Bartas's). But he cannot. His *literally*
penetrating indagations elide the issue of interpretation, and in any case
he does not wish to claim that the hidden level is the "real" or more
important one. (That is what the old symbolic or emblematic reading of
the creatures had claimed; once the meaning of a creature was agreed
upon, there was little need for further concern with its physical characteristics.) He does wish to claim, however, that it is the more *exciting* one.

We can now see why Boyle's allusion to the trope is followed by a
passage in praise of dissection:

One would think . . . that the conversing with dead and stinking carcasses (that
are not only hideous objects in themselves, but made more ghastly by putting
us in mind, that ourselves must be such) should be not only a very melancholy,
but a very hated employment. And yet . . . there are anatomists, who dote upon
it; and I confess its instructivenesse hath not only so reconciled me to it, but so
enamoured me of it, that I have often spent hours much less delightfully, not
only in courts, but even in libraries, than in tracing in those forsaken mansions,
the inimitable workmanship of the omniscient Architect . . . now, I confess, I
could with more delight look upon a skillful dissection, than the famous clock
at *Strasburgh*.[71]

Dissection seems to legitimate the claim of a difference between surface
(dead and stinking carcasses) and deeper meaning (the Creator's inimitable workmanship) and thereby evokes a fundamental Western preoccupation. In fact, however, there is no difference in "meaning" between
them. The surface and the inner structure (assuming one could satisfac-
torily separate them) both comprise the mansion. Both reveal the
Creator's workmanship. Boyle has not, one feels, worked out precisely
how the two "levels" are related, but the imprecision is freeing.

The chief rhetorical advantage of speaking of the world as a book
may well be that it allows Boyle to justify his attention to the "abstruse"
phenomena, in which category he includes phenomena that have previously been ignored on the grounds that they are base or common.
Claiming the necessity for a close reading of the book of the world
licenses Boyle to investigate even the "most despicable productions of
nature."[72] The need to justify a very material probing no doubt responds
to profound cultural anxiety. Among the opinions recorded in Samuel

Hartlib's *Ephemerides* is a vigorous expression of disapproval and distaste for this aspect of the experimental project: "To mangle tyrannise etc over the Creatures for to trie exp[e]riments or to bee imploid so filthily about them as to weigh pisse etc as Verul[amus] p[re]scribes is a meere drudgery curiosity and Impiety and no necessity for it."[73] By equating "close reading" with "deep probing," Boyle seeks to disarm such attacks. There *is* a necessity for trying experiments, he maintains; if each verse of the Scriptures demands the studious attention of God's people, then so too does the metaphoric equivalent of each word of God's *other* book. It is a principle that undermines received hierarchies of importance, leaving readers free to find their own patterns.

That we cannot understand each "word," Boyle asserts in *A Free Enquiry into the Vulgarly Receiv'd Notion of Nature*, is the fault of the reader, not the writer.[74] There, in extensive and somewhat labored detail, he explains that the book of the world is an exceedingly difficult text:

And, indeed, the admirable wisdom and skill, that, in some conspicuous instances, the divine Opificer has displayed in the fitting of things for such ends and uses, for which (among other purposes) He may rationally be supposed to have designed them, may justly persuade us, that his skill would not appear inferior in reference to the rest also of his corporeal works, if we could as well in these, as in those, discern their particular final causes. As if we suppose an excellent letter about several subjects, and to different purposes, whereof some parts were written in plain characters, others in cyphers, besides a third sort of clauses, wherein both kinds of writing were variously mixed, to be heedfully perused by a very intelligent person; if he finds, that those passages, that he can understand, are excellently suited to the scopes, that appear to be intended in them, it is rational as well as equitable in him to conclude, that the passages or clauses of the third sort, if any of them seem to be insignificant, or even to make an incongruous sense, do it but because of the illegible words; and that both these passages, and those written altogether in cyphers, would be found no less worthy of the excellent writer, than the plainest parts of the epistle, if the particular purposes, they were designed for, were as clearly discernable by the reader.[75]

Boyle recommends both confidence and humility to the reader. Proceed as if every passage is valuable, he urges, but admit that there are passages you cannot understand. He might well offer the advice to readers of the paragraph above, which seems designed to embody his point: it is necessary to live with indeterminacy, but let that be a spur to the work of understanding – and of imaginative creation. Certainly Boyle's thinking about indeterminacy has generated a new version of Browne's "encoded" text of the world.

This reading practice is profoundly opposed to a symbolic or emblematic reading of God's other book. For emblematists, the function of a creature's physical attributes (observed or imagined) is to point to its meaning. Boyle's reading practice does not allow the "intelligent and philosophical peruser" to lose sight of the creature's body. To study it is to look, literally, at ever smaller, ever more "unobvious," body parts. When he speculates about what dissection and microscopy *might* reveal, when he extends the limits of what is known to an imaginative apprehension of what is not yet known, Boyle engages in something very like poetic creation. The vivid exercise of his imagination occurs precisely at the point at which he admits he does not know or he cannot see. The appeal of his famous description of "those little mites, that are bred in mouldy cheese" in *The Usefulness of Experimental Natural Philosophy* is not entirely dissimilar to the appeal of Mercutio's description of Queen Mab. It has everything to do with what Boyle *cannot* see through the lens of the microscope.

Now let us but consider, how strangely skilful and delicate a workmanship must be employed to contrive into so narrow a compass the several parts internal and external, requisite to make up this little animal; how many must go to the texture of the eyes, and other organs of sense; how many to the snout (which he has, not unlike a hog) and the several parts of it; how many to the stomach and guts, and the other inward parts addicted to the digestion of aliment, and exclusion of excrements; and, to be short, how inimaginably subtle must be the animal spirits running to and fro in nerves suitable in such little legs: and if, as we have observed them to multiply by eggs, the little creatures be hatched in those little eggs, after the manner of divers other oviparous animals, how much smaller than a hatched mite must be a mite upon the animation of its delineated parts?[76]

In sentiments echoing those of Thomas Browne, Boyle avers that *anyone* can admire God's wisdom in "[t]hose vast exotick animals, which the multitude flocks to see, and which men give money to be allowed to gaze on," the verb *flocks* associating the multitude with the exhibition.[77] Such "conspicuous" creatures are worthy of admiration – but not as much as the silk worm and the cheese mite.

Boyle thus inverts, as Browne does, the traditional hierarchy of importance in the realm of creatures, and although the inversion itself had long since become a convention, the specific "creeping things" that Boyle cites are *not* conventional. The theoretical position he establishes by means of the trope of the world-as-book frees him from many conventional assumptions. He clearly feels that certain readers of the created world have advantages over others; training and equipment (e.g., the microscope) count for a great deal. Yet his claims for such readers are surprisingly modest. Boyle himself displays a marked humility before the text of the world, avowing that its every "word" is worthy of his attention, perhaps especially those words hitherto deemed trivial or base. This interpretive democracy results, in part, from the anti-hermeneutical thrust of his writing: he questions the relationship between "surface" and "depth." The questioning carries with it a potential for re-conceiving traditional categories of social and political value. If he and Thomas Browne ignore this potential, John Milton does not.

CHAPTER 3

The place of experimental reading

The earliest human utterance represented in *Paradise Lost* is a demand that Creation declare its Creator. It appears in book VIII as a self-quotation in Adam's account for Raphael of his first moments of life. Upon waking, Adam recalls, he gazed at the sky, looked at the landscape and its creatures, and then "perused" and "surveyed" his own body, "limb by limb" (*PL*, VIII.258–68). His study of the created world leads to his first utterance:

> Thou sun, said I, fair light,
> And thou enlightened earth, so fresh and gay,
> Ye hills and dales, ye rivers, woods, and plains,
> And ye that live and move, fair creatures, tell,
> Tell, if ye saw, how came I thus, how here?
> Not of my self; by some great maker then,
> In goodness and in power pre-eminent;
> Tell me, how may I know him, how adore,
> From whom I have that thus I move and live,
> And feel that I am happier than I know. (*PL*, VIII.273–82)

The self-quotation ends here. The Adam of book VIII resumes the narrative:

> While thus I called, and strayed I knew not whither,
> From where I first drew air, and first beheld
> This happy light, when answer none returned,
> On a green shady bank profuse of flowers
> Pensive I sat me down; (*PL*, VIII.283–87)

The clause in line 285, "when answer none returned," is surprising, for it is not entirely true.[1] Adam himself has answered his question. Tell me how I got here, he charges the creatures, and he himself responds, "by some great maker." But of course Adam has answered only the first of his questions ("how came I thus, how here?"). There are two questions in the passage. The second one – how may I know the Creator, how adore him? – does not receive an answer, not here, not yet, at least not an answer that Adam perceives as an answer.

Adam's first speech, scholars agree, is one of several evocations in *Paradise Lost* of Psalm 19, which begins:

1 The heavens declare the glory of God; and the firmament sheweth his handywork.
2 Day unto day uttereth speech, and night unto night sheweth knowledge.
3 *There is* no speech nor language, *where* their voice is not heard.

Dayton Haskin has traced the intricate steps by which Calvin and other early modern commentators on the psalm developed the "metaphorical possibilities of 'declaring' and 'proclaiming'" and came "to understand the opening verses as a celebration of God's *writing* in nature."[2] The implication of the third verse, which might have checked the optimistic tenor of the first two, was treated in a variety of ways. The interpolated words of the King James Version (indicated by italics), the metaphoric transformation of declaring to writing (making silence less worrisome), and the common conviction that the Fall had rendered opaque what had previously been clear – by these means, notes Haskin, "the commentary manages to evade the interesting possibility that at verse 3 the psalm momentarily modulates into a lament that God's Word goes unheard because of qualities inherent in the cosmic language itself."[3] Milton did *not* evade the possibility, argues Haskin: *Paradise Lost* "represents the world-as-book as having been already difficult to read before the Fall," a fact symbolized, he points out, in the tangled undergrowth and perplexing paths of paradise.[4] We will see that it is symbolized, too, in the "silence" that greets Adam's request for the creatures to declare their Creator.

"How may I know him, how adore" is a question not to be answered simply, immediately, or finally. He who would know the Creator in the Creation, the silence breathes, must embrace a process of seeking, a practice of reading. The quest does not yield an answer; it yields ever-new perspectives on the question. These emerge over time, develop, and change. By the time Adam sings the morning hymn with Eve, he has learned to hear and see the creatures' declaration of the Maker. He and Eve address the sun in the same words he had first used, but to vastly different effect:

Thou sun, of this great world both eye and soul,
Acknowledge him thy greater, sound his praise
In thy eternal course, both when thou climb'st,
And when high noon hast gained, and when thou fall'st. (*PL*, v.171–74)

Adam no longer demands that the sun tell him how to know and praise the Creator. He has read the sun's declaration of the Creator in its rising and falling; he knows that declaring and praising the Creator are one; and he has learned that in articulating the sun's praise, he himself praises the Creator.

Still later, Adam proposes another reading of the sun, a reading which he prefaces by saying to Raphael, "something yet of doubt remains / Which only thy solution can resolve" (*PL*, VIII.13–14). He proceeds to suggest that nature has committed "disproportions" by causing the sun to move around the earth. He thereby implicitly criticizes the Ptolemaic system. Raphael's response to Adam's observations is ambiguous, if not equivocating. It has led critics to state that Milton did not know whether the Copernican or the Ptolemaic system was correct and so could not allow the archangel to declare for either. But in fact, Raphael's reading of heaven is at one with his reading of creeping things: it is open-ended and richly indeterminate. It is indeed structurally unresolvable, designed *not* to meet Adam's demand for a "solution" to "resolve" his doubtful reading (and the etymological cousins make his demand doubly insistent). The opening words of Raphael's response to Adam – "To ask or search I blame thee not, for heaven / Is as the book of God before thee set" (*PL*, VIII.66–67) – are so familiar that one may easily overlook the fact that *ask* and *search* have no object. Raphael commends the *process* of poring over God's book; he declines to halt the process by providing a solution for Adam (which would in any case be *Raphael's* solution).

Milton's representation of the book of the world embraces the entailments of the metaphor in a distinctive way: *Paradise Lost* suggests that the value of God's other book lies not in its provision of conclusive answers but in its openness to constant rereading and reviewing. Pronouncing the "right" answer to the cosmological controversy would make Raphael's reading of the book of heaven prescriptive, and the poem makes it clear that while the creatures have meaning, they do not have *a* meaning. Indeed, the poem represents the book of the world as responding to the same interpretive practices that the Bible responds to, as Milton came to understand them. In a recent contribution to the ongoing debate about the role of Protestantism in the emergence of modern science, Peter Harrison argues that changes in modes of reading the Bible at the Reformation are responsible for the changes in the *metaphorical* reading of the natural world that emerged in the seventeenth century. Protestants' renunciation of allegory in favor of the literal, historical sense of the Scriptures, he suggests, had the unforeseen consequence of cutting short a potentially endless chain of reference, in which word refers to object, and object refers to other objects. The literalist mentality of the reformers thus gave a determinate meaning to the text of scripture, and at the same time precluded the possibility of assigning meanings to natural objects . . . In this way the study of the natural world was liberated from the specifically religious concern of biblical interpretation, and the sphere of nature was opened up to new ordering principles.[5]

This post-Reformation way of reading the world, states Harrison, culminates in the rise of physico-theology, a species of natural theology which finds evidence for the Creator's beneficence in the design of every feature of Creation.[6]

The earliest phase of physico-theology, however, properly belongs to the end of the seventeenth century.[7] When Harrison states that "[t]he rise of physico-theology in the seventeenth century ensured the survival of the medieval image of 'the book of nature,'" he elides a step in that survival, that is, what happened to the trope in the middle decades of the century, as the new philosophy searched for ways to articulate itself.[8] Physico-theology, with its "depths and banalities," slips at times into easy moralizing and labored exposition of the trope;[9] Browne, Boyle, and other experimentalists mint it anew at every allusion. Moreover, the premise that a literalist, Reformed reading "gave a determinate meaning to the text of scripture" is one that must be qualified in the case of John Milton. Indeed, it is essential to recognize the importance that Milton assigned to biblical indeterminacy. The "plain" sense of the Scriptures, as Milton understood it, has a closer relevance to the new philosophy than Harrison's thesis suggests.

In his indispensable study of Milton's interpretive procedures, Dayton Haskin demonstrates how complex and various were Bible-reading practices in the seventeenth century.[10] Among these, the "experimental" reading of the mid-century deserves particular attention. The term *experimental* in this context, Haskin explains, refers to the element of personal feeling or experience that many came to regard as the essential feature of reading the Scriptures.

Associating their religious experience with a dynamic sense that their lives involved recurring tests, people used the word "experimental" to characterize the sincerity and intensity of their devotion. They spoke about the emotional impact of the "experimental" knowledge they got from the Bible and opposed this to a knowledge (sometimes called "historical" knowledge) derived from "mere testimony or conjecture."[11]

Experimental devotion was associated with finding one's biblical "place," that is, with finding a passage of the Bible which offered one, through analogy with one's own condition, the assurance of being elected – or the threat of not being elected. That a "place" could seem to imply the reader's reprobation came to be for Milton *prima facie* evidence that the reader had misapplied or misunderstood the passage. For him, "conferring places," or interpreting one place through comparison with others, was an essential part of experimental devotion.

Haskin locates three stages in Milton's evolving understanding of what the conference of places entailed. From his early assumption that he could understand obscure places by comparing them to plain or transparent places, to the growing sense that obscure places were numerous indeed but could be resolved by appealing to the primary biblical rule of charity (rather than to the traditional "analogy of faith"), Milton came at last to regard the Bible "as a divinely authorized collection of fragments."[12] In this mature stage of his hermeneutical development, while holding that conferring places can "tease out secrets that had long been buried in scriptural texts," Milton acknowledges that the process of interpreting is continual and so accepts without anxiety genuine ambiguity in the Bible.[13] Milton's transformed experimental reading practice embraces indeterminacy, asserting that the attempt to know one's eternal destiny on the basis of a single biblical place is futile and misguided. This new mode of experimental reading, Haskin notes, refuses to "fix meaning but allows for places to play off one another," so that "the truly exemplary person is not the one who achieves an assured position but rather one who refuses to impose a totalizing pattern."[14]

An understanding of Milton's experimental reading of the Bible illuminates his poetry in unexpected ways, as Haskin goes on to demonstrate.[15] He shows that in *Paradise Regained* Mary's pondering "these things in her heart" is an act of experimental devotion: "Milton and Mary alike . . . collect, compare, and recombine texts in a continuing search for meanings that cannot be permanently fixed."[16] He observes that in *Samson Agonistes* Milton declines to provide "a control that fixes or stabilizes the workings of the allusions to New Testament literature" and in so declining, helps "undermine a dogmatic cast of mind by prompting readers to reflect upon the historical limitations within which the biblical texts had come to be written."[17] Turning finally to *Paradise Lost*, he suggests that Adam and Eve are meant to read the world as Milton reads the Word, experimentally. He argues, as we noted above, that verbal complexity is *not* an unfortunate result of the Fall, but that the necessity for interpretation is present even in the prelapsarian garden, signaled by its "shrubs and tangled bushes" (*PL*, IV.176) and its "wanton growth . . . tending to wild" (*PL*, IX.211–12).

The Fall of Adam and Eve is shown to have greatly intensified an interpretive burden that was already there . . . Milton's poem does not represent prelapsarian experience simply as wholeness, postlapsarian as doubleness: doubleness and ambiguity are there for Adam and Eve to encounter from the beginning. They are a constituent of paradise, an aspect of its *copia* and an epitome of the distinctively human "place" which is Eden, a "Wilderness of sweets" offering "enormous bliss."[18]

Bearing the burden of interpretation, he concludes, is represented as a glorious challenge in *Paradise Lost*. We might restate this: to understand that the necessity for interpretation is endless, and that the endless deferring of certainty is necessary, is to understand the condition of being alive. When Eve determines to know absolutely, to fix interpretation, she indeed reaches for death.

The fact that Milton's poem represents the world as a text for Adam and Eve to read has been noted by many scholars, often with a glance at the traditional nature of the trope. But Dayton Haskin's work has made it clear that Milton's attention to the methodology of reading reshapes and revitalizes the trope. Traditional exhortations to read the book of the world mean by *read* something akin to "repeat the lessons learned by rote." The new experimental reading, which Milton makes central to Adam and Eve's life in paradise, demands a creative and ongoing engagement with the text. Thus Raphael does not interpret the minims' script for Adam and Eve; they must interpret it for themselves – and continue to review and perhaps revise their interpretation. Construing meaning is a labor that is coterminous with life. In the postlapsarian world, the labor is sometimes arduous; in the garden of Eden, it is always delightful. *How* delightful has not yet fully engaged the attention of scholars. Adam and Eve's prelapsarian life has, on the whole, been more readily mined for its intimations of mortality than valued as a fully realized representation. Yet when we hurry through paradise to get to the Fall, we miss the extraordinary text which is the prelapsarian world. It is a text which perfectly reflects its historical moment, the middle decades of the seventeenth century, when the mature development of Milton's experimental reading of the Bible coincided with the new experimental philosophy's dramatic and excited opening of "wide vistas" on the natural world.

It is the thesis of this book that the natural world represented in *Paradise Lost* yields its interpretive riches upon an experimental reading, and that comprising those riches are the reveries, discoveries, and uncertainties of experimental philosophy in its first, exhilarating decades. By the end of the century, those parts of experimental philosophy most relevant to Milton's representation of the garden of Eden, the study of plants and animals, had trimmed their speculative sails and retreated into physico-theology; and "experimental" devotion, like many other enthusiasms, was laid aside as a relic of the revolutionary age.[19] But for a brief period in the middle of the seventeenth century, experimental philosophy and experimental devotion coincided and were forged together by a poet who glimpsed in their union a new version of paradise. It may well be that what called Milton's attention to the compatibility of experimental phi-losophy and experimental devotion was the tendency of the former to articulate its project in terms of reading the book of the world. Certainly, in appropriating the traditional metaphor, the new philosophers refash-ioned it in ways that parallel Milton's refashioning of an experimental reading of the Bible. Both sorts of experimentalism validated and con-ditioned the experience of the individual: each assigned unprecedented value to the individual's perspective while stipulating that it submit itself to review and reassessment, that it acknowledge its provisionality and avoid equating itself with the truth, and that it renounce claims to pos-sessing absolute or overarching knowledge.

Such a renunciation opened for Milton many opportunities for the work of the Holy Spirit and the scientific imagination in *Paradise Lost*, as we will see in the following chapters. The animals and plants of the garden of Eden are simultaneously represented as "authorized frag-ments," verses in the glorious book of the world which need to be read experimentally, *and* as the subjects of the experimentalists' investiga-tions, creatures about which natural history was posing many new ques-tions and discovering some new answers. We need now to consider, in turn, the two "chapters" in the book of the world that Milton draws upon most extensively for depicting the garden of Eden in *Paradise Lost*, the two fields of natural history that eventually became known as zoology and botany. The study of animals was not as advanced in the seventeenth century as the study of plants; Thomas Browne devotes more time in *Pseudodoxia Epidemica* to animal lore than to plant lore because the former was more plentiful and more fantastic. There is a corresponding difference in Milton's treatment of animals and plants in *Paradise Lost*. Animals tend to appear more often in parodic and satanic contexts, for the legends accumulating around them may be shown to exemplify superstition and ignorance. Plants, already inscribed in a more naturalistic discourse, are available for speculative and visionary treatment in the poem. Around both animals and plants there was in the seventeenth century a sense of great excitement. As Joseph Levine remarks, it is not entirely inappropriate to use the term *revolution* with regard to natural history, for

across the seas there came in great boatloads, thousands of specimens of seeds and plants, insects and animals, many previously unknown, enough to fill the cabinets and botanical gardens of the collectors with still other new worlds of nature. The suddenness of these discoveries and the consequences to precon-ceived opinion were certainly revolutionary.[20]

Yet, at a time when Europeans were marveling at the strange new animals arriving from Asia, Africa, and America, Milton's representa-tion of Creation appears to ignore them.

There are no dodos in Milton's garden of Eden, nor opossums, flying squirrels, armadillos, or iguanas. Scholarship has not been particularly interested in their absence. Those scholars who have studied the repre-sentation of animals in *Paradise Lost* have concentrated on them as a means of characterizing Satan and Adam. In studies of Satan, critical attention has focused on Milton's use of animal similes and the archangel's enclosure in the body of the serpent. In studies of Adam, criticism has generally limited itself to considering his ability to name the creatures when they pass before him.[21] Barbara Lewalski argues that an understanding of the beasts leads Adam to an understanding of himself: "God brings the creatures two by two before Adam in subjec-tion, and 'endues' him with knowledge of their natures, but Adam con-cludes from this experience that he can find neither happiness nor contentment in the Garden without a mate of his own kind."[22] Elaborating on Lewalski's argument, John Leonard suggests that Adam's growing self-understanding in book VIII depends specifically upon his appreciation of human language.[23] God's invitation to Adam to choose a mate from among the beasts is a test of that appreciation, Leonard explains:

Adam passes the test by holding fast to rational conversation as the true end of language. The animals provide Adam with abundant opportunities to talk about Creation, but this talking *about*, even in natural language, is not enough. Adam wants someone to talk *to* . . . Adam's real trial turns out not to have been the giving of "fit and meet" names to the lower species, but the judging of what is fit and meet for himself.[24]

Lewalski's and Leonard's arguments assume that Adam's naming of the animals has, in fact, little to do with animals. They are deemed to be useful to Milton primarily for the purpose of representing human beings.

Historically, however, "the giving of 'fit and meet' names to the lower species" *was* a "real trial" in the seventeenth century. "Animal" is not a timeless, universal category but a historically particular one. In the mid-seventeenth century, the traditional symbolic construing of animals was beginning to lose its cultural dominance, although zoology as such is unrecognizable in the period. Interest in the animal *body* was initially simply an extension of the interest in the animal's *meaning* and hence was focused on the strange or notable individual. The anatomical study of animals began only slowly to grow in importance during the second half of the century. Michel Foucault dramatizes the change as occurring when *historia* turns into *historia naturalis*. By *historia*, he means the old "discourse of hermeneutics" that translates the "hidden virtues" of animals; by *historia naturalis*, the new "discourse of description" that transcribes their "visible structures."[25] The year 1657, marking the publication of Joannes Jonston's *Historia naturalis*, serves Foucault as a symbolic date for the change. It signifies "the sudden separation, in the realm of Historia, of two orders of knowledge henceforward to be considered different."[26] But the separation was not sudden. Nor does Jonston's natural history belong unambiguously on the modern side of the divide between old and new science. John Ray's critical remark in *The Ornithology*, that we do not need any more epitomes of Gesner and Aldrovandi, "such Epitomes being already made by *Johnston*," suggests that Jonston's work was not seen to be progressive in its own day.[27]

Jonston's *Historia naturalis* is the last in a line that begins with Conrad Gesner's illustrated *Historia animalium*, published between 1551 and 1557. The study of animals burgeoned after Gesner. Inspired by and often dependent upon Gesner's work, a succession of massive, illustrated animal histories appeared over the next hundred years. Medieval bestiaries, modeled on the *Physiologus*, are relatively brief. The animal histories of the late Renaissance, adopting the expansive mode of Pliny and Aristotle, are vast.[28] Those of Gesner, Ulisse Aldrovandi, Edward Topsell – and Jonston – have been called "pandects" and "humanist encyclopedias."[29] Those of Pierre Belon, Guillaume Rondelet, Jacob Bondt, and Willem Piso are briefer only because they confine themselves to a single "species" or geographical area.[30]

The aim of these animal histories is to collect all the available learning on each animal they treat. They are therefore characterized by a complex mingling of *kinds* of information. The descriptions of domestic animals contain detailed and precise observations about eating habits, reproductive cycles, common diseases, and so on. Entries on wild European animals contain observational knowledge and lore in varying proportions, depending upon the degree of fear the animal elicits. (There are more legends about wolves than squirrels.) Non-European animals familiar from classical antiquity and the Bible, especially those which are part of the bestiary tradition, are treated in terms of their inscription in elaborate symbolic systems: "*Hieroglyphics, Emblems, Morals, Fables, Presages,* or ought else appertaining to *Divinity, Ethics, Grammar,* or any sort of Humane Learning," as John Ray notes disapprovingly in 1678.[31] With some exceptions, the entries on "new" animals from Asia, Africa, and America are relatively bare in terms of lore and symbolism.[32] They consist largely of physical description, ranging from the vague to the detailed. The major exceptions – and they comprise an important category in terms of Milton's representation of the natural world – are animals such as the crocodile, which were familiar from ancient and medieval literature, but which Europeans encountered in the flesh in the sixteenth and seventeenth centuries.[33] The clash between the creature of the imagination and the living animal produces some of the most colorful passages in the animal histories – and some of the most extraordinary illustrations.[34]

The heterogeneity of the information contained in the animal histories is epitomized by the mixed provenance of the illustrations. When Foucault claims that "what is *missing*" from Jonston's natural history is "[t]he whole of animal semantics," he ignores Jonston's illustrations.[35] Many of these display, in Foucault's terms, a lingering involvement with the discourse of hermeneutics, as revealed in their rendering of monstrous and hence portentous individuals.[36] A griffin appears at table 49 (fig. 2), although there is no accompanying text for the image, and a martigora, at table 52. Tables 10 and 11 portray several kinds of unicorns or monoceroses. These plates signal the kinship between Jonston's natural history and those of the sixteenth century.[37] Peter Dance, for instance, notes of the plates for Rondelet's *De piscibus marinis* that while some "are good enough for many of the fishes depicted to be identified with certainty," others display creatures such as the bishop fish that "never had living counterparts."[38] Many of the latter were copied from Gesner.

2 Griffin, from *Historia naturalis* (1650) by Joannes Jonston; the hybrid monster in the natural history. Reproduced by permission of the British Library.

They represented creatures that had come to be too familiar to be omitted; the reading public evidently expected to find them in an encyclopedic animal history.

In the more usual case of actual animals, even a fresh rendering based on eye-witness observation does not necessarily replace an outmoded but familiar image, an aspect of Renaissance natural history which William Ashworth's work has done much to illuminate. Copies of Albrecht Dürer's rhinoceros appeared regularly in animal histories until the end of the seventeenth century. F. J. Cole notes that in the second edition of Piso's *De Indiae utriusque re naturali et medica* (1658), a picture based on an eye-witness account was used for the rhinoceros entry, with the comment that the new image corrected the mistake of attributing armor and scales to the beast.[39] Nonetheless, a descendant of Dürer's rhinoceros appears prominently on the title-page, apparently a sort of advertisement of the book's contents. James Ackerman argues that the economics of printing in the sixteenth and seventeenth centuries perpetuated the tendency to use older images. Once an authoritative illustration was in circulation, publishers were loathe to exchange it for a new rendering: "Not only was it easier to reproduce a plate in the workshop than to portray anew a specimen or a cadaver, but this procedure could be carried out by the publisher's blockcutters without recourse to expensive artists."[40] Thus the plates from Gesner's *Historia animalium* were copied repeatedly for subsequent animal histories, including Jonston's. This conservative drag on illustrations became critical when, as in the seventeenth century, knowledge about animals was rapidly changing. Because printers altered texts more quickly than they altered illustrations, the discrepancy increased between the verbal descriptions and the accompanying images, which were often copies of copies of much older originals. William Ashworth observes that the persistence of older images casts at least some doubt on Elizabeth Eisenstein's assertions that printing strengthened the authority of experiential knowledge.[41] Eisenstein argues that "once fresh observations drawn from nature could be duplicated in printed books, they became available to scattered readers who could, at long last, check books against nature and feed back corrections with new observations to be incorporated into later editions."[42] The process she describes undoubtedly occurred for the *texts* of early modern animal histories, but not necessarily for their *illustrations*. The latter might well reinforce traditional notions about an animal even when the verbal description of the animal questioned or disputed those notions.

The appeal of the animal histories is therefore, at least in part, the appeal of the curiosity cabinets and menageries of the period: to gaze in wonder at the strangeness of animals, or, as David Murray explains, "to create surprise rather than to afford instruction."[43] At cabinets like that of the Tradescants in South Lambeth, called The Ark, Peter Mundy remarked that a visitor "might in one daye behold and collecte into one place more Curiosities then hee should see if hee spent all his life in Travell."[44] The animals in such collections were, in Mundy's phrase, "reall, although dead and dryed."[45]

Seventeenth-century English tourists could also see, alive, some of the Asian, African, and American beasts they read about. Wild and exotic animals were kept in the garden menageries of the great Italian princes and held to be among the sights that contemporary tourists could not miss.[46] William Parker assumes that Milton would have done as other tourists did during his trip to Italy in 1638–39. "Doubtless," Parker remarks, "he went to see the Duke's wild beasts."[47] London was hardly less advanced than Italy in the display and commodification of wild beasts. At various times during the reign of the first two Stuarts, wolves, lions, and other great cats could be seen at the Tower; and an emu, a giraffe, camels, and cormorants, in St. James's Park. Still other creatures could be viewed for a small fee in the private homes of wealthy merchants. John Ray mentions that he saw one female and two male cassowaries, or emus, "at Mr. *Maydstons*, an *East-India* Merchant in *Newgate-Market*, brought out of the *East Indies*."[48] Nor should one forget what Charles Raven calls "the large stranded species which found their way into the London [fish] market" – which, if not alive, were only recently dead.[49]

Plants "dead and dryed" and methodically arranged were not easily available for observation in seventeenth-century England, where the *hortus siccus* was relatively uncommon.[50] Gardens and illustrated herbals were the favored means of displaying plants. The plants that the ancient world had possessed, the early modern period coveted. Karen Reeds has spoken of "[t]he labor of collating classical botanical texts with nature [that] flourished in the sixteenth century."[51] This labor continued well into the seventeenth century, and to it must be added the immense project of describing plants of the New World and working out their relationship to plants of the Old World.[52] The labor manifested itself in the publication of illustrated herbals and other books on gardening and cultivation, "roughly five times as many," states Blanche Henrey, as had been published in the previous century.[53] John Gerard's *Herball, or General Historie of Plants*, first published in 1597 and revised forty years later by Thomas Johnson, is perhaps the best-known herbal of this period or any other in England.[54] Gerard's herbal and that of John Parkinson, *Theatrum Botanicum*, published in 1640, were called by the nineteenth-century botanist, James E. Smith, "the two main pillars of Botany in England till the time of Ray."[55] Parkinson's *Paradisi in Sole Paradisus Terrestris* is "the first English gardening book," notes Charles Raven.[56] Published in 1629, it considers in turn flower gardens, kitchen gardens, and orchards, and testifies, notes Raven, "to the development both of plant-breeding and of exploration" in the early modern period.[57] These are merely the most compendious and the most popular of the English botanical encyclopedias circulating in Milton's day. Competing with them in popularity were the herbals of continental naturalists such as Otto Brunfels, Leonard Fuchs, Jerome Bock, Andrea Cesalpino, Rembert Dodoens, Charles l'Ecluse, Matthias de L'Obel, Jean Bauhin, and Gaspard Bauhin.[58]

The labor of collating classical texts with nature and of describing American, Asian, and African plants new to Europeans quickly transformed itself into a passion for collecting. The seventeenth century was an age of curiosity cabinets and herbaria, botanical gardens and *jardins de plaisir*. Not surprisingly, there was a thriving European trade in plants, particularly exotic ones.[59] Enterprising plant collectors such as the Tradescants, gardeners to monarchs and nobles, were as valuable to their patrons for obtaining plants from abroad as for laying out gardens at home.[60] Naturalists, physicians, and apothecaries (who cannot be entirely distinguished) were also enthusiastic collectors and cultivators of plants, for plants were the chief source of medicine in the early modern period and therefore worthy of the most careful study. This is undoubtedly the reason that botany assumed its modern form more quickly than zoology did. The correct identification of hellebore or deadly nightshade mattered in a way that the correct identification of an armadillo did not. Because an accurate assessment of a plant's healing qualities affected people's lives immediately, and because plants were on the whole more easily available for study than animals, the plant lore of the early modern period is somewhat less fantastic than the animal lore. Much of it attests to a desire for effective medicine. The energy that propelled early modern naturalists to search for plants described by the ancients and to bring back "new" plants from Asia, Africa, and the Americas – and their willingness to believe that those plants had properties far superior to the herbs in their own kitchen garden – often stems from a deep and understandable longing for good health.

The reproduction of botanical illustrations made possible by the printing press plays an important role in the identification of plants in the sixteenth and seventeenth centuries.[61] Aided no doubt by the greater ease with which an artist could observe plants, botanical illustrations generally conform more closely to modern notions of scientific accuracy than do zoological illustrations. As with illustrations of animals, however, authoritative illustrations of plants tended to be copied and recopied by different printers until they had lost their resemblance to the originals. Even the best herbals thus contain a mixed assortment of illustrations, ranging from crude to highly sophisticated renderings. Moreover, seriously hindering both the identification of plants and the dissemination of botanical knowledge in the seventeenth century was the absence of a standard system of nomenclature and classification. One of the most striking features of early modern herbals is their inclusion of many vaguely distinguished varieties of a single kind of plant. In many cases, common or traditional names of plants point to imagined similarities between New World and Old World plants, or between European and biblical plants (as far, at least, as the latter could be known). Some common plant names allude to the doctrine of signatures; others embody the symbolic systems (religious, political, and erotic) in which plants had long been inscribed.[62] For the botanically minded naturalist, the seventeenth is a century of what Donald Worster has called "taxonomic chaos."[63]

For the botanically minded poet, however, it is a nominal cornucopia. The exuberant and flourishing profusion of plant names in the period provides Milton with an opportunity to revitalize traditional representations of herbs, trees, and flowers. Paradoxically, the revitalizing is accomplished in *Paradise Lost* by means of a bare and unmodified naming of plants. Precisely *because* they are unadorned, these names release into the poem a rich discursive and cultural heritage, a fact not fully recognized by scholars who speak merely of Milton's compressed, abbreviated, or sublimated depiction of the natural world.[64] In the mid-seventeenth-century confluence of discursive streams, the simplest and hence most unrestricted naming allows the widest reference. Such naming forms the basis of Milton's experimental representation of the botanical natural world, as we will see.

In his *Historie of the World*, Sir Walter Raleigh takes issue with the notion "that by *Paradise* was meant the whole earth."[65] The precise geographical location of paradise was, in the Renaissance, the subject of "furious controversy," as Alastair Fowler notes (*PL*, IV.209–16n).[66] He also notes that Milton "contrives to include both" of the favored options for paradise (in Chaldea or near Mt. Niphates) and "neatly succeeds, also, in accommodating yet another competing theory" (that paradise was "'under the Equinoctiall'"). By excluding none of the favorite possibilities for the location of paradise, the poem avoids committing itself to any of them even as it respectfully acknowledges them. This strategy leaves open – or, rather, is carefully designed not to preclude – exactly the possibility that Raleigh rejects: that by "paradise" is meant the whole earth. The poem does not insist upon this interpretive option. But it is made attractively available by the fact that every plant named in paradise has an eastern and western, an ancient and modern, variety. The plants represented in Milton's garden, that is, grow in the fertile area where the seventeenth century's knowledge of classical and biblical antiquity overlaps with its contemporary experiences and experiments in the New World and the Old. The poem's depiction of cedars and roses, fig trees and balm, results from a careful reconciliation of these discursive empires.

Most powerful of all these discourses is that of experimentalism, in this sense: it establishes a controlling decorum of naturalistic representation. Legends about their fantastic qualities hover around the plants growing in paradise, but they are never allowed to settle. No plant in Milton's garden of Eden, including the tree of forbidden fruit, has magically curative or destructive properties. This is not to say that the representation of flora in *Paradise Lost* is staid or unadventurous. The opposite is true. But paradise is not a garden of rare or unique individuals. The glory of Milton's garden of Eden lies in the way the common and unindividuated tree, herb, or flower comprehends in itself the botanical richness of all ages and climes. This is not the spurious or exaggerated quality imposed upon a plant by lore and legend; it is the uncommon beauty inhering in the common creature, increasingly revealed by the new experimental understanding of the natural world. The political conclusions Milton draws from this new understanding of the botanical world, like those he draws from the new understanding of the zoological world, differ from the political conclusions of many of the experimentalists, firmly established at the heart of Restoration England. Nonetheless, the very freedom with which the poem revitalizes the representation and the significance of the common creature is a sign of the impact of the new philosophy, which is as notable in the mid-seventeenth century for the multiplying of questions as for the promulgation of new theories. In its depiction of the natural world, the poem occasionally plays with possibilities that experimentalism admits it cannot disprove, yet it never strays beyond the bounds set by experimentalism's growing faith in the orderly and rational functioning of the universe. The poem's depiction of the garden of Eden, in short, is governed by the same combination of skepticism and open-mindedness that characterizes the experimentalists' reading of the natural world, and by the same willingness to defer certainty and accept indeterminacy that characterizes Milton's experimental reading of the Scriptures.

The remainder of this book will consider the fusion of experimental devotion and experimentalist insight in the poem's representation of fauna, in part two, and flora, in part three. Part two begins with a consideration of the mustiest bits of animal lore in *Paradise Lost*, lore associated with Satan, before moving on to the animals celebrated in Raphael's account of Creation. Chapter 4 locates in the grotesque serpents of book x the results of a superstitious construing of Creation, of a failure to let the spirit inform the letter of God's other book. In chapter 5, we will see that the satanic griffin and leviathan display the monstrous effects of a non-experimental reading, when fragments of the text of the world are cemented rather than "conferred." Chapter 6 depicts the conventional chain of being as providing both an interpretive principle for reading the book of beasts and a new way of thinking about classification, one of the persistent concerns of the new natural history. In the portraits of the bee and the ant, discussed in chapter 7, we discover the possibility of a reformed natural analogy that applies new experimentalist knowledge to a conventional political construing of creatures. Turning to plants in part three, we will look first at the tree of forbidden fruit and the tree whose leaves clothe Adam and Eve, observing in chapter 8 that experimental reading and experimentalist insight agree in construing both the unknown and the too familiar with scrupulous care. In the poem's unadorned listing of the trees of the garden, considered in chapter 9, we see how the conferring of literal and figurative places magnifies the book of the world. The representation of Eve's roses, re-read in chapter 10 in light of contemporary experiments with color, suggests a transformed symbolic role for the natural world. In the poem's representation of Edenic balm, considered in chapter 11, we are shown the glory and the wonder inherent in the ordinary experience of the natural world.

Let us end part one with another look at "creeping things." Hooke's praise of *"a new visible World"* in the preface to *Micrographia* is often taken to herald the experimentalists' belief that to see is to know, a belief that led ultimately to what David Michael Levin has called the "hegemony of vision." But Hooke's praise of optic lenses does not make an easy equation between seeing and knowing. He acknowledges that that which is seen must be interpreted. To see a structure does not allow direct access to knowing any more than reading words does, for the interpreting mind must represent what it sees. Thus Hooke admits that while his aim has been to discover the "true appearance" of each object and then to make a "plain representation" of it, the process has entailed some difficulty:

of these kind of Objects there is much more difficulty to discover the true shape, then of those visible to the naked eye, the same Object seeming quite differing, in one position to the Light, from what it really is, and may be discover'd in another. And therefore I never began to make any draught before by many examinations in several lights, and in several position to those lights, I had discover'd the true form. For it is exceeding difficult in some Objects, to distinguish between a prominency *and a* depression, *between a* shadow *and a* black stain, *or a* reflection *and a* whiteness in the colour. *Besides, the transparency of most Objects renders them yet much more difficult then if they were* opacous. *The Eyes of a Fly in one kind of light appear almost like a Lattice, drill'd through with abundance of small holes; which probably may be the Reason, why the Ingenious* Dr. Power *seems to suppose them such. In the Sunshine they look like a Surface cover'd with golden Nails; in another posture, like a Surface cover'd with Pyramids; in another with Cones; and in other postures of quite other shapes.*[67]

Understood literally, "*many examinations in several lights*" may describe one of the central tenets of the experimental philosophy; understood figuratively, it may describe Milton's reformed practice of experimental Bible-reading. The phrase points to the difficulty and the excitement of studying a complex, fragmented text, to the inevitable necessity for interpretation and re-interpretation, and to the pleasures of imaginative and disciplined construing in the face of indeterminacy. Experience fully informed by "many examinations in several lights" lies behind Milton's representation of the natural world in *Paradise Lost*.

PART II

Reforming animals

CHAPTER 4

Milton's complicated serpents

The metamorphosis of Satan and his fellows into serpents in book x of
Paradise Lost occurs with a flourish of proper nouns:

> now all were transformed
> Alike, to serpents all as accessories
> To his bold riot: dreadful was the din
> Of hissing through the hall, thick swarming now
> With complicated monsters head and tail,
> Scorpion and asp, and amphisbaena dire,
> Cerastes horned, hydrus, and ellops drear,
> And dipsas (not so thick swarmed once the soil
> Bedropped with blood of Gorgon, or the isle
> Ophiusa) but still greatest he the midst,
> Now dragon grown, larger than whom the sun
> Ingendered in the Pythian vale on slime,
> Huge Python, and his power no less he seemed
> Above the rest still to retain;   (*PL*, x.519–32)

With the exception of the dragon, the scorpion, and the asp, the monstrous serpents in this passage tend to produce some uneasiness in scholars. Chapters 12 and 20 of Revelation have rendered the dragon
commonplace as a figure for Satan;[1] the scorpion and the asp are familiar from numerous biblical verses as images of vindictiveness and
destruction.[2] The amphisbaena, cerastes, hydrus, ellops, and dipsas are,
in contrast, distinctly obscure as infernal figures. Typically, scholarly
uneasiness shows itself by omitting them from critical discussion. Even
Michael Lieb's otherwise full and sensitive treatment of the metamorphosis is silent about the amphisbaena and its fellows.[3] Merritt Hughes,
however, offers a cautious justification in his edition of *Paradise Lost*:
"Like all Milton's serpents, the fabulous *Amphisbæna*, which had a head
at each end, was understood to be real and symbolic."[4]

The phrase, "real and symbolic," is borrowed from Kester Svendsen's
discussion of "imaginary animals" in *Paradise Lost*. "Every culture of the

least sophistication knows the dragon," Svendsen asserts, "and from Beowulf to Milton, English literature accepts it as both real and symbolic."[5] If one agrees with Svendsen that "most of [Milton's] science is traditional and conventional, a literary as well as scientific commonplace," then the presence of the amphisbaena can be explained by noting that the passage in book x echoes Du Bartas's description of creeping things in *The Divine Weeks and Works*:[6]

> Alas, why didst thou on *this day* Create
> These harmefull Beasts, which but exasperate
> Our thorny life? O, weart thou pleas'd to forme
> Th'innammel'd Scorpion, and the Viper-worme,
> Th'horned *Cerastes*, th'*Alexandrian* Skink,
> Th'Adder, and *Drynas* (full of odious stinke)
> Th'Eft, Snake, and *Dipsas* (causing deadly thirst)
> Why hast thou arm'd them with a rage so curst?
> Pardon, good God, pardon me, 't was our pride,
> Not thou, that troubled our first happy tide,
> And in the childhood of the world, did bring
> Th'*Amphisbena* her double banefull sting. (*Divine Weeks*, I.vi.185–96)

If, on the other hand, one construes Milton as being aware that the new philosophy had cast such creatures into doubt, then citing Du Bartas as a source is *not* an explanation for the amphisbaena. It is still necessary to ask why Milton echoes a predecessor in a passage that seems so manifestly to endorse antiquated lore.

Alastair Fowler answers this question in an unexpected way. In contrast to the prevailing critical diffidence about the serpents of book x, he robustly declares that they "are actual species, and M[ilton] is grappling with the problem how Providence can allow them to exist" (*PL*, x.524–26n). Fowler's insistence that they are actual species attests to his desire to salvage Milton for the "scientific" seventeenth century, a project I am wholly in sympathy with. The salvaging, however, cannot be carried out as Fowler suggests. The phrase "actual species" posits as its opposite that which is mythological or fabulous. But divisions between actual and mythological creatures, and even the conceptual basis for such divisions, were still evolving in the mid-seventeenth century. By insisting upon the "actuality" of the serpents in book x, Fowler obscures the history inscribed in Milton's representation. *Amphisbaena* may *now* refer to an actual species, but that is because the ancient name of an unidentifiable creature is being applied to a modern identification.[7] G. C. Druce, for instance, argues that the third-century amphisbaena of

Nicander is the legless lizard "discovered" in the nineteenth century.[8] A convincing and imaginative identification of this sort may validate the zoological acumen of classical antiquity; it may also suggest that at certain points in history, the term *amphisbaena* had a specific physical referent. But it does not necessarily assist us in knowing what a sixteenth- or seventeenth-century writer means by *amphisbaena*. The intellectual problem for the natural historians of Milton's era was that the creatures (sometimes) described with zoological accuracy by (some of) the ancients had been in the intervening centuries almost wholly subsumed under a richly elaborated symbolic system that attached only secondary value to an animal's observed physical characteristics. Ulisse Aldrovandi's entry on the amphisbaena (fig. 3) in his *Serpentum, et draconum historia*, published in 1640 though written some years earlier, reveals that the transition from a discourse of hidden meanings to a discourse of visible structures (to use Foucault's terms) did not happen easily nor suddenly. The entry concedes that the amphisbaena might be any one of the following, depending upon which authority one consulted: a fish; a one-headed serpent that can move forwards and backwards, or whose tail moves as if it were a head; a two-headed "freak" or defect of nature; a naturally born two-headed serpent; or a fabulous legend.[9]

Paradoxically, when Fowler explains that Milton "is grappling with the problem how Providence can allow [such serpents] to exist," he raises precisely the specter of old-fashioned thinking which he is trying to lay. The question Fowler attributes to Milton is essentially the one that Du Bartas asks: "Alas, why didst thou on *this day* Create / These harmefull Beasts, which but exasperate / Our thorny life?" Du Bartas characteristically answers with a moral platitude: "'t was our pride." Neither the question nor the answer is directly relevant to Satan's metamorphosis in *Paradise Lost*. Du Bartas's serpents belong to the earth; they are works of the Sixth Day of Creation. Milton's serpents belong to hell; they are part of what Isabel MacCaffrey calls the "hidden, monster-haunted world of dark perplexity."[10] That difference makes *all* the difference. The passage in book x is not interested in explaining "Why God created such noysome and dangerous creatures," as a marginal gloss on Du Bartas's poem puts it.[11] On the contrary, the effect of echoing the Bartasian passage in an infernal context is to call into question the epistemological status of the serpents.

Some among Milton's contemporaries are explicit in voicing doubts about the existence of two-headed serpents. During his journey to India in 1633, Peter Mundy saw what was said to be a (dead) amphisbaena –

Amphisbæna Greuini.

3 Amphisbaena, from *Serpentum, et draconum historia* (1640) by Ulisse Aldrovandi; "one
 head at both extreames," more monstrous than Geryon or Cerberus.

"vulgarly held to have 2 heads, att each end one," he notes in his journal
– and studied it closely.[12] It "seemd to have 2 heads indeede," he reports,
"both ends being alike; but for all I could deserne, it had but one reall."[13]
Afterwards, apparently reflecting further on the creature as he revised
his manuscript, he made a marginal note of his reaction to Du Bartas's
claims: "In the Commentaries on Dubartas in french in page 267 are
these words, 'Amphisbenae is as much as to say as double marcheur or
going both waies, a serpent supposed to have 2 heads *but not soe*.'"[14]
Thomas Browne, too, considers the amphisbaena a problem worthy of
attention, devoting a chapter of *Pseudodoxia Epidemica* to it.[15] He declares

in the first place that no species whatsoever is known to have multiples of "the principall parts, the liver, heart, and especially the braine" (*PE*, 217). When a plurality of heads does occur, the animal is not "an animall of one denomination; for properly that animall is not one" (*PE*, 218).[16] It is not a species, that is, but an accident. In any case, having two anterior ends is a logical impossibility, and so Browne declares against the amphisbaena: "therefore this duplicity was ill contrived to place one head at both extreames, and had beene more tolerable to have setled three or foure at one, and therefore also Poets have been more reasonable then Philosophers, and Geryon or Cerberus, lesse monstrous then Amphisbæna" (*PE*, 218). The term "duplicity" is one of Browne's punning epiphanies: the alleged doubleness of the monster is a piece of (self-)deception on the part of those who allege it.

Browne's notion of monstrosity in the chapter is complex and sophisticated. Katharine Park and Lorraine Daston have argued that over the course of the sixteenth and seventeenth centuries, there is a clear development "from monsters as prodigies to monsters as examples of medical pathology."[17] They note that along the developmental way, intermediate positions are occupied by the purveyors of wonder books, or "catalogues of strange instances or hidden properties of animals, vegetables, and minerals," and by Francis Bacon and his experimentalist program, which held that "the most penetrating insights into the inner workings of nature were to be gleaned from the close study of anomalies."[18] Browne's discussions of the amphisbaena and similarly dubious creatures in *Pseudodoxia Epidemica* capture another kind of transitional moment before the achievement of the eighteenth-century "medicalization of monsters."[19] Browne's term *contrived*, especially, implies that *some* wonders or anomalies are attributable directly to human invention, the result (if one wishes to be charitable) of human misapprehension. He implies that "monster," as it is a category which must be construed, can also be contested.

Browne thus does not take for granted the existence of monsters in the form in which they are reported to a credulous public. In an extraordinary turn of thought, he implies that there ought to be order and regularity even in monstrosity.[20] Even nature's "Anomalies" or "monstrous productions" must obey her laws (*PE*, 219, 218). The amphisbaena, with a head at each end, does not; Geryon and Cerberus, monsters of poetic fiction, do. The abnormalities attributed to the latter two are those we would expect of a defective birth, Browne argues, and this part of his argument confirms Park and Daston's theory.[21] The abnormalities of Geryon and Cerberus, that is, are normal:

double formations do often happen unto multiparous generations, more especially that of Serpents, whose productions being numerous, and their Eggs in
chaines or links together, (which sometime conjoyne and inoculate into each
other) they may unite into various shapes, and come out in mixed formations;
but these are monstrous productions, beside the intention of Nature, and the
statutes of generation, neither begotten of like parents, nor begetting the like
againe, but irregularly produced do stand as Anomalies in the generall booke
of Nature. (*PE*, 218–19)

Here, "monstrous" means congenitally defective, and "Anomalies" are
"accidentall effects," creatures which cannot reproduce their like and
hence do not deserve the name of a species, or "one denomination."
The monstrosity of the amphisbaena, however, is *not* normal. The
amphisbaena represents an unnatural construing of abnormalities. It is,
in short, a *monstrous* monster.

By the time Milton published *Paradise Lost*, the improbability of the
amphisbaena's existence had been well aired. *Pseudodoxia Epidemica* was
in its third edition by 1658, and though Browne's reflections may well
have set out the strongest case against the amphisbaena, even
Aldrovandi's richly inconclusive entry (and the similarly inconclusive
entries in the natural histories of Topsell and Gesner) constituted a kind
of evidence against it. In Du Bartas's epic catalog of 1567, the amphisbaena is unexceptional. In Milton's catalog of 1667, the presence of the
amphisbaena cannot but attract attention. The occurrence of the creature in book x, in other words, is not innocent.

We need to ask whether Milton's catalog is in fact a parody of Du
Bartas's. Certainly there are other signs of parody. Even Alastair Fowler,
in claiming that "the serpents are actual species," glosses over the fact
that not all the creatures in the list *are* serpents, actual or fabulous. In
contrast to modern editors, Richard Bentley was indignant about this.
Bentley's commentary on the metamorphosis in book x deserves quoting
in its entirety. It raises pertinent questions about natural history even as
it heaps blame upon a non-existent editor:

Our Editor, who for many Pages had in vain sought, where he might intrude
something of his own, found here a fit Opportunity: for the Devils being turn'd
into *Serpents*, he whips into the Text all the Serpents that he knew. But he begins
very unluckily, *Scorpion and Asp*. Is the Scorpion then a *Serpent?* and one of the
Hissers here? If ever he can hiss, it should be now, this ignorant Editor. Ay, but
Ellops drear, an Adjective of Poetical Terror. Not so very *drear* neither: for *Ellops*
is no Hissing Serpent, but a Mute Fish; and one of the most admir'd too, the
Acipenser. He has already discover'd himself: so that we'll leave him, and tack
together the Author's genuine Verses:

With complicated Monsters head and tail:
But still the greatest He, and in the midst,
Now Dragon grown. His Pow'r no less he seem'd
Above the rest still to retain.

Our Editor, instead of an *Insect* and a *Fish*; might have easily had good store of Serpents to fill up with, *Presters, Basilisks, Rattlesnakes*, &c. But had he given the whole List out of *Aldrovandus* without Error; yet it had been all trifling here, neither Learning nor Poetry.[22]

Let us put aside for the moment what is clearly most annoying to Bentley, i.e., the inclusion of an insect and a fish in a list of "serpents," and turn to the "good store of Serpents," which, he claims, Milton *could* have used, "*Presters, Basilisks, Rattlesnakes.*"

The prester and especially the basilisk have an obvious and well-established symbolic reference to Satan. The bite of the prester, associated with a scorching whirlwind, was said to kill by inducing "heat" and swelling. Its poison finally suffocates the victim, Topsell reports, "as it were by fire."[23] The basilisk is more lethal still. Ansell Robin observes that "[i]f any animal has been worked to death in the service of literature, it is the basilisk."[24] The bestiarists report that its hiss, smell, appearance, breath, and touch are all fatal.[25] The crown or crest on its head signifies the sovereignty of the creature, which reigns by virtue of the fact that it frightens away other serpents. Given the clear symbolic usefulness of the basilisk to Satan, we may indeed wonder with Bentley why it does *not* appear in book x.

The other possibility Bentley mentions, the rattlesnake, raises very different representational issues, for the rattlesnake was a New World serpent and precisely identifiable. John Evelyn records in his diary that he "saw at Dr. *Joylifes*, two *Virginian* rattle-snakes a live" on September 19, 1657. They produce their rattling, he notes, by means of "certaine gristly Skinns curiously joynted, yet loose, like the *Vertebra* or back bone; & transparant as parchment."[26] Although he surmises that they rattle in order to warn other creatures away, Evelyn attaches no *symbolic* value to the rattle or the snake. Even Robert Hubert, who manages to insert a bit of lore into his account of the rattlesnake in his catalog of "rarities," makes no attempt to moralize the creature:

A *Boicininga*, or *Rattle Snake*; Nature has formed him with a rattle at his tayle that men might avoyd the danger of his biting; for being once bitten by him, a Man dyes in halfe an houre unlesse he hath of the rattle snake roote, for to apply a little of it to the offended place, and by eating a little of it also.[27]

Bentley's "*Presters, Basilisks, Rattlesnakes*" suggests that he would have preferred Milton's serpents to be either more or less symbolic than they are. One can understand his point. Editors have been able to suggest only faint symbolic appropriateness for the monstrous serpents, or rather, for a few of them. Merritt Hughes, consulting Aldrovandi, suggests that the amphisbaena is a symbol of "inconstancy and adultery"; "the *Cerastes* symbolizes the devil and lust for power"; and the bite of the dipsas induces a thirst "like the thirst of Tantalus in hell."[28] But other creatures in Milton's catalog resist this symbolizing approach, especially the indeterminate ellops. Indeed, a closer look at the ellops soon explains Bentley's indignation at its appearance among a gathering of serpents. Hughes suggests that the ellops is "perhaps originally the swordfish."[29] The editors of the *OED* hesitate. The first definition, on the sole authority of *Paradise Lost*, book x, is "a sort of serpent"; the second definition is "a kind of fish mentioned by ancient writers."[30] Ansell Robin more sensibly remarks that the ellops "is a vague reptile about which neither Milton nor anyone else had much information."[31] After considering the ellops, one feels some sympathy with at least half of Bentley's declaration: the list is certainly not "Learning." But let us assume, *pace* Bentley, that that is the *point* of the list. Bentley, as Christopher Ricks remarks, "has a great gift for getting hold of the right thing – by the wrong end."[32]

If *Paradise Lost* x.519–32 does indeed parody a Bartasian catalog, the parodic element resides in a designed defectiveness. Twentieth-century readers may have some difficulty in spotting the defectiveness of Milton's catalog. Nonetheless, a list of "serpents" in 1667 that lumps together the scorpion, the monstrous amphisbaena, and the mute and inglorious ellops is not a respectable encyclopedic list. It is on the contrary monstrously heterogeneous. Bentley's indignation suggests that readers closer to Milton's own day would have realized that something was wrong with the list. The parodic element here is delicately dependent upon a precise historical context, when new discriminations among kinds of living creatures were beginning to emerge from the welter of encyclopedic collections. To an age that was becoming sensitive to the problem of classifying amphibia and reptiles especially, it was clear that the traditional names for "serpents," which rival a nest of vipers in their complicated writhings and interrelationships, were contributing hugely to the epistemological mystification. The massing of serpent names in book x makes exactly this point. Fowler's statement that Milton "is grappling with the problem how Providence can allow [such creatures] to exist" entirely misses the historical turmoil surrounding their naming and existence. Thus Browne can claim that an attempt to determine "the kinde or species" of the serpent in Genesis is to "continue the delusion of the Serpent" (*PE*, 539).[33] When Du Bartas asks why God created amphisbaenas, his question reflects no anxiety about what amphisbaenas *are*. When Milton, a hundred years later, turns the companions of the Father of Lies into amphisbaenas, we need to think in terms of the construction of fictions and fables.

In a lengthy consideration of the causes of common error in *Pseudodoxia Epidemica*, Browne devotes two chapters to "the last and common promoter of false Opinions, the endeavours of Satan" (*PE*, 58). Browne makes the general point that Satan is "the first contriver of Error, and professed opposer of Truth" (*PE*, 58). Then in a remarkable and difficult passage, he connects the apprehension of the true God with a clearsighted and unperplexed knowledge of the physical world and its laws:

unity is the inseparable and essentiall attribute of Deitie; And if there be more then one God, it is no Atheisme to say there is no God at all. And herein though Socrates onely suffered, yet were Plato and Aristotle guilty of the same truth, who demonstratively understanding the simplicity of perfection, and the indivisible condition of the first causator, it was not in the power of earth, or Areopagy of hell to work them from it. For holding an Apodicticall knowledge, and assured science of its verity, to perswade their apprehensions unto a plurality of gods in the world, were to make Euclide beleeve there were more then one Center in a Circle, or one right Angle in a Triangle; which were indeed a fruitlesse attempt, and inferreth absurdities beyond the evasion of hell. (*PE*, 60)

If, that is, the Creator indeed declares himself in the Creation, then it is essential to disentangle the understanding of that Creation from errors and falsities. Francis Bacon had expressed the principle more polemically in *The Advancement of Learning*:

And as for the conceit that too much knowledge should incline a man to atheism, and that the ignorance of second causes should make a more devout dependence upon God which is the first cause; first, it is good to ask the question which Job asked of his friends, *Will you lie for God, as one man will do for another, to gratify him?* For certain it is that God worketh nothing in nature but by second causes; and if they would have it otherwise believed, it is mere imposture, as it were in favour toward God; and nothing else but to offer to the author of truth the unclean sacrifice of a lie.[34]

Bacon's principle is clear: to "lie," to accept falsities, about the natural world is to deceive oneself about the nature of God.

This principle finds expression in *Paradise Lost*. Satan and his crew, who deceive themselves about the nature of God, are made in book x to embody falsities about God's natural world. The significance of the serpentine metamorphosis is that the fallen angels are *not* inscribed in a discourse of "actual species." They are inscribed in specious actuality, entangled in a discourse of superstition and half-truths. They are the very embodiment of the way human error construes the Creation. These are indeed "complicated" monsters: the past-participial adjective points both to their writhing bodies and to superstition's knotted thwarting of science, the "knowing" of God and the world. Satanic usage perverts the diction that ought to declare and magnify the Creation into diction that confuses, obscures, and terrifies. It is possible that fear is the most debilitating of superstition's many consequences. Complicated and twisted together (as Adam's fears are massed together in a monstrous soliloquy later in book x), the serpents' names have a terrifying sound. But only *en masse*. Considered separately and dispassionately, the creatures are not particularly frightening. The hydrus may be a venomous water snake, as Hughes suggests, but it may also be an otter;[35] and even *dragon* may mean merely a large worm.

As the great dragon, Satan is the very embodiment of error and ignorance, the enemy to what Milton calls in *The Doctrine and Discipline of Divorce* "the industry of free reasoning."[36] The embodiment of course brings Satan into conformity with the Scriptures. The dragon is introduced in the twelfth chapter of Revelation:

3. And there appeared another wonder in heaven; and behold a great red dragon, having seven heads and ten horns, and seven crowns upon his heads.
4. And his tail drew the third part of the stars of heaven, and did cast them to the earth:

The identification with Satan is made explicit a few chapters later: "the dragon, that old serpent, which is the Devil, and Satan" (Revelation 20.2).

As Spenser had done in book 1 of *The Faerie Queene*, Milton connects the apocalyptic dragon to Error in *The Doctrine and Discipline of Divorce*.[37] There he represents Custom joining with Error, a headless dragon, in an unholy union:[38]

To persue the Allegory, Custome being but a meer face, as Eccho is a meere voice, rests not in her unaccomplishment, untill by secret inclination, shee accorporat her selfe with error, who being a blind and Serpentine body without a head, willingly accepts what he wants, and supplies what her incompleatnesse went seeking. Hence it is, that Error supports Custome, Custome count'nances Error.[39]

Indeed Milton goes on to represent the defeat of the dragon of error as the fundamental meaning of the Reformation:

Then was the Sacred BIBLE sought out of the dusty corners where prophane Falshood and Neglect had throwne it, the *Schooles* opened, *Divine* and *Humane Learning* rak't out of the *embers* of *forgotten Tongues*, the *Princes* and *Cities* trooping apace to the new erected Banner of *Salvation*; the *Martyrs*, with the unresistable might of *Weaknesse*, shaking the *Powers* of *Darknesse*, and scorning the *fiery rage* of the old *red Dragon*.[40]

If Milton's prose repeatedly asserts a general connection between error and the serpent-dragon, it also locates idolatry as the iron bridge between them. Idolatry, as reification, implies choosing the static over the dynamic, fixity over process. Such reification, Milton implies, occurs particularly in the use of symbols and signs, even verbal signs, among which are names. Idolizing names stultifies rather than enables thought. Thus in *Of Reformation* Milton compares the citing of authorities to the worship of Moses's serpent:

And heerewithall I invoke the *Immortall* DEITIE *Reveler* and *Judge* of Secrets, That wherever I have in this Booke plainely and roundly (though worthily and truly) laid open the faults and blemishes of *Fathers*, *Martyrs*, or Christian *Emperors*; or have otherwise inveighed against Error and Superstition with vehement Expressions: I have done it, neither out of malice, nor list to speak evill, nor any vaine-glory; but of meere necessity, to vindicate the spotlesse *Truth* from an ignominious bondage, whose native worth is now become of such a low esteeme, that shee is like to finde small credit with us for what she can say, unlesse shee can bring a Ticket from *Cranmer*, *Latimer*, and *Ridley*; or prove her selfe a retainer to *Constantine*, and weare his *badge*. More tolerable it were for the *Church* of God that all these Names were utterly abolisht, like the *Brazen Serpent*; then that mens fond opinion should thus idolize them, and the Heavenly *Truth* be thus captivated.[41]

Reciting the names of Bishops Cranmer, Latimer, and Ridley, Milton charges, has become a substitute for what he explains in *De Doctrina Christiana* is God's demand that we "puzzle out a religious creed" for ourselves.[42] The process implicit in "puzzle out" – a wary but determined, open-minded and ongoing, search – stands in sharp contrast to the confident passivity implied by wearing a badge.[43]

Satan's metamorphosis in book x represents his falling into precisely the error that he himself most encourages: the reification of the sign. He

becomes his own idol.[44] His fate follows hard upon and is a manifestation of his habit of interpreting signs literally. Immediately before his
metamorphosis, he boasts of deceiving man with an apple:

> him by fraud I have seduced
> From his creator, and the more to increase
> Your wonder, with an apple;   (*PL*, x.485–87)

The boast signals what Milton might call "apprehension, carnall" or a
propensity to deny the spirit that inheres in the letter.[45] Satan is an unfit
reader of Creation: to call the forbidden fruit a mere apple attests to an
inadequate hermeneutics.[46] For his denial of the spirit, incorporation in
the (dead) letter is appropriate.

The representation of Satan in book x is thus structured in direct
opposition to what Milton sees as God's mode of representing himself
in the Scriptures. Although "God, as he really is, is far beyond man's
imagination, let alone his understanding," God has helped human
understanding, Milton argues, by providing descriptions of himself in
the Bible.[47] These contain all that it is requisite for human beings to
know about him:[48]

It is safest for us to form an image of God in our minds which corresponds to
his representation and description of himself in the sacred writings. Admittedly,
God is always described or outlined not as he really is but in such a way as will
make him conceivable to us. Nevertheless, we ought to form just such a mental
image of him as he, in bringing himself within the limits of our understanding,
wishes us to form.[49]

Milton's words point to a tension between biblically justified confidence
in imagining God and the need for humble recognition that God is
beyond human understanding. It is a productive tension, in Milton's
view. It yields all the benefits that can be gained from a willingness to
submit figural expression to constant and prayerful reflection. In contrast to its depiction of God, the Bible is more restricted in its depiction
of Satan, interpreting the serpent of Genesis primarily by the dragon of
Revelation. Milton would surely have regarded this single or fused image
as the appropriate figural mode for the adversary of the ineffable and
inexpressible God. Idolatrous reification – the serpent-dragon that drags
its belly in the dust of the material world – necessarily stands in opposition to the God who is spirit. The metamorphosis of Satan in book x of
Paradise Lost is an imaginative rendition of the Bible's portrait of Satan
and the error he represents.

The error has implications for the reader of the poem. Reification construes the material or verbal sign as sufficient in itself, hence "freeing" idolatrous readers from the obligation to reflect, to meditate, to ponder verbal incarnation in their hearts. It is the error that Browne inveighs against over and over in *Pseudodoxia Epidemica*, the error of receiving literally that which was intended figuratively. Thus Browne deplores the fate of the "Hieroglyphical doctrine of the Ægyptians":

although in many things, they exceeded not their true, and reall apprehensions, yet in some other they either framing the story, or taking up the tradition, conduceable unto their intentions, obliquely confirmed many falsities, which as authentick and conceded truths did after passe unto the Greeks, from them unto other Nations, and are still retained by some symbolicall writers, Emblematistes, Heraldes, and others. (*PE*, 56)

Milton knew as surely as Browne did that the fate of the hieroglyphs is the potential fate of all figurative language. The poet (or scientist) who would attempt to delineate "what surmounts the reach / Of human sense . . . By likening spiritual to corporeal forms, / As may express them best" (*PL*, v.571–74), runs the risk of confirming falsities in unfit readers. Browne's defense against the human tendency to reify the sign is to engage in careful, reasoned argument against it, case by case. Milton's is to make its consequences imaginatively visible to readers, so that those guilty of reifying the sign are themselves reified and made to embody their error.

In the fallen angels' transformation into the serpents of vulgar and common error, Milton represents the very mode by which the error of literalness abuses the spirit of understanding. There is a final illustration of that mode in book x, when Adam calls Eve a "serpent" (*PL*, x.867). The insult associates Eve with Satan, implying that the Fall is entirely Eve's fault and excusing Adam from the effort of trying to understand his own culpability. It also shows fallen humanity in the throes of conceiving nature in terms of human characteristics, for nature and human understanding of nature fall simultaneously in the poem. More seriously, however, it shows Adam seizing upon and beginning to reify a metaphor, which (if held to) would destroy the possibility of forgiveness and reconciliation between husband and wife. Precisely this sort of permanent rupture occurs in *Samson Agonistes*, when Samson not only accepts but elaborates the Chorus's description of Dalila as "a manifest serpent by her sting" (*SA*, 997). Samson's response takes up the theme:

> So let her go, God sent her to debase me,
> And aggravate my folly who committed

To such a viper his most sacred trust
Of secrecy, my safety, and my life.   (*SA*, 999–1002)

Construing Dalila as a poisonous beast justifies Samson's violent rejection of her. James Turner has commented on the contrast between this
rejection and the reconciliation of Adam and Eve:

> In the closing books of *Paradise Lost* we follow the painstaking reconstruction of
> trust, forbearance, and mutual loyalty in the face of unprecedentedly destruc-
> tive emotions, and we see two individuals struggling with but resisting the very
> desire that Milton so richly indulges in his other marital writings – the tempta-
> tion to expel and annihilate the other.[50]

Such annihilation is made easier when figurative use hardens into superstitious literalness. In Samson's imagining of her, Dalila herself not only
becomes a viper, but her "fair enchanted cup, and warbling charm"
threaten him with similar, bestial metamorphosis. The error which
Satan embodies, it would seem, is a contagious one: in book x, *all* the
fallen angels are "transformed / Alike, to serpents" (*PL*, x.519–20).

The contagion lies in the delusion that "puzzling out" is no longer
necessary, that the interpretive task can be and has been completed. But
the world with its creatures, like the Bible, is represented in *Paradise Lost*
as a "divinely authorized collection of fragments," in Dayton Haskin's
phrase, and the interpretation of fragments is by its nature never complete and never wholly certain. Reading such a text requires the humility to submit one's conclusions to continual reassessment; without it, the
fragments of the world's text are cemented into immobility, and conclusions harden into superstition.

CHAPTER 5

New uses for monstrous lore

The most dominant zoological feature of the curiosity collections of the sixteenth and seventeenth centuries was probably the animal fragment. Catalogs of the collections reveal a high proportion of parts of animals among the natural rarities.[1] The fact that the Tradescants list their "Whole Birds" separately suggests that these are particularly notable features of The Ark. The *Musæum Tradescantianum* also contains a list of "Beaks, or Heads" of birds, among them a "Cassaway, or Emeu, Griffin, Pellican, Shoveler, and thirty other severall forrain sorts."[2] Collectors of natural rarities in fact often had to make do with "Heads Horns Beaks Clawes Skins Fethers," as John Tradescant acknowledges in a letter of 1625.[3] These inedible parts were not infrequently what remained after a specimen had become a meal on the long voyage back to Europe.[4]

Given the high proportion of fragments in the natural history collections of the period, Giuseppe Olmi urges caution when we find naturalists or collectors claiming to have a creature under direct observation.

In most cases, in fact, they were dealing not with whole animals but with parts of them, often very small and insignificant parts . . . Not only was the naturalist in no position to carry out anatomical dissection, therefore, but he could not even have had an overall conception of the appearance of the whole animal. Hence, in this context the fragment acted simply as a token of an exotic animal, concerning which wider ideas were extremely vague.[5]

Olmi's warning needs to be qualified in the case of fabulous animals. It is precisely because visitors *did* have an idea of what the animal looked like that a collector could display a horn or beak and label it as a unicorn's or a griffin's. The value of such displays relied upon the complicit imagination of visitors. Even in the case of exotic actual animals, collectors and visitors could be expected to have seen images of the creature, images often fanciful and anatomically inaccurate. The problem

99

for naturalists may not have been that wider ideas about an animal were vague, but that they were fixed – and experimentally unreliable. Fragments could easily be construed to confirm the existence of very strange animals.

Fragments could also be used, however, to *check* such construing. Milton's comparison of Satan to a griffin in book I and a leviathan in book II of *Paradise Lost* incorporates the experience of the animal fragment into the poem in a way that debunks rather than confirms superstitious construing. In this way, the poem draws upon and refashions the traditional symbolic richness of fabulous creatures while denying their actual, bodily existence. It is a daring representational strategy, worthy of an "adventurous song," and it makes untenable the claim that its very inclusion of mythical beasts means the science of the poem is old-fashioned.

In book II of *Paradise Lost* Satan is likened to a griffin as he moves through Chaos toward earth:

> As when a gryphon through the wilderness
> With winged course o'er hill or moory dale,
> Pursues the Arimaspian, who by stealth
> Had from his wakeful custody purloined
> The guarded gold: so eagerly the fiend
> O'er bog or steep, through straight, rough, dense, or rare,
> With head, hands, wings or feet pursues his way,
> And swims or sinks, or wades, or creeps, or flies: (*PL*, II.943–50)

Alone among critics in giving any thought to the reality of the griffin, Svendsen argues that "the respectability of the scientific detail is irrelevant" in this and other such passages, "for in metaphor everything is true."[6] By "scientific detail," Svendsen seems to mean the way in which the creature is represented. For him, as indeed for most critics, the griffin belongs so wholly to fabulous legend that questions about its body simply do not arise.

Yet there is much evidence for the seventeenth century's troubled uncertainty about the reality of the griffin. "Griffins," declares Sir Hamon L'Estrange, "are but a Poeticall fiction," yet he mentions having seen a griffin's claw in Sir Robert Cotton's library.[7] Alexander Ross maintains that griffins exist but have moved to inaccessible parts of Scythia and other such regions and so are rarely seen.[8] Jonston's *Historia naturalis*, as we noted earlier, simultaneously declares and disavows the creature's existence, as no text accompanies the plate of the griffin at table 49 (fig. 2). John Wilkins refuses to make linguistic provision "for *fictitious Animals*, as *Syren*, or *Mermaid, Phoenix, Griffin, Harpy*," in his proposals for a new philosophical language, since they are "but bare names, and no more."[9] But the Tradescants' catalog lists a griffin among its "Beaks, or Heads" of birds. Of course, what they displayed could not demonstrate the griffin's reality. A part cannot prove the whole of a hybrid, and parts were all of a griffin that visitors to curiosity cabinets could ever see, a head or a beak in the Tradescants' museum, claws and eggs in other collections.[10] Would visitors have imagined that they were seeing, in the fragment before them, part of a creature with wings and the body of a lion?[11] Or did they understand "Griffin" as an eagle or vulture? When would they have begun to notice that although some collections contained whole pelicans, no collection ever contained a whole griffin?

Even if we assume that by 1667 the griffin had been largely relegated to fable, the propriety of using the creature in a simile is still open to question. Its inclusion in *Paradise Lost* breathes new life into something the new philosophy was struggling to smother. The Great Instaurator himself had set out the principle that metaphor, not even but especially, is obliged to respect accuracy. In *The Advancement of Learning* Bacon warns of the danger posed to knowledge by the persistent repetition of familiar tropes containing outdated and erroneous knowledge. To counter this habit, he urges the creation of "*a calendar of popular errors*": "I mean chiefly, in natural history such as pass in speech and conceit, and are nevertheless apparently detected and convicted of untruth; that man's knowledge be not weakened nor imbased by such dross and vanity."[12] Repeating superstitious and fabulous material about the natural world is dangerous, *even in metaphor*, Bacon declares, "for as things now are, if an untruth in nature be once on foot, what by reason of the neglect of examination and countenance of antiquity, and what by reason of the use of the opinion in similitudes and ornaments of speech, it is never called down."[13] In Bacon's opinion, to use "similitudes and ornaments of speech" containing "an untruth in nature" is equivalent to perpetuating error.

Given the Baconian warning about similitudes and the creature's doubtful bodily existence, it is clear that the decision to compare Satan to a griffin in book II of *Paradise Lost* courts certain risks. Balancing the risks, however, is the griffin's enduring vitality as a symbol, based in part on the creature's malleable moral status and in part on contemporary readers' thorough familiarity with its story. Without clarifying the former, Du Bartas disregards the latter, and retells the story in exhaustive detail in *The Divine Weeks and Works*. His narrative may serve as a model for poetic and scientific outdatedness against which to set Milton's new experimental mode of symbolizing.

> In the swift Ranke of these fell Rovers, flies
> The *Indian Griffin* with the glistring eyes,
> Beake *Eagle-like*, backe sable, Sanguine brest,
> White (Swan-like) wings, fierce tallents, alwaies prest
> For bloody Battailes; for, with these he teares
> Boares, Lyons, Horses, Tigres, Bulls, and Beares:
> With these, our Grandames fruitfull panch he pulls,
> Whence many an Ingot of pure Gold he culls,
> To floore his proud nest, builded strong and steepe
> On a high Rock, better his thefts to keepe:
> With these, he guards against an Armie bold
> The hollow Mines where first he findeth gold,
> As wroath, that men upon his right should rove,
> Or theevish hands usurp his *Tresor-trove*.
>   O! ever may'st thou fight so (valiant Foule)
> For this dire bane of our seduced soule,
> And (with thee) may the *Dardane* Ants, so ward
> The Gold committed to their carefull Guard,
> That hence-forth hope-less, mans fraile mind may rest-her
> From seeking that, which doth it's Maisters maister:
>   (*Divine Weeks*, I.v.713–32)

Du Bartas's griffin is notable for its fierce guardianship of gold, a trait which, however, slides perilously close to avarice here. Indeed, a marginal note at "valiant Foule" – "Detestation of Avarice, for her execrable and dangerous effects" – points ambiguously to both the griffin and fallen humanity.[14] Du Bartas clearly means to suggest that the griffin protects humanity from its own worst impulses. But the passage does not fully succeed in its aim, and it is finally impossible to decide if the griffin symbolizes avarice or the guarding against avarice.

In his *Historie of the World*, Sir Walter Raleigh provides a more scientifically and politically skeptical account of the griffin and the Arimaspians. Reporting what various classical authors have recorded about a one-eyed people, he announces that he believes none of them. Yet he suggests a literal basis for the story, "as all fables were commonly grounded upon some true stories or other things done": "I take it that this name signifying *One-eyed* was first given them by reason that they used to weare a vizard of defence, with one sight in the middle to serve both eyes; and not that they had by nature any such defect."[15] He then refashions the symbolic significance of the griffin legend.

That if those men which fight against so many dangerous passages for gold, or other riches of this world, had their perfect senses, and were not deprived of halfe their eye-sight (at least of the eye of right reason and understanding) they would content themselves with a quiet and moderate estate; and not subject themselves to famine, corrupt aire, violent heate, and cold, and to all sorts of miserable diseases.[16]

His reshaping of the legend's symbolic significance apparently responds to Raleigh's experience of colonial activities in the New World. He is not interested in questions about the griffin's body.

The representation of the griffin in *Paradise Lost*, however, proposes for the creature a new symbolic function based precisely on the monstrosity of its body. Milton's dialogue with traditional representations of the griffin, that is, can be fully understood only in relationship to new developments in natural history, as exemplified by Thomas Browne's treatment of the griffin in *Pseudodoxia Epidemica*. Like Raleigh, Browne suggests for the creature a renovated symbolic role. This represents an important departure from Bacon's principles. Browne brings to his Baconian "rejection of fables and popular errors" a characteristically reforming spirit. Even as he regards his collection of fables with a skeptical eye, he suggests, as Raleigh does, rational origins for them and so partially rehabilitates them. Many fallacies have evolved, Browne declares, from taking literally instances of "Æquivocation and Amphibology" which the ancients meant figuratively: "which enigmatical deliveries comprehended usefull verities, but being mistaken by literall Expositors at the first, they have been mis-understood by most since, and may bee occasion of error to verball capacities for ever" (*PE*, 24). He is especially critical of painters and poets for "trimly advancing the Ægyptian notions of Harpies, Phœnix, Gryphins, and many more" (*PE*, 56) and encouraging humanity to convert "Metaphors into proprieties" (*PE*, 23).

Browne urges a reversal of this process. Unlike Bacon, he sees an exemplary usefulness even for the errors of natural philosophy – once they have been shown to be errors. "[I]mpossible falsities," he argues, may contain "wholesome moralities, and such as expiate the trespasse of their absurdities" (*PE*, 55). The Egyptians' hieroglyphics were originally constructed to convey "hidden conceits"; may they not now be stripped of the falsifying literalness with which ignorant generations have endowed them and be restored again to their status as symbols? Perhaps the "alphabet of things" can be re-invested with significance – if not with its original hieroglyphical significance, then with appropriate new significance. Thus Browne concludes his discussion of the griffin by speculating on its possible contemporary usefulness as a symbol:

So doth it well make out the properties of a Guardian, or any person entrusted; the eares implying attention, the wings celerity of execution, the Lion-like shape, courage and audacity, the hooked bill, reservance and tenacity. It is also an Embleme of valour and magnanimity, as being compounded of the Eagle and Lion, the noblest animals in their kinds; and so is it applyable unto Princes, Presidents, Generals, and all heroick Commanders, and so is it also borne in the Coat-armes of many noble Families of Europe. (*PE*, 200–01)

This survey of the griffin's symbolic potential, moving as it does from ears to wings to torso to beak, arises from what Browne views as its most notable feature and the infallible sign of its fictiveness: its composite nature. His discussion of the griffin, in fact, begins with its composite-ness:

That there are Griffons in Nature, that is a mixt and dubious animall, in the fore-part resembling an Eagle, and behinde the shape of a Lion, with erected eares, foure feet and a long taile, many affirme, and most I perceive deny not . . . if examined by the doctrine of animals, the invention is monstrous, not much inferiour unto the figment of Sphynx, Chimæra, and Harpies. (*PE*, 199)

Browne goes on to make a careful distinction between such hybrid monsters and flying creatures such as the bat, which are "of mixed and participating natures, that is, between bird and quadruped" (*PE*, 199).

Natural hybrids like the bat are creatures whose "parts," as Browne explains, are "so conformed and set together that we cannot define the beginning or end of either, there being a commixtion of both in the whole, rather then an adaptation, or cement of the one unto the other."[17] Browne offers here what might be called a positive version of the mixed creature, that is, a creature which is mixed but not monstrous, for ambiguous or hybrid creatures are usually defined as monstrous in the Renaissance. Recent studies have concentrated on the gradual secularization of the monstrous over the course of the sixteenth and seventeenth centuries, as the term moved from denoting prodigies to denoting developmental abnormalities.[18] But *monster* encompasses a larger and more diverse body of bodies, so to speak, than such studies suggest. The ancient notion of a monster as a creature composed of two or more animal forms – what Browne refers to as "an adaptation or cement" – is

still alive in the sixteenth and seventeenth centuries. "Legged like a man
. . . and his fins like arms," Caliban is, in the eyes of Stephano and
Trinculo, a "most delicate monster."[19] Browne himself mentions
"Sphynx, Chimæra, and Harpies" in addition to the griffin as monstrous
inventions. The term *monster* was also used of actual creatures which
seemed in some way double-natured. Thus John Guillim in his *Display of
Heraldrie* classifies the reremouse, or bat (a "bird" which suckles its young),
with other *"exorbitant Animals* . . . those *Creatures formed* or rather *deformed*
with the confused shapes of *Creatures* of different kinds and qualities."[20]
Guillim includes in this section the griffin, wiverne, cockatrice, reremouse, harpy, mermaid, and "whatsoever other double shaped *Animall* of
any two or more of the particular kindes before handled."[21] It is likely
that Ambroise Paré designates the ostrich and the crocodile as monsters
not because they were rare, as Katharine Park and Lorraine Daston have
suggested, but because they seem to be composed of qualities belonging
to more than one "kind."[22] Such monsters are, unsurprisingly, the same
creatures that most disrupted biblical and classical categories. Calling
them "monsters" is perhaps merely a direct voicing of the anxiety generated by their ambiguous or transgressive status. Browne's careful distinction between the bat and griffin, however, suggests a new way of
approaching mixed creatures. Rather than lumping all mixed creatures
together as monsters, awkward additions to otherwise stable categories,
he in effect divides them into two groups. "Middle and participating"
creatures, like the bat, should be regarded as a distinct kind, as a finished
or perfected part of Creation. But "adapted" or "cemented" creatures,
like the griffin, ought indeed to be regarded as monstrous.

The simile of book II of *Paradise Lost* represents Satan as just such "an
adaptation or cement of prominent parts." We are shown not a whole
body but a sequence of bodily parts: "head, hands, wings or feet." It is
as if, flying through Chaos, Satan becomes dis-composed, exchanging an
integrated form for bodily parts uncouthly stuck together to make a
griffin. The monstrous product of an imagined act of self-creation – we
were "self-begot, self-raised / By our own quickening power" (*PL*,
v.860–61), he claims – he is without form, and spiritually void.

Appropriately, Satan's griffin-like movement through Chaos is heterogeneous and opportunistic: he "swims or sinks, or wades, or creeps, or
flyes," a mixture of modes as far removed as possible from the orderly
and disciplined use of the material world intended by the Creator at
Creation.

> earth in her rich attire
> Consummate lovely smiled; air, water, earth,
> By fowl, fish, beast, was flown, was swum, was walked
> Frequent;   (*PL*, vii.501–04)

Chaos itself is represented as a confusion of elements, an anarchy of factions constantly grouping and regrouping, a disintegrated landscape experienced as a succession of threatening micro-environments: "bog or steep . . . straight, rough, dense, or rare." Rhetorically, the simile is a cement of monosyllables, discrete nouns, adjectives, and verbs.[23] At every level the simile insists upon compositeness, for what turns out to be finally most usable about the griffin as simile is the lack of integrated form. Omitted from Raphael's list of animals brought into being at the Creation, the griffin belongs wholly to Chaos; it "exists" only in the realm of the uncreated, a mass of fragments stuck uncouthly together. By equating the composite with that which is without true form, the simile effectively exposes the griffin as materially or bodily non-existent.[24] In other words, the very proof of the griffin's fictiveness – its monstrous and hence un-real confusion of parts – is the basis of the simile.

Milton's treatment of the griffin suggests a more innovative use of "similitudes and ornaments of speech" than Bacon had envisioned, one which does not perpetrate untruths but analyzes them. In this enterprise Milton is clearly allied with Thomas Browne. But the symbolic use to which Milton puts the griffin signals his political disagreement with the conservative Browne. What Browne views with complacency – that the griffin, "borne in the Coat-armes of many noble Families of Europe," "doth . . . well make out the properties of a Guardian, or any person entrusted" – Milton regards with grim irony. What is called "guardianship" may be instead the rapacious guarding of material self-interest. (In the case of noble families, such material is all too often walled up in mighty palaces, "builded strong and steepe / On a high Rock, [the] better [their] thefts to keepe.") As the griffin pursues his gold, Satan pursues his way, gold and way having been lost through a notable failure of "*wakeful* custody," for neither the griffin nor Satan knows what is truly worth guarding. Griffin and fiend are audacious and fierce, but only in guarding their own good, which is to misconstrue the good. They are greedy guardians, an oxymoron in the economy of the spirit, where avarice is loss.

Kester Svendsen notes the implied charge of rapacity when Milton refers to officials of the ecclesiastical courts as "a corporalty of griffonlike Promooters, and Apparitors" in *Of Reformation*.[25] There is a more apposite reference to the griffin in *History of Britain*. Milton writes there of a human griffin, "*Griffin* Prince of South *Wales*," who, guilty of "frequent inrodes and robberies" and proficient at seizing "much booty" and "great spoils," is a rapacious thief whom "no bonds of faith could restrain."[26] The species of activity at which all griffins seem to excel – hoarding, collecting, cementing, guarding – is precisely what renders the griffin and the noble families it represents *unfit* to be guardians. The simile in book II pointedly undermines Browne's suggestions about the griffin's symbolic role, implying that value does not inhere naturally in things, not even in gold.

Ancient symbol of devotion to other gods, the gold hoarded by the griffin has no absolute value, the simile implies. Value is culturally produced or manufactured. Hence gold in the passage is implicitly reduced to its unrefined, un-formed, original state, "ore." The sound is repeated insistently in the passage: in *course* and *moarie*; in the two contractions of *over*; and in the reiterated conjunction *or* in lines 948–50. Value derives, the simile implies, from imposing shape on the unformed and fragmented material of the world, and that which can be shaped can be reshaped. Milton thus turns the skepticism of the new philosophy to new political uses. With its re-thinking of what had been held to be scientific truth, experimentalism had begun to demonstrate that even the "natural" world is a product of human construing. So too, then, the political world: that which is construed can be reconstrued. The principle is suggested even more pointedly in the comparison of Satan to a leviathan in book I, where the superstitious fictions of natural history are equated with the political fictions of the state, and the value that is construed is claimed to be natural.

In the canto devoted to the House of Astragon in *Gondibert*, William Davenant imagines a collection of relics improbably featuring a whale in the place usually reserved for the crocodile:

This dismall Gall'ry, lofty, long, and wide;
Was hung with *Skelitons* of ev'ry kinde:
... a whale is high in Cables ty'd,
Whose strength might Herds of Elephants controul;[27]

In actuality, collectors resorted to a less ambitious mode of displaying their whale fragments. The small drilled hole evident in the scapula of the Tradescants' whale, surmises Robert Gunther, "probably indicates that the bone was formerly hung up on a wall."[28] The 1656 catalog lists

among the Tradescants' holdings "A Whales skin. tayle. jawes. ribs. back-
bone. bladder. eare-bone. pupilla, as big as a pease."[29] These fragments
were undoubtedly impressive to visitors, since everyone knew what
whales – or at least pictures of whales – looked like. Images of whales
could be found on sign boards, on maps, in Bibles, and among the illustrations of the natural histories. So ubiquitous are they that Thomas
Browne discusses them in the fifth book of *Pseudodoxia Epidemica*, devoted
to the consideration "Of many things questionable as they are described
in Pictures." Browne himself concentrates on the whale's spouting of
water.

According to common pictorial convention, the jets of water spouted
by whales resemble ostrich plumes. Browne muses: "Wee cannot but
observe that in the picture of Jonah and others, Whales are described
with two prominent spouts on their heads; whereas indeed they have but
one in the forehead, and terminating over the windepipe" (*PE*, 416).
Browne's point is that the characteristic spouting of whales is part of
their respiratory system. In the 1658 edition of *Pseudodoxia Epidemica* he
notes with regret a missed opportunity to investigate in detail the breathing mechanism of a spermaceti whale beached "not many years since"
on the Norfolk coast: "The sphincters inserving unto the Fistula or
spout, might have been examined, since they are so notably contrived in
other cetaceous Animals" (*PE*, 262, 274). Unfortunately, the "abomina-
ble scent" of the dead whale did not permit such close examination.
Evelyn's examination of the whale beached at Greenwich in 1658 did
not aspire to such detail, though he marks on his sketch of the whale the
"Tunnells through which, shutting the mouth, the water is forced
upward, at least 30 foote, like a black thick mist."[30]

Milton's representation of the leviathan in book 1 of *Paradise Lost*
seems far removed from Browne or Evelyn's concern with physiological
exactness. As Bishop Newton observes, "Milton describes it . . . partly as
a *fish* and partly as a *beast*, and attributes *scales* to it."[31] The Hebrew word
transcribed as *leviathan* simply denotes a large water animal or sea
monster, and Renaissance scholars debated whether this meant that it
was a crocodile, serpent, or whale. Newton finally, though somewhat
hesitantly, concluded that Milton "took it rather for a *whale* (as was the
general opinion) there being no crocodiles upon the coasts of Norway,
and what follows being related of the whale, but never, as I have heard,
of the crocodile."[32] Indeed, what has been of overwhelming interest to
scholars is the story "related of the whale, but never . . . of the crocodile," that is, the tradition that interprets the leviathan of the Bible as an

allegory of the devil.[33] Roland Frye notes that the tradition was visually reinforced well into the seventeenth century. The simile in book I, it is generally agreed, invokes the tradition and gives it a proleptic twist. Frye explains:

Just as Leviathan lured seamen to anchor on the seeming security of his great bulk, only then to plunge to the bottom of the sea and destroy them, so Satan had already lured his angelic followers to Hell and would so lure many deceived men and women in future ages.[34]

The reason for the mariners' mistake, somewhat obscured by Frye's summary, is that the leviathan looks like an island. The twelfth-century bestiary translated by T. H. White is clear on this point.

The animal lifts its back out of the open sea above the watery waves, and then it anchors itself in the one place; and on its back, what with the shingle of the ocean drawn there by the gales, a level lawn gets made and bushes begin to grow there. Sailing ships that happen to be going that way take it to be an island, and land on it. Then they make themselves a fireplace. But the Whale, feeling the hotness of the fire, suddenly plunges down into the depths of the deep, and pulls down the anchored ship with it into the profound.[35]

Some accounts attribute the whale's sounding to malice rather than to reflex. But they are consistent in blaming the mistake of the mariners on the whale's resemblance to an island, a safe landing place. The emphasis here is thus upon Satan's deceitfulness; he beguiles human beings into a false sense of security and so destroys them.

The leviathan of *Paradise Lost*, book I, however, does not look like an island. Floating on the burning lake, Satan is in bulk as huge as

> that sea-beast
> Leviathan, which God of all his works
> Created hugest that swim the ocean stream:
> Him haply slumbering on the Norway foam
> The pilot of some small night-foundered skiff,
> Deeming some island, oft, as seamen tell,
> With fixed anchor in his scaly rind
> Moors by his side under the lea, while night
> Invests the sea, and wished morn delays: (*PL*, I.200–08)

This leviathan is not covered with grass and shrubs but has instead a "scaly rind." Although scales were attributed to the leviathan of legend, Milton and his contemporaries almost certainly knew that whales did not have scales. A piece of whale's "skin" was displayed at The Ark, and Evelyn reports of the Greenwich whale that it was "black skin'd like Coach-leather."[36] The adjective *scaly* suggests merely the appearance of scales, which is, however, enough to subvert the premise of the legend. Even at night, a scaly or scale-covered hump does not closely resemble a grassy island. Only the strong desire for "wished morn" could sustain such delusion; the deception occurring in this retelling of the story is the self-deception of the pilot. The story is no longer about *Satan's* capacity to deceive. It has become a story about the capacity of human beings to deceive themselves – about, among other things, the devil's capacity to deceive.

The other leviathan in *Paradise Lost*, described by Raphael in book vii, is clearly a whale. But its physical traits are perhaps more unsettling than the "scaly rind" of the satanic leviathan:

> there leviathan
> Hugest of living creatures, on the deep
> Stretched like a promontory sleeps or swims,
> And seems a moving land, and at his gills
> Draws in, and at his trunk spouts out a sea.   (*PL*, vii.412–16)

"Stretched like a promontory" has been taken to be another echo of the legend invoked in book i. But a promontory gets its name from the fact that it projects or stands out. It is a dramatic feature of the landscape, which can in no way be mistaken for an island rising gently out of the sea. The implication of deception has been erased from this passage. The fanciful part of the old lore is not subverted here, as in book i, but simply dismissed, while the underlying analogy (whale/land) is not only endorsed as valid but graphically elaborated.

Undoubtedly, however, the "gills" and particularly the "trunk" of the leviathan in book vii are its most puzzling features (though not even Dr. Bentley expressed uneasiness about them). Their presence in the description appears to make the traditional point, that the whale is to fish as the elephant is to quadrupeds: each is the largest of its kind. In this reading, natural history takes second place to the requirements of symbolic representation. Yet the problem of how the whale breathed was a topic of great interest to Milton's experimentalist contemporaries, as indicated by Thomas Browne's desire to investigate "[t]he sphincters inserving unto the Fistula or spout." To assign a "scaly rind" to a figure for Satan – that is, to assign a fiction to the Father of Lies – seems appropriate. To assign gills and trunk to a whale praised as part of God's good Creation is more puzzling. Perhaps the column of water rising from the spout is being imagined as a figurative trunk. But if that were so, then surely (to emulate Dr. Bentley) "at his trunk" would be "as a trunk"? The

4 Orc, from *De piscibus . . . et de cetis* (1613) by Ulisse Aldrovandi, showing two prominent spouts.

pictures of whales (or whale-like "orcs") that Browne refers to occasionally show creatures having "two prominent spouts on their heads" (fig. 4).[37] Are these perhaps truncated trunks, which Milton reduces to one? It becomes difficult to avoid the suspicion that wordplay is at work in this passage – as if the trunk and gills of the whale are a *jeu de mots*, the verbal equivalent of the whale's *jet d'eau*. Because we remember "the unwieldy elephant," who, to make Adam and Eve smile, "wreath'd / His lithe proboscis" (*PL,* IV.345–46), we assume that the "trunk" of the leviathan, "Wallowing unwieldy" (*PL,* VII.411), is also an external trunk. We are encouraged to make that assumption, perhaps, and then to think again. A trunk can be external, but it can also be internal. In anatomical usage, a trunk is the "main line of a blood vessel, nerve, or other such structure."[38] The whale's main air pipe or trunk is what Thomas Browne means by its "Fistula or spout" (for spouts, too, can be internal).[39] Milton's punning use of *trunk,* that is, conjures up the venerable correspondence between elephant and leviathan even as it incorporates into Raphael's description natural history's latest observations on whales.

Attributing gills to the whale is perhaps understandable in a way that attributing a trunk to it is not. In Robert Hubert's curiosity cabinet, a seventeenth-century visitor could see something called "a finne of one of the Gills" of that "*Whale* that was taken up at *Greenwich*, a little before *Cromwel's* death."[40] Aristotle, however, had stated very clearly that the whale and the dolphin "have a blow-hole but no gills,"[41] and Pliny, associating whales with dolphins, says that the latter "cannot breathe under water."[42] Not that Aristotle and Pliny's is an authority upon which an experimentalist would have built an absolute trust. A fundamental principle of the new knowing, set out by Browne in *Pseudodoxia Epidemica*, is that "a resolved prostration unto Antiquity," and indeed "the resignation of our judgements upon the testimony of any Age or Author whatsoever," is "a powerfull enemy unto knowledge" (*PE*, 40). Browne himself, however, implicitly confirms the assertions of Aristotle and Pliny, for in his discussion of whales, he mentions a windpipe and does *not* mention gills. But what seems on Milton's part to be a disregard for the best current opinion on cetacean physiology is, it seems likely, another play on words. There are at least two possible plays. *Gills*, used figuratively, refers to the area around the mouth, chin, and jowls. Whales might thus be said to take in water through their figurative though not their literal gills. A second play on words involves a different substantive development of the word *gill* (from the Old Norse *gil*, a deep valley), meaning a small tributary stream, the tributary, in fact, of a trunk river.[43] There is a double reason to suppose that Milton might have been alert to this meaning of *gill*. It occurs in a relevant context in a work that he undoubtedly knew, *The Sacred Philosophie of the Holy Scripture*; and the surname of the author of the work is Gil.[44] This is of course Milton's old teacher at St. Paul's, Alexander Gil. In *The Sacred Philosophie*, Gil declares in a simile that "the great rivers are nothing else but the gathering together of waters from many smaller fountains and gilz."[45] Milton's description of the leviathan in book VII may thus be paying a witty compliment to Gil by using his sentence and his name to magnify the image of the whale as a "moving land."

Let us look again at Raphael's description:

> there leviathan
> Hugest of living creatures, on the deep
> Stretched like a promontory sleeps or swims,
> And seems a moving land, and at his gills
> Draws in, and at his trunk spouts out a sea.   (*PL*, VII.412–16)

The hugeness of the whale is dramatically confirmed here. His gills and trunk, with their reference to river systems, allow Milton to image the whale as a wide tract of land, perhaps an entire country or subcontinent, crossed by myriad small streams which flow into a vast trunk river, which rushes finally into the sea. The Milton who imagines such a leviathan is more playful than he is generally allowed to be. This is a Milton who enjoys evoking and then gently debunking an old legend, or planting a compliment to an old teacher in an account of the Fifth Day of Creation, a man who does not mind painting a trunk on a whale for the sake of a pun. If this seems to flout our notions of what is seemly in the serious author of a serious poem, we need to ask ourselves what the alternative is. Is it more farfetched to believe that Milton would carefully elaborate an intricate and topical pun, or that he thought whales had gills and a trunk? The construction of a playful Milton may cause us to have to confront the genuine strangeness of an era long gone, which is unsettling, but the construction of a scientifically backward Milton encourages us to be condescending, if not to the man, at least to the era.

Given the difference in their representation, it is significant that Milton uses the term *leviathan* for both the sea monster in book I and the whale in book VII. Uppermost in both depictions are questions about how to construe a creature enmeshed in superstition, a fact which suggests an implied allusion to Hobbes's *Leviathan*, a work centrally concerned with ideology's construing of the state. Hobbes explains that he drew his title from Job:

Hitherto I have set forth the nature of Man, (whose Pride and other Passions have compelled him to submit himselfe to Government;) together with the great power of his Governour, whom I compared to *Leviathan*, taking that comparison out of the two last verses of the one and fortieth of *Job*: where God having set forth the great power of *Leviathan*, calleth him King of the Proud. *There is nothing*, saith he, *on earth, to be compared with him. He is made so as not to be afraid. He seeth every high thing below him; and is King of all the children of pride.*[46]

John Steadman has argued that Hobbes is drawing upon a minor though well-established exegetical tradition which associated *leviathan* with a multitude of people having a king at its head.[47] But the monstrous sea beast is not irrelevant to Hobbes's title. In the context of his political philosophy, the leviathan can signal that which is the product of human construing, but which is so irresistible as to appear natural and therefore to have God's blessing. Nigel Smith has pointed to the crucial role of artificiality in Hobbes's conception of the body (whether the human body or the body politic). The concept of the artificial or the constructed, Smith observes, is carefully set out and delimited in Hobbes's answer to Davenant's Preface to *Gondibert*:

Beyond the actuall workes of nature a Poet may now go; but beyond the conceaved possibility of nature never. I can allow a Geographer to make, in the Sea, a fish or a ship, which by the scale of his mappe would be two or three hundred mile long, and thinke it done for ornament, because it is done with out the precincts of his undertaking; but when he paynts an Elephant so, I presently apprehend it as ignorance, and a playne confession of *Terra incognita*.[48]

Hobbes "permits the vastly disproportionate representation of whales on maps," Smith remarks, because they are "cartographers' conventions."[49] In politics as in epic representation, Hobbes prefers the artificial to be naturalized. The usefulness of the leviathan lies in the fact that, as a sea-beast of legend, it is not truly natural, so Hobbes can attribute qualities to it which cannot be checked against reality. It is as if Hobbes is metaphorizing a metaphor.

Milton's representation of two leviathans in *Paradise Lost* exposes the basis of Hobbes's strategy, exposes the appearance of naturalness as just that – an appearance. Milton's point is perhaps something like this: the mythical leviathan has some features of the natural (cetacean, crocodilian, or serpentine), but the overall entity is fictional. It has a kind of claim to being natural, but in fact it is monstrous and thus can be mobilized for ideological purposes. The construing of Leviathan is thus a model for the workings of ideology. The presence of the two, deliberately different, leviathans in *Paradise Lost* makes the point that there is nothing "natural" without the mediating work of the human understanding. But precisely because it is necessary to construe in order to understand, we are not limited to those myths that have been produced before us; we can re-form our myths. *Leviathan* may once have meant a multitude of subjects with a king at its head, just as it once meant a treacherous anchorage for our faith. But the mid-century's expanded understanding of the animal body and its focused attention on the process by which that animal body has been made to "mean" liberate new metaphorical possibilities.

CHAPTER 6

From rarities to representatives

> the fiend
> Saw undelighted all delight, all kind
> Of living creatures new to sight and strange.
>
> (*PL*, IV.285–87)

When the Son views Creation, he finds that it is "entirely good" (VII.549); when Satan views Eden's creatures, he finds them strange. Denying that God is the Creator, Satan is bound to be surprised by evidence of divine creativity. "That we were formed then say'st thou?", he demands of Abdiel during the rebellion in heaven. "And the work / Of secondary hands . . . ? Strange point and new!" (V.853–55). *Strange*, that is, measures Satan's estrangement from God; it does not measure God's creatures. The corollary is that the creatures of paradise are *not* strange. This in turn suggests that Milton's representation of them is part of a growing mid-century resistance to parading the strangeness of animals for purposes of profit, prestige, or moralizing.[1] The vogue of the curiosity cabinet was far from over when Milton published *Paradise Lost*, but its role was changing. The fate of the collection owned by Robert Hubert is instructive. In 1666, the Royal Society urged its members to contribute their curiosities to the Society's Repository, where they would be kept "better and safer, than in their own private Cabinets."[2] In the same year the Society purchased Hubert's collection, whose catalog (published in 1664) clearly assumes that readers will find strangeness titillating. On two consecutive pages of the catalog, these entries appear:

A strange horne of a *Virginia Deere*.
A strange horne of a *German* Raine *Deere*.

 * * *

A Male and Female *Barbarouses* heads, either of them are as big as a Swines head; it is a strange beast of the Deserts of *East India* . . .
A strange Tuske of a great Boar . . .

Besides the things above mentioned, there are in a chest great variety of strange
bones, teeth and clawes of many different Creatures.[3]

Strange functions here as an advertisement, the verbal equivalent of
Dürer's rhinoceros on a title-page: it seems intended both to tantalize the
public and to reassure them that they will find in the collection the familiar strangeness of animals. In 1681 the Royal Society commissioned
Nehemiah Grew to draw up an inventory of its Repository. Comparing
Grew's revised descriptions with Hubert's original ones, Michael Hunter
notes that Grew imposes essentially "scientific" criteria "on a collection
which remained inspired by the criteria of rarity and curiosity."[4] Hunter
argues that the movement away from private collections to those owned
and maintained by institutions results from a decline in the popularity of
the "cult of rarity" and an increased valuing of the notion of representative individuals.[5] The latter is fundamental to taxonomy, a project
which would preoccupy natural history for the next hundred years.

If Milton's representation of Edenic creatures is part of a trend away
from regarding animals as strange spectacles, we have to ask why
Raphael mentions the crocodile among the beasts of the earth created
on the Sixth Day. The crocodile is the signifier of strangeness *par excel-
lence* in early modern Europe, a commonplace among the exotica. It is
the last beast of the earth to appear; after naming it, Raphael moves on
to describe creeping things:

> out of the ground up rose
> As from his lair the wild beast where he wons
> In forest wild, in thicket, brake, or den;
> Among the trees in pairs they rose, they walked:
> The cattle in the fields and meadows green:
> Those rare and solitary, these in flocks
> Pasturing at once, and in broad herds upsprung.
> The grassy clods now calved, now half appeared
> The tawny lion, pawing to get free
> His hinder parts, then springs as broke from bonds,
> And rampant shakes his brinded mane; the ounce,
> The libbard, and the tiger, as the mole
> Rising, the crumbled earth above them threw
> In hillocks; the swift stag from underground
> Bore up his branching head: scarce from his mould
> Behemoth biggest born of earth upheaved
> His vastness: fleeced the flocks and bleating rose,
> As plants: ambiguous between sea and land
> The river horse and scaly crocodile.   (VII.456–74)

In this relatively brief passage, Raphael in fact names several "strange" individuals: in addition to the crocodile, there are four great cats (lion, lynx, leopard, tiger), an elephant, and a hippopotamus. The passage, that is, does not mount an obvious challenge to the cult of rarity or to other features of a traditional picture of Creation. It does not mount an *obvious* challenge. But the challenge is there, if we choose to highlight it. Milton writes the (represented) book of the world as he understood the Bible to have been written: to encourage "experimental" reading, that is, ceaseless interpretive activity, the conferring of places, and the acceptance of indeterminacy. Raphael's natural history can be read as confirming conventional ideas; more interestingly, it can be read as questioning them. A reader who chooses the first interpretive option does not lose anything. (Both interpretive options are founded on and lead to a fundamental truth, that the world has been created for the good of humankind by a beneficent Creator.) The question is not what would be lost, but what would not be gained, from a conventional reading of the book of the world. Let us return to the passage above and ask why Raphael names certain individuals, particularly the crocodile. Before we do so, however, we need to know what Raphael means by his "scaly crocodile." As Lepidus puts it, "What manner o'thing is your crocodile?"[6]

The crocodile was ubiquitous in sixteenth- and seventeenth-century collections of rarities.[7] Indeed, pieces of crocodile hide from the Tradescants' exhibits are still in existence.[8] In prints included in the catalogs of many collections, the crocodile is often the most prominent creature in the room, usually depicted hanging from the ceiling, as in the frontispiece to the catalog of Ferrante Imperato's collection in Naples (fig. 5).[9] John Evelyn visited Imperato's collection in February, 1645, and mentions in his diary the "extraordinary great Crocodile" he saw there.[10] In Renaissance animal encyclopedias, the crocodile always occupies an important place – no matter where that place is. There was much uncertainty about how to classify the creature. Gesner and Aldrovandi place it in the second category of quadrupeds, among the oviparous beasts. Though he follows Gesner in so much else, Topsell disregards this category altogether. Evidently thinking of it as a "creeping thing" in shape and movement, he classes the crocodile with "Serpents," along with other "non-blooded" creatures such as the bee, the chameleon, the toad, and the earthworm.[11] Among the hexameral poets, Tasso lumps the crocodile (as well as the hippopotamus) with fish, placing its creation on the Fifth Day, when the water was told to generate life.[12] Du Bartas assigns the crocodile's creation to the Sixth Day, calling it a "Serpent"

5 *Dell'historia naturale* (1599) by Ferrante Imperato, frontispiece, showing the
"extraordinary greate Crocodile" seen by John Evelyn.

and, clearly impressed by its ferocity, groups it with such other noxious
creepers as the dragon, scorpion, and viper.[13]
   The writers of Renaissance natural histories may be said to organize
rather than to classify the animal world. By the middle of the seventeenth century, the organization was in some disarray. Zoological
classification traces its early modern origins to the publication of John
Ray's *Ornithology* in 1676 and his work on fish, mammals, and insects in
the following two decades.[14] "With extraordinary sagacity," notes
William Wightman, "[Ray] recognized the feet and the teeth [of
mammals] as having the greatest significance."[15] Whereas Ray devised
a definition of *species*, Renaissance encyclopedists, remarks Ernst Mayr,
had been concerned with "what we would now call behavior and
ecology," i.e., adaption to habitat.[16] If the moralizing tradition of the
bestiaries is responsible for the emphasis on animal behavior, as Mayr
claims, then the first chapter of Genesis and Aristotle's *Historia animalium*
are responsible for the emphasis on ecology. Genesis's division of
animals into those of water, air, and land (the latter comprising two
kinds, beasts and creeping things) neatly coincides with Aristotle's

emphasis upon the four elements (the element of fire playing a negligible role in classical animal ecology).[17] Renaissance naturalists could hardly be expected to ignore this confluence of authority. From Gesner to Aldrovandi, they typically borrow Aristotle's distinctions – between "blooded" (viviparous quadrupeds, oviparous quadrupeds, birds, whales, fish, and serpents) and "nonblooded" animals (insects and most kinds of marine animals) – for the major subdivisions of their natural histories.[18] Below the level of these taxa, however, organizational diversity flourishes. Two schemes appear with some frequency: alphabetical arrangements, and arrangements based on an animal's importance, as indicated by its size, rarity, or symbolic meaning. Gesner puts his viviparous quadrupeds in strict alphabetical order. Aldrovandi begins with the lion, follows it with the leopard, lynx, and tiger, then moves on to the bear, wolf, gulo, and hippopotamus.[19] His *Ornithologia*, eccentrically organized even by Renaissance standards, uses such categories as birds of mixed nature (including the bat), legendary birds (including the sphinx), birds that sing sweetly, water birds, and birds with hard beaks.

The fact that John Ray rejects Aristotle's division into oviparous and viviparous animals – "because in the strict sense all animals come from eggs" – gives some indication of his boldness in reforming the classificatory chaos of the late Renaissance.[20] Remarkably, Ray combines devout Christian belief with an apparently untroubled independence from the zoological tradition based on Genesis. Cuvier's claim that he was "the first zoologist to make use of comparative anatomy" is fully justified, remarks Charles Raven.[21] Ray proposed classifying animals according to differences in their respiratory systems, though he was willing, Raven notes, to accept the traditional division into "Land-animals, Birds, Fishes, Insects." But he "definitely condemns that into Land-animals, Water-animals and Amphibians" on the grounds that the latter "unite what ought to be separated and separate what obviously belong together."[22] Ray thus observes that whales, conventionally grouped with fish, "evidently agree with viviparous Quadrupeds in everything except hair, feet and the element in which they live."[23] This is to say that the whale is not a water-animal but a land-animal who happens to dwell in the water, a conception which figuratively releases the whale from the habitat to which it had been confined for centuries.

Raphael's narrative of Creation can be demonstrated to share the impulse (though not the method) of Ray's new system of classification: it separates what ought to be separated, and unites what ought to be united. The grounds for this assertion are not self-evident. Raphael's

naming of strange individual beasts, in an overall structure based on biblical divisions (fish of the sea, fowl of the air, beasts and creeping things
of the earth), appears to depend on the two concerns that Mayr
identifies with the "old" natural history, behavior and ecology. These
concerns spectacularly coincide in the crocodile. In addition to its indeterminate species, the crocodile was attractive to Renaissance naturalists
for its eccentric behavior, known from the literature of classical antiquity
and the tradition of the bestiaries. The crocodile came to western
Europe richly draped in lore: 'twas "a strange serpent" indeed, as
Lepidus concludes. The opportunity to see it in the flesh, albeit dried,
must have been irresistible. Everyone knew of the crocodile's rapacious
cruelty and its hypocritical tears, of its teeth and its tonguelessness, of
"the little Bird *trochilus*" and the wily ichneumon.[24] The hexameralists
felt obliged to draw a moral from the tale. Thus Du Bartas, recounting
at some length the stratagem by which the ichneumon safely enters the
crocodile's mouth and proceeds to gnaw his entrails, concludes: "(good
Lord) th'hast taught Mankind a Reason / To draw life out of Death, and
Health from Poyson" (*Divine Weeks*, I.vi.283–84).

The crocodile of *Paradise Lost*, book VII, resembles Du Bartas's crocodile only in the epithet "scaly." Otherwise, it has been stripped of lore and
lessons.[25] While Du Bartas requires a thousand lines to rehearse the standard eccentricities of the creatures, Milton requires a little over a hundred
for Raphael's "abbreviated catalogue," as Arnold Williams has called it.[26]
Elaborating on his comment, Barbara Lewalski describes Raphael's
account of Creation as "a brief hexaemeral epic," which "eschews the
lengthy catalogues and the encyclopedic lore characteristic of the genre,
offering instead a sharply focused description of the wonders and pro-
cesses of creation."[27] But the historical as well as the formal significance
of the brevity needs to be recognized. For this recognition, a Foucauldian
notion of rupture is not sufficiently historical. We need instead to think
about the consequences for representation when epistemes collide.
Traditional lore does not simply disappear from the representation of
animals as overripe fruit drops off a tree. The shape and pressure of what
Milton refrains from saying can still be felt in Raphael's Creation narrative. To respond to the layered richness of the text, we need to acknowledge both that the lore is no longer present and that its penumbra is. To
choose as the culminating beast the crocodile, whose story every seventeenth-century reader knows, and then to refer solely and briefly to its
ecology, "ambiguous between sea and land," is to produce a line of verse
heavy with significance both for what is said and for what is not said.

Raphael attributes to the crocodile a dual allegiance to land and water, an allegiance also attributed to the "river horse," the etymological meaning of *hippopotamus*. We recall that John Ray disliked the imprecision of the category "amphibians." For the old natural history, the category was essential; transitional creatures were necessary to make the scale of nature continuous. A. O. Lovejoy explains the genesis of the Great Chain of Being as lying in the fusion of the Platonic notion of the world's fullness with the Aristotelian notion of continuity.[28] What Lovejoy named the "principle of plenitude" dictates that *every* rung of the ladder of Creation must be occupied.[29] The crocodile epitomizes the transitional creature for Renaissance natural history, and Raphael's list, which saves the crocodile for last and draws pointed attention to its doubleness, apparently endorses the notion of plenitude and, by implication, the traditional, hierarchical scale of nature. We will return later to the scale of nature. First, we need to look more closely at the crocodile as the exemplar of nature's plenitude. That reading is available, perhaps *too* available. The crocodile's double role seems overdetermined. It is both amphibious and ambiguous; it is paired with another amphibious ambiguity (or oxymoron), the "river horse"; by virtue of its position in Raphael's list, it is ambiguous not only between sea and land but also between beast and creeping thing. Its very name can be applied to amphibious and non-amphibious species, to *Crocodilus vulgaris* or to what Topsell calls "the land Crocodile of *Bresilia*" (clearly a lizard) and "the Crocodile of the Earth called *Scincus*, a Skink."[30]

A closer look at Raphael's account of the Fifth and Sixth Days' work reveals that a merging or reconciliation of water, air, and land – whether literal or figurative – is the norm for most of the creatures. Prominent in Raphael's description of "the fowls of the air" are the water fowl. We first see the swan, for example, as she "rows her state" in lakes and rivers; only then do we read that, deciding to "quit / The dank," she "tower[s] / The mid aerial sky" (*PL*, vii.438–42). In the description of the leviathan, a figurative coalescing of sea, land, *and* air occurs: tempesting the ocean, the leviathan moves in the sea like a continent, spouting out another sea (*PL*, vii.412–16). Its "gills" and "trunk" connect it with fish of the sea and beasts of the earth (elephants).[31] A more subdued and perhaps more unexpected figure of sea and land reconciled is presented by the fish, who, "single or with mate / Graze the sea weed their pasture, and through groves / Of coral stray" (*PL*, vii.403–05). "Not," states Alastair Fowler, "merely a piscatory modulation of the pastoral mode," for the description of grazing fish points to the "ideological bearing" of diet (*PL*, vii.404n). He means of course that postlapsarian fish will devour each other. They will; but, anticipating the Fall, Fowler does not linger over the significance for Milton's paradise of what he dismisses as "piscatory pastoralism." As Fowler knows, Raphael's image of fish grazing in pastures of seaweed and straying through groves of coral nods at the venerable system of universal analogies, the idea that different realms of creation correspond at every point.[32] That the system is *not* fully fleshed out in the archangel's account of Creation is the most important fact about it, a fact which Fowler's hasty dismissal erases.

Thomas Browne subjects one aspect of the system of analogies to skeptical consideration in *Pseudodoxia Epidemica*: "That all Animals in the land are in their kinde in the Sea" (*PE*, 262), that is, schools of fish are to the sea what herds of cattle are to the earth. Another aspect of the analogical system holds that "the vegetable is an animal living head down" and "a plant is an upright animal."[33] When Raphael tells Adam that "the swift stag from underground / Bore up his branching head" (*PL*, vii.469–70), the adjective *branching* suggests that antlers reiterate, in the animal realm, the branches of trees – just as coral reiterates them in the mineral realm, under the sea.[34] The assumed correspondence between plants and animals emerges again in Raphael's description of flocks rising as plants from the soil, a wittier simile than may at first appear. The expectation of creaturely correspondence is responsible for some of the more fanciful entries that regularly appear in Renaissance natural histories. Among them is the Scythian lamb, also called the vegetable lamb of Tartary, or the barometz.[35] Looking very like a sheep draped over an upright stick in the ground, a barometz can be seen to the left of the central tree in the frontispiece of John Parkinson's *Paradisi in Sole Paradisus Terrestris* (1628) (fig. 6). Thomas Browne gives the creature short shrift, *strange* here being the equivalent of a raised eyebrow:

the Boramez, that strange plant-animall or vegetable Lamb of Tartary, which Wolves delight to feed on, which hath the shape of a Lamb, affordeth a bloudy juice upon breaking, and liveth while the plants be consumed about it; and yet if all this be no more then the shape of a Lamb in the flower or seed, upon the top of the stalk, as we meet with the formes of Bees, Flies and Dogs in some others, he hath seen nothing that shall much wonder at it. (*PE*, 298)[36]

Browne clearly regards the vegetable lamb as fancy's child. Milton's subtle allusion to it indicates a skepticism and a sense of humor no less marked than Browne's.

Raphael's "fleeced the flocks and bleating rose, / As plants" evokes but does not insist upon the vegetable lamb. Nothing in Raphael's

6 *Paradisi in Sole Paradisus Terrestris* (1629) by John Parkinson, title-page, showing the barometz or vegetable lamb of Tartary.

description expresses commitment to it as an actual creature. On the contrary, a reader's knowledge of the vegetable lamb enriches the verse as a reminiscence enhances the present moment. It is to be savored and then let go. Similarly, we can acknowledge that coral groves and branching antlers weave a web of analogies in the passage. But the web is finespun and delicate; it will not support a fully elaborated system, a system which would end by constraining the reader. As it is, Raphael's light touch leaves the reader free to look, or not to look, for other resemblances. When he argues against the theory that all creatures on land have their counterparts in the sea, Thomas Browne observes that the theory imposes limits on God's creativity:

> by this assertion wee restraine the hand of God, and abridge the variety of the creation; making the creatures of one Element, but an acting over those of another, and conjoyning as it were the species of things which stood at distance in the intellect of God, and though united in the Chaos, had several seeds of their creation: for although in that indistinguisht masse, all things seemed one, yet separated by the voyce of God, according to their species they came out in incommunicated varieties, and irrelative seminalities, as well as divided places; and so although we say the world was made in sixe dayes, yet was there as it were a world in every one, that is, a distinct creation of distinguisht creatures, a distinction in time of creatures divided in nature, and a severall approbation, and survey in every one. (*PE*, 264)

As Browne points out, imposing a strict system of analogies undoes the primary work of Creation, which he represents in the passage above as the work of dividing and distinguishing. We recall John Ray's objection to uniting what ought to be separated and separating what ought to be united. Raphael's narrative, by delicately sketching patterns of relatedness among creatures of different realms, releases them from strict confinement to a single habitat and hence from an enforced cohabitation with the wrong kind.

The work of Creation in *Paradise Lost* is represented as a balance between two impulses: dividing and distinguishing, and integrating into wholeness. The Son's initial creative act demonstrates that balance. The circumference he draws around the universe simultaneously separates it from Chaos and forms it into a discrete whole.[37] Just so, Raphael's representation of the Fifth and Sixth Days' work sets distinctions among the creatures within an integrating order. We may call that order the scale of nature, or with Lovejoy call it the Great Chain of Being, as long as we remember that to name it is not necessarily to understand its workings in *Paradise Lost*. Allusions to the *scala naturae* occur throughout the poem, most explicitly in book v, when Raphael compares the structure of the universe to a plant. In conventional form, the Great Chain of Being is static. Because it assumes that each creature has an ordained place, it reinforces established political and social hierarchies. As scholars have frequently observed, however, Milton's construing of "the scale of nature" is dynamic – "as dynamic as any evolutionary system of more recent times," remarks Alastair Fowler (*PL*, v.469–90n). A number of studies have demonstrated that this dynamic scale of being has important consequences for Milton's political and theological views. It has important consequences, too, for Milton's natural history, as Adam's response to Raphael's plant metaphor suggests:

> Well hast thou taught the way that might direct
> Our knowledge, and the scale of nature set
> From centre to circumference, whereon
> In contemplation of created things
> By steps we may ascend to God.   (*PL*, v.508–12)

Two images are juxtaposed here, the scale and the circle. If we identify Adam's *circumference* with the Son's (*PL*, VII.231), it will be clear that Adam understands from Raphael's words that there is not one scale of nature but many, perhaps an infinite number. He seems to picture them radiating out from God's throne as ribbons stream out from a maypole. The contemplator of created things can start at any point (i.e., any creature) on the "circumference" and ascend from there to God.

The difficulty with even the dynamic scale of nature perceived by Fowler and others is that it remains linear and there is only one line. Because creatures occupy a "lower" or "higher" place in relation to other creatures, comparisons of worth are inevitable, though usually disguised. The debate about whether Adam should have insisted that Eve stay by his side in book IX is of course a question about whether Adam's authority is higher than Eve's. To assume that Raphael has much to teach Adam and little to learn from him is to assume that angels are superior to human beings. Such comparisons assess the "inferior" in terms of the "superior," which means that they do not fully see either. The inadequacy of using comparisons for knowing a creature's worth becomes clear in the animal realm. Is an elephant superior to a whale? Is a crocodile superior to a butterfly? The questions are nonsensical. Adam's response to Raphael draws a new picture of the scale of nature, one which assigns absolute rather than relative worth to each creature and which strips away the worst implications of "knowing one's place."

As Raphael's plant does, so each creature *in itself* offers the contemplator the means to ascend step by step to God. This reformed *scala* releases
"place" from fixity, in the sense both of habitat and of social position.
Hence the animals in Raphael's description of Creation move freely
between water and air, land and water. They are equally mobile as
symbols of place.

"Note that the animal named first," remarks Fowler of Raphael's list,
"is the sovereign of beasts" (*PL*, vii.463–70n). But he overlooks the verb
calved.

> The grassy clods now calved, now half appeared
> The tawny lion, pawing to get free
> His hinder parts, then springs as broke from bonds,
> And rampant shakes his brinded mane; the ounce,
> The libbard, and the tiger, as the mole
> Rising, the crumbled earth above them threw
> In hillocks   (*PL*, vii.463–69)

Characteristically, the passage gestures toward a conventionally hierarchical natural history, giving pride of place to the lion and three other
"noble," heraldic beasts, the lynx, leopard, and tiger. However, just as
the verb makes the calf the equal of the lion, so the simile makes the
mole the fellow of "the ounce, / The libbard, and the tiger." Similarly,
the homely *brinded*, appearing in the company of the heraldic epithet
rampant, implicitly likens the lion to the common domestic cat.[38]

The sovereign of beasts also heads the list of those animals Satan sees
frisking around Adam and Eve when he enters the garden of Eden:

> Sporting the lion ramped, and in his paw
> Dandled the kid; bears, tigers, ounces, pards,
> Gambolled before them, the unwieldy elephant
> To make them mirth used all his might, and wreathed
> His lithe proboscis; close the serpent sly
> Insinuating, wove with Gordian twine
> His braided train, and of his fatal guile
> Gave proof unheeded   (*PL*, iv.343–50)

The lion and the kid together form a conventional symbol of prelapsarian innocence, and scholars have noted "countless visual representations" of Eden relevant to this scene.[39] But a lion rampant, even while
dandling a kid, remains a symbol of human sovereignty. (Medieval
herald-painters "held that the lion must ever be ramping."[40]) What kind
of sovereign does a dandling lion represent? A sovereign worthy of paradise, a true sovereign, the passage above seems to answer, which implies

that sovereignty symbolized by a proud and fierce lion is sovereignty mis-conceived.[41] The process of freeing animals from their symbolic places culminates in Raphael's description of "creeping things," literally the lowest of animals. The implication is clear: ramping is not inherently superior to creeping.

By releasing creatures from their conventional syntax, Milton implies that the book of the world is, like the Bible, a text to be read experimentally. The experimental reading he proposes coincides in important ways with an experimentalist reading: it implicitly questions prevailing arrangements of the animal kingdom; it is skeptical but not contemptuous of certain venerable histories; it treats representative features rather than monstrous uniqueness as its proper subject; it admits ignorance. The coinciding can hardly have been accidental. Milton seems to have been unusually attuned to the intellectual currents of his day – and unusually gifted at adapting them to and letting them inflect his own purposes. Thus, Raphael's dynamic portrayal of animals in constant movement suggests that the creatures, like biblical "places," must be constantly "conferred," not reified in a static hierarchy, but continually combined and recombined, their new patterns illuminating hitherto hidden meanings. With its carefully distanced allusions to commonplace notions, Raphael's account of Creation implies that readers who study the book of nature can acknowledge conventional readings but must not embrace them merely because they are conventional. Behemoth, "biggest born of earth," is only *probably* an elephant. Raphael's narrative helps us see that reading God's beneficence in the book of the world is a pleasure and a responsibility that never comes to an end. He does so by incorporating "strange" individuals into his account. In their recalcitrant strangeness, they remind us that absolute interpretive certainty can never be achieved – and that the necessary indeterminacy generates creativity. The crocodile epitomizes the richness of an unresolvable ambiguity within the Creator's orderly control of the whole. Its species, its behavior, its habitat – none of these is certain. In its indecipherability, it represents a new way of knowing Creation.

CHAPTER 7

Rehabilitating the political animal

Raphael's description of creeping things culminates in two specific instances, the ant and the bee.

>   First crept
> The parsimonious emmet, provident
> Of future, in small room large heart enclosed,
> Pattern of just equality perhaps
> Hereafter, joined in her popular tribes
> Of commonalty: swarming next appeared
> The female bee that feeds her husband drone
> Deliciously, and builds her waxen cells
> With honey stored: (*PL*, VII.484–92)

Large issues are at stake in the representation of these tiny creatures. Established since classical and biblical antiquity as privileged sites of analogy, the royalist bee and the republican ant were recruited into the ideological wars of the mid-seventeenth century. At about the same time, they became, with other insects, the first objects of microscopical investigation. There is some tension between these two roles. Regarding them as political analogies tends to reinscribe animals in the symbolizing tradition characteristic of the "old" natural history – and into an "old" political debate apparently concluded at the Restoration. Regarding insects as objects of observation tends to limit their importance to their bodily structures. As Catherine Wilson notes, the "exact" or microscopical part of the new natural history "was as impoverished in cultural terms as it was enriched in observational terms."[1]

The tension between the two epistemologies creates a complex representational problem for the Creation narrative in *Paradise Lost*. Timothy Raylor has called attention to Samuel Hartlib's "excision of analogy and correspondence" from his mid-century treatise on bee-keeping, *The Reformed Common-wealth of Bees* (1655).[2] He notes that Hartlib's "severing of the analogical from the practical" may be regarded "as a precursor of the attempt by the Royal Society to exclude ideological issues from natural philosophical enquiry – a move likewise designed to avert religious and political controversy."[3] Milton would not have regarded averting such controversy as being one of the aims of "heroic song." On the other hand, to fix the "meaning" of ants and bees is an interpretive practice at odds with his experimental reading of God's Scriptures. Milton's solution to the representational crux is complex, subtle, and demanding. It requires readers to "confer" passages in *Paradise Lost* as they would "places" in the Bible and thereby reveals another dimension of the fitness that he asks of his readers. There are three "places" specifically concerned with ants and bees in the poem: the narrator's comparison of the fallen angels to bees in book I; the description of the ant in book VII; and immediately following it, the description of the bee. The exercise demands from the reader, as if from a microscopist, attention to minute features of these texts.

Pairing ants and bees as complementary models of industry and government is a commonplace of classical and Renaissance literature.[4] Bacon famously pairs them as examples of mysterious knowledge in the fifth book of *The Advancement of Learning*:

Who showed the way to the bees, that sail through such a vast sea of air to fields in flower far removed from their hive, and back again? Who taught the ant to bite the grains of corn that she lays up in her hill, lest they should sprout and so disappoint her hope?[5]

What had been complementary became oppositional in the mid-seventeenth century, as ant and bee were pressed into analogical service for republicans and royalists. Paul Hammond has commented that *all* attempts at the mid-century to fashion political rhetoric were fraught with difficulty, for "textual communities" were no longer coherent. What had been a common language of political debate became fragmented: "traditional genres were wrested to new purposes, strange idiolects flourished, and notions of likeness and difference, community and foreignness, connection and separation, were newly experienced and continually redefined."[6] Also fragmented at the mid-century was a body of shared assumptions about the natural world. Hence the use of natural analogies was thrown into disarray. Even venerable analogies were affected by the turmoil, which, in the case of bees and ants, took the form of an ever-clearer recognition that a great deal about their behavior was *not*, in fact, understood.

What was not understood about the beehive was the function of the large, unique bee almost universally called the "king." The mistake in gender indicates why its function remained mysterious. Despite the mystery, the presence of a bee which could be construed as a king explains the reason for the hive's popularity as a royalist political analogy. Indeed, writers of all political persuasions assumed the hive had a monarchical government; their debate centered on whether it was an absolute or contractual monarchy, the latter often called, somewhat confusingly, a "commonwealth."[7] Thomas Mouffet retains a "King" to whom the governed grant authority while reserving "their Prerogative of Election."[8] In *A Theatre of Politicall Flying-Insects* (1657), Samuel Purchas calls the chief bee a "commander" or a "prince," revisionist terminology, perhaps, for a revised monarchy.[9] Thus "the beehive was widely taken to demonstrate the naturalness of Stuart-style absolutism" in the seventeenth century, an assumption voiced again after 1660.[10] Raylor observes that the revived claim was made "most notably in the work of the royal 'Bee Master', Moses Rusden, whose *Further Discovery of Bees* (London, 1679) depicts on its frontispiece a crowned bee surmounted by the royal arms."[11]

Though the exact function of the monarch bee was in doubt, royalist analogy-makers were able to point to bees' manufacture of honey as evidence that the monarchical organization of the hive was a productive one. The ability to make honey was also cited as evidence of the superiority of bees to ants. The basis for this strand of the analogy had been laid in classical antiquity by Pliny, who observes (in Philemon Holland's translation) that ants "labour and travell in common, as the Bees doe."[12] But bees "make their own meat," while ants merely store what they have gathered. John Evelyn puts it more succinctly: "The Ants indeed for themselves but the Bee for others."[13] Robert Boyle repeats the distinction in a comparison between those who take instruction from books of devotion and those who take instruction from the book of nature. The difference, he explains, is as that

betwixt an ant, that contributes nothing either to the production or improvement of the corn she lays up and feeds on, but only carries away that, which she finds ready formed into its little granary or repository; and the industrious bee, who, without stealing from flowers anything that can prejudice them, does not only gather, but improve and transform her food.[14]

Boyle alludes here to the parable of the talents (Matthew 25.14–30) to underline the superiority of bees to ants. The bee, in Boyle's telling, is analogous to the servant who invests his talents, increasing his five talents to ten. The ant is analogous to the servant who merely hides his single talent in the earth.

The pairing of bees and ants in *Paradise Lost* contests the prevailing equation of the monarchical state with productivity, the republican state with selfish individualism. The contestation is vigorous but indirect; it depends upon readers' willingness to confer "places" and to attach significance to what the text refrains from saying. Turning first to the comparison of the fallen angels to bees in book 1, we notice that there is no mention of honey, that crucial indicator of bees' productivity. The simile appears in connection with Pandaemonium, whose "spacious hall"

> Thick swarmed, both on the ground and in the air,
> Brushed with the hiss of rustling wings. As bees
> In spring time, when the Sun with Taurus rides,
> Pour forth their populous youth about the hive
> In clusters; they among fresh dews and flowers
> Fly to and fro, or on the smoothed plank,
> The suburb of their straw-built citadel,
> New rubbed with balm, expatiate and confer
> Their state affairs. So thick the airy crowd
> Swarmed and were straitened;   (*PL*, 1.767–76)

The most striking fact about the populous youth who congregate outside the citadel is that, although they are busy – flying to and fro, expatiating and conferring – they are not working. *Suburb*, moreover, just hints at licentious behavior, another kind of unproductive business.[15] Since they do not work, they cannot be worker bees, which suggests that this hive is composed solely of drones. J. B. Broadbent describes them as "amateur politicians" who "gossip, while the real work of government goes on inside."[16] But the simile gives no hint of "real work" going on anywhere here. There is only expatiating and conferring. Alternately swelling with self-importance and huddling close (a movement which reiterates their physical expansion and contraction), these bees embody immoderate and wasteful activity.[17] They are not the "clean, chaste, pious and industrious" creatures of tradition.[18] Indeed, they possess none of the attributes for which bees had been extolled for centuries as a pattern for productive human behavior, a lack summed up in their failure to produce honey.[19]

The omission of features one would normally expect to find in a bee analogy points to the bees' importance for political debate. Other than honey, the most significant omission here is of course the monarch bee, the hive's unmentioned and unmentionable center. Milton translates what natural philosophy did not understand – i.e., the monarch bee's role in the hive – into a figure of corrupt idleness. It is an idleness so absolute that it affects the populace even though the monarch is invisible or absent. It reveals itself, that is, in the idle and dissolute behavior of the populace. Milton's disapproval of a state of idleness can best be measured by his admiration for the industrious nation he had once imagined England to be. In *Areopagitica* he envisions London as a "vast City; a City of refuge, the mansion house of liberty," filled with people "sitting by their studious lamps, musing, searching, revolving new notions and idea's wherewith to present, as with their homage and their fealty the approaching Reformation: others as fast reading, trying all things, assenting to the force of reason and convincement."[20] The obverse of the vast industrious city is the citadel or "little city" of drones in book i. In its mixture of politics and licentiousness, idleness and plotting, the similic hive embodies the relatedness of moral and political corruption. A government which is itself ill-governed cannot but breed undisciplined and dissolute followers, expensive and idle hangers-on, who consume rather than contribute to the wealth of the kingdom. The bees in book i are closer to "A darksome cloud of locusts swarming down" (*PL*, xii.185) than to the insects admired by Charles Butler in *The Feminine Monarchie* for their "co[n]tinual labour and consenting order."[21] The springtime swarming of the infernal bees thus becomes an ominous sign of destruction rather than the sign of industrious activity for which the beekeeper watches with eager anticipation. The "hiss" of wings that ushers in the bee simile at *PL*, 1.768 magnifies the threat of the swarm, for it is the preeminent sound-symbolic term for serpents.[22] Michael Lieb calls it "the Satanic 'Word' incarnate."[23]

Neither the perfume sprinkled on a courtier's handkerchief nor the balm rubbed on the bees' plank overcomes the stench of a dissolute court. The simile in its context in book i insistently links foul air and bad politics. For centuries it had been a tenet of bee-keeping that hives must be placed where the air is pure and fresh, if not actually sweet-smelling. Foul air, it was affirmed, made bees ill or killed them.[24] In his *Theatre of Politicall Flying-Insects*, however, Purchas denies this and other received opinions on bees:

They are not offended with red coloured cloaths as some affirm, nor yet inebriated with sweet oyntments, no nor much offended with stinking favours: I have known twenty Hives together stand against a dunghil divers years, and thrive and prosper well.[25]

Milton's infernal bees are likewise not "much offended" by the corrupt atmosphere of Pandaemonium, produced by the burning of "naphtha and asphaltus" (*PL*, 1.729).[26] Through the smoky stench of pitch, the simile connects Pandaemonium to Babylon, notable for its abundance of "Asphalta or Bytumen," as Diodorus Siculus reports. Outside the city walls "is an overture of the earth" from which "issueth . . . an ill smell, as it were of Sulphur, which kills the Creatures that pass by."[27] The infamous symbol of luxury and despotic monarchy, Babylon's "stinking favours" waft over Pandaemonium and the infernal hive. Whereas Purchas and Mouffet attempt to save the beehive for political analogy by downplaying its absolutist potential, Milton subtly emphasizes that potential by associating the hive of Pandaemonium with the tyrannies of ancient Babylon.[28]

The hive in book 1 is finally impervious, flimsily impervious, to efforts at reform and reconstruction. The bees' "straw-built citadel" is not merely an ironic oxymoron. The construction of beehives was undergoing a revolution in the seventeenth century. In *The Reformed Commonwealth of Bees*, Samuel Hartlib published Christopher Wren's drawing of a multi-storeyed hive. One of Wren's earliest known architectural designs, it calls for glass plates between wooden storeys and a casing of stone (fig. 7). Observing that Wren's hive "was expensive to produce (requiring the skills of a cabinet maker)," Timothy Raylor wonders if "the multi-storeyed hive" could ever "have been a commercial success."[29] It did, in any case, excite a great deal of interest. John Evelyn, too, tried his hand at designing beehives of wood and glass, sketches of which may be seen in the manuscript of his *Elysium Britannicum*. But the infernal hive of *Paradise Lost* is a house of straw, symbol for Milton of all that is morally worthless, a structure outmoded and incapable of reformation.[30]

The only explicit connection between the infernal simile and the newly created bees of book VII is, appropriately enough, the term *swarming*.

> swarming next appeared
> The female bee that feeds her husband drone
> Deliciously, and builds her waxen cells
> With honey stored: (*PL*, VII.489–92)

In fact, *swarming* does not feel entirely appropriate here. The term seems incommensurate with the singular of kind ("swarming, the female bee

The Common-wealth of Bees.

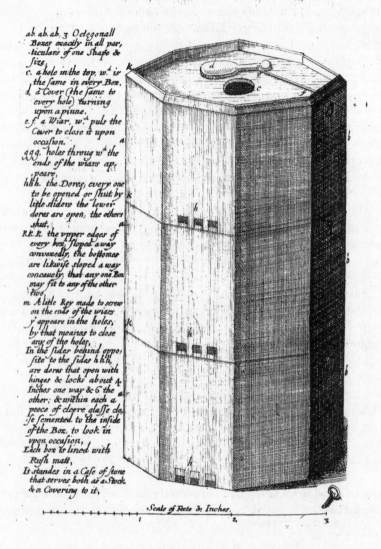

ab. ab. ab. 3 Octegonall
Boxes exactly in all par,
ticulars of one shape &
sise,
c. a hole in the top, w.ᶜʰ is
the same in every Box,
d. a Cover (the same to
every hole) turning
upon a pinne,
e.f. a Wiar, w.ᶜʰ puls the
Cover to close it upon
occasion,
g.g.g. holes throug w.ᶜʰ the
ends of the wiars ap,
peare,
hhh. the Dores, every one
to be opened or shut by
litle sliders the lower
dores are open, the others
shut,
R.R.R. the vpper edges of
every box sloped away
convexedly, the bottomes
are likwise sloped away
concauely, that any one Box
may fit to any of the other
two,
m. A litle Rey made to screw
on the ends of the wiars
y.ᵗ appeare in the holes,
by that meanes to close
any of the holes,
In the sides behind oppo,
site to the sides h h h,
are dores that open with
hinges & locks about 4
Inches one way & 6 the
other; & within each a
peece of cleere glasse cla,
se semented to the inside
of the Box, to look in
vpon occasion,
Each box is lined with
Rush matt,
It standes in a Case of stone
that serves both as a Stock
& a Covering to it,

Scale of Feete & Inches,

7 Hive of glass, wood, and stone, designed by Christopher Wren, from *The Reformed
Common-wealth of Bees* (1655) by Samuel Hartlib.

appeared"). The disproportion thus hinted at is carried further in the relationship depicted. The female bee clearly studies "household good," but she is yoked in marriage to the type of dissolute, unchaste idler revealed by the simile in book 1.[31] Raphael's differential treatment sketches a portrait of what Milton in his divorce tracts had viewed solely from a man's perspective, "*a matrimony found to be uncurably unfit.*"[32] But the portrait also has political implications. The structure of the early modern family was widely regarded as being analogous to that of the state: as the husband is to the wife, so the monarch is to the people.[33] Raphael's term, "husband drone," is therefore a subversive oxymoron along the lines of "luxurious monarch." The buried political analogy suggests that a worthy people can be shackled to an unworthy monarch and that, while productivity is possible under these conditions, it will of necessity be limited and narrowly directed. In view of the traditional claims about bees making honey and ants (merely) storing grain, it is notable that Raphael's female bees *store* their honey.

The productivity of the ant-hill is best summed up in the word *parsimonious*, implying a careful dispersal at the opposite pole from *swarming*. A principle of parsimony governs the very diction in which Raphael praises the ant:

> First crept
> The parsimonious emmet, provident
> Of future, in small room large heart enclosed,
> Pattern of just equality perhaps
> Hereafter, joined in her popular tribes
> Of commonalty: (*PL*, vii.484–89)

In the second edition of *The Readie and Easie Way*, published in 1660, Milton praises the polity of the "pismire" in similar terms:

which evidently shews us, that they who think the nation undon without a king, though they look grave or haughtie, have not so much true spirit and understanding in them as a pismire: neither are these diligent creatures hence concluded to live in lawless anarchie, or that commended, but are set the examples to imprudent and ungovernd men, of a frugal and self-governing democratie or Commonwealth; safer and more thriving in the joint providence and counsel of many industrious equals, then under the single domination of one imperious Lord.[34]

Parsimony and providence are the virtues of the ants' commonalty. They are paired with another, magnanimity, a quality which Milton borrows from Virgil's description of bees in the fourth *Georgic* and reassigns to ants.[35] Virgil's magnanimous bees are gallant and warrior-like;

Milton's magnanimous ants are parsimonious. "Parsimonious magnanimity" is *not* an oxymoron. As Milton explains in *The Readie and Easie Way*, only the great-hearted *can* be parsimonious, for they alone know how to refrain from (*parcere*) soft and corrupting luxury:

for of all governments a Commonwealth aims most to make the people flourishing, vertuous, noble and high spirited. Monarchs will never permitt: whose aim is to make the people, wealthie indeed perhaps and well fleec't, for thir own shearing and the supplie of regal prodigalitie; but otherwise softest, basest, vitiousest, servilest, easiest to be kept under; and not only in fleece, but in minde also sheepishest.[36]

Better to be a pismire than a sheep.

As Mouffet notes in his *Theater of Insects*, there are three English words for ant: "*Ant, Emmet, Pismire.*"[37] Mouffet uses the terms indiscriminately; Milton does not. The surprising number of words beginning with *p* in Raphael's description of the ant (*parsimonious, provident, Pattern, perhaps, popular*) draws attention to the very absence of *pismire*. In terms of stylistic register, *emmet*, neither as common as *ant* nor as colloquial as *pismire*, confers a certain dignity on the little creature. It also leaves the reader free to imagine an unexpressed alliterative possibility. Among the creeping things named by Raphael, the emmet is first, alone in its eminence. There is "bad eminence" in *Paradise Lost*, which is Satan's (*PL*, II.6); "bright eminence," which is the unfallen angels' (*PL*, IV.44); and "pre-eminence," which is God's (*PL*, V.661). The eminence of the emmet is the true creaturely eminence of humility. Such humility is worthy of high place, as John Guillim recognizes in his *Display of Heraldrie*. Proposing an "*Escocheon of Eleven Emmets*" (fig. 8), he explains: "By the *Emmet* or *Pismire* may be signified a man of great labour, wisedome and providence in all his affaires, and of a pregnant and ready memorie."[38] Milton's analogical use of the ant is less explicit than Guillim's, or, rather, it is more dependent upon the reader's active involvement in the interpretive process. By "conferring" the simile in book I with the description in book VII, readers can see that Raphael's praise of the bee bears out rather than contradicts the simile's implied charge of luxury and corruption against the hive. By "conferring" the praise of the emmet and the praise of the bee, readers can see how narrowly conceived the latter's productivity is. What is explicit in Milton's analogical use of the ant is softened by *perhaps*, dual in its reference. It indicates uncertainty about whether human beings will someday have enough wisdom to recognize a pattern for themselves in the commonalty of ants; it also indicates uncertainty about the future use of analogical thinking based upon animal behavior.[39]

8 "*Escocheon* of Eleven Emmets," from *A Display of Heraldrie* (1638) by John Guillim; the ant signifies "a man of great labour, wisedome and providence in all his affaires."

The increase in zoological knowledge in the seventeenth century inevitably destabilized conventional animal analogies. Let us return to Robert Boyle's rather surprising charge that the ant "contributes nothing to the production or improvement" of the grain it stores. (Why should it?) His criticism may have its origin in an opinion dating back at least to Pliny. Ants were believed to bite off the ends of the grain they stored to prevent it from sprouting. Boyle reports this story, though admittedly with some degree of skepticism, in *Disquisition about Final Causes*:

For it is known, that these little creatures do in the summer hoard up grains of corn against the winter. And their sagacity is the more considerable, if it be true, what divers learned persons affirm, that they eat or bite off the germens of the grains of corn they lay up, lest the moisture of the earth exposed to the rains should make it sprout. But whatever become of this tradition, these insects do some other actions, resembling sagacity and industry.[40]

The skepticism may be due to the fact that Thomas Browne reports in *Pseudodoxia Epidemica* that he had "made tryall" and discovered that cutting off the ends of grain does *not* prevent its germination (*PE*, 285–86). Moreover, he reveals, he had also dug up ant-hills during the winter and found . . . very little.

But the prudence of this animal is by Knawing, peircing, or otherwise, to destroy the litle nebbe or principle of germination. Which notwithstanding is not easily discoverable; it being no ready business to meet with such grains in Anthills; and he must dig deep, that will seek them in the Winter. (*PE*, 286)

The delicacy of this last injunction is characteristic of Browne's philosophical caution. He casts doubt on a piece of traditional lore yet admits, in effect, that he cannot offer a better explanation. Lacking therefore a solid reason for dismissing the ant's reputed providence, he retains it. Indeed, he repeats the praise in a later chapter on the cicada, whose life is "so short in Summer, that for provision it needs not have recourse unto the providence of the Pismire in Winter" (*PE*, 372). In the alliteration of *provision*, *providence*, and *Pismire*, there is the gentlest touch of irony, so gentle that it does not stand in the way of one who might wish to repeat Browne's praise of the ant's providence and ignore his doubts about the providential method. Nonetheless, it may be that Browne's success in undermining animal lore stands behind Raphael's hint that animal analogies may not remain in use in the future.

A political reading of the hive and the ant-hill is neither ignored nor enforced in *Paradise Lost*. It is available to readers who are willing to "confer places" in the poem and ponder what they find there. The representational strategy of the poem encourages a canny and responsible reading practice. It is tempting to imagine that Milton recognized in Robert Hooke's *Micrographia* – that landmark work of mid-century experimentalism – another text amenable to experimental reading. There is no evidence that Milton ever looked through the lenses of a microscope; by the time Hooke "shewed a microscopical observation of a pismire" to the Royal Society in October, 1663, Milton had long been blind.[41] He could have heard, however, that the drawing of the ant (fig. 9) is one of the most striking illustrations in *Micrographia*, and that the only part of the bee shown pictorially is the sting (fig. 10). The two drawings – the ant "cas'd over with a very strong armour," making it capable of prodigious labor, and the sting of the bee, instrument of annoyance to human flesh – might well serve as corroborating instances of Milton's reformed mode of natural analogy.[42]

Schem. XXX II

9 Ant, from *Micrographia* (1665) by Robert Hooke, "cas'd over with a very strong armour."

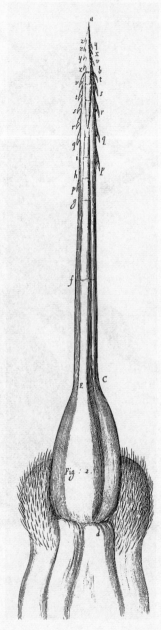

10 Sting of bee, from *Micrographia* (1665) by Robert Hooke; "a weapon of offence."

PART III

Transplanting the garden

CHAPTER 8

Naming and not naming

Eve, as she recalls for him, first spies Adam "fair indeed and tall, / Under a platan" (*PL*, IV.477–78). Her simple naming of the tree exemplifies the decorum of botanical representation in *Paradise Lost*. The platan, or plane tree, is one of the trees that John Evelyn recommends cultivating in England.[1] In his *Sylva, or A Discourse of Forest-Trees* (1664), a work which according to Blanche Henrey "exerted a greater influence on forestry" in England than any other book of the century, Evelyn extols "the incomparable and shady *Platanus*":[2]

> *that* so beautiful and precious *Tree*, which we reade the *Romans* brought out of the *Levant*, and cultivated with so much industry and cost, for its stately and proud head only; that they would *irrigate* them with *Wine* in stead of *Water*, and so priz'd the very *shadow* of it, that when afterwards they transplanted them into *France*, they exacted a *Tribute* of any of the *Natives* who should presume but to put his *head* under it. *Pliny* tells us there is no *Tree* whatsoever which so well defends us from the *heat* of the *Sun* in *Summer*, nor that admits it more kindly in *Winter*.[3]

The plane tree shaded Plato's Academy in Athens, and for Pliny it is foremost among trees, the first temple of the gods.[4] It was brought to Italy, Pliny notes, "only [i.e., solely] for the shade that it giveth."[5] On Crete, he declares, it is an evergreen.[6] The Bible also contributed to the ancient reputation of the plane tree, Ecclesiasticus 24.16 being commonly taken as an allegorical reference to the Messiah: "I . . . am exalted as a plane tree by the water."[7]

Particularly gratifying to the seventeenth century was the fact that the plane tree of the ancients was still extant and identifiable, though in countries remote from Europe. Parkinson states that it

> groweth not naturally in any Country of *Europe*, but in *Asia*, *Syria*, *Egypt*, and *Africa* . . . it is found with very few in our Christian world, and those onely great lovers of rarities, being very tender, not enduring without extraordinary care and keeping, the cold of our climate.[8]

However, he reports the existence of a New World variety, the "Virginian" or "West-Indian" plane tree, which, he notes, has recently been brought to England by John Tradescant.[9] These are undoubtedly the "one or two yong ones at this time growing with Mr Tradescant" that Johnson mentions in his edition of Gerard's *Herball*.[10]

Given the rich cultural history of the plane tree, Eve's concise "under a platan" momentarily bestows upon Adam the wisdom of Plato and the grace of Christ. It also allows us to glimpse ordinary human desire at work in the midst of an extraordinary situation: Adam, eagerly anticipating God's last best gift, the first woman on earth, waits for her in the cool shade of a tree. His platan links the antiquity of paradise with the gardening enthusiasms of Milton's own day. Because *platan* is geographically unspecific (or, as we would say today, because the genus includes an oriental and an occidental species), Adam's tree forms a bridge between the familiar paradise of the old world and the newer paradises of America. Adam's tree *may* be one of the evergreen planes mentioned by Pliny, as there are otherwise no deciduous trees in paradise, but the poem does not insist upon it.[11] Nor does the poem insist upon the legends that associate the platan with idolatry, though these may be recalled in Adam's postlapsarian and abortive plan to rear an altar wherever the divine presence has appeared in the garden.[12] One of those places, Adam says to Michael, is "under this tree" (*PL*, XI.320). Eve's simple naming of the tree, in other words, brings into play an array of associations that vastly enlarges the symbolic and naturalistic ground covered by the garden. None of these associations is insisted upon; they are raised and disappear again as a ripple moves across the surface of the water. As we will see, Milton's "experimental" reading of botanical Creation, corresponding as it does with an experimentalist respect for the natural world, imparadises the whole world, but with an exceedingly light touch.

Before we turn in the following chapters to Milton's treatment of other "ordinary" paradisal plants, let us consider the two most renowned plants in *Paradise Lost*, the tree of forbidden fruit and the tree whose leaves furnish Adam and Eve's first garments. They are apparent exceptions to a representational strategy that seeks to wed experimentalist restraint with imaginative freedom. The tree of forbidden fruit remains, it would seem, too generically unspecified to partake in any way of experimentalism; the banyan tree, too precisely identified to be reshaped by the imagination. Yet if we consider Milton's strategy of naming them (which includes misnaming, renaming, and not naming them), we can see that even plants deeply inscribed in sacred mythology are treated also as botanical entities. While the poem's treatment of the forbidden fruit demonstrates the perils of an incautious construing of the natural world, the treatment of the fig tree demonstrates the benefits of a daring one.

Referring to speculation about the identity of the forbidden fruit, Thomas Browne comments in *Pseudodoxia Epidemica* on the importance of allowing to remain unresolved those issues of which "there is no determination in the Text" (*PE*, 537):

Since therefore after this fruit curiosity fruitlessely enquireth, and confidence blindly determineth, we shall surcease our Inquisition, rather troubled that it was tasted, then troubling our selves in its decision; this only we observe, when things are left uncertaine men will assure them by determination. (*PE*, 539)

Browne applies the same hermeneutic principle to reading the Bible and reading the book of Creation: to wrest determination from indeterminacy is a misreading of the text, and such misreading leads to misunderstanding the Creator. For rhetorical purposes, however, even Robert Boyle can speak of the forbidden fruit as an apple. In his "Discourse against Swearing" (published posthumously in 1695), Boyle asks, "What trifle could appear slighter than the eating of an apple? Yet this petty seeming peccadillo lost *Adam* paradise."[13] Milton famously calls the forbidden fruit an "apple" in *Areopagitica*: "It was from out the rinde of one apple tasted, that the knowledge of good and evill as two twins cleaving together leapt forth into the World."[14] But *Areopagitica* was published more than twenty years before *Paradise Lost*. Not only is the representational decorum of the tract very different from that of the poem; conceptions about the natural world had changed between 1644 and 1667. In the poem, in which the nature of the created world is of central importance, Milton consistently uses botanical terms with precision and care. In the case of the fruit of the forbidden tree, precise and careful usage means *refraining* from naming.

The poem's first detailed description of the fruit of the forbidden tree belongs to the serpent. He says to Eve:

> on a day roving the field, I chanced
> A goodly tree far distant to behold
> Loaden with fruit of fairest colours mixed,
> Ruddy and gold: I nearer drew to gaze;
> When from the boughs a savoury odour blown,
> Grateful to appetite, more pleased my sense
> Than smell of sweetest fennel or the teats

> Of ewe or goat dropping with milk at even,
> Unsucked of lamb or kid, that tend their play.
> To satisfy the sharp desire I had
> Of tasting those fair apples, I resolved
> Not to defer; (*PL*, ix.575–86)

(Typically, it is Satan who repeats antiquated lore about the natural world, i.e., that serpents love fennel and milk from the teat.) Commenting on Satan's feigned desire "Of tasting those fair apples," Thomas Newton remarks almost impatiently, "There is no knowing for certain what the forbidden fruit was. The common notion is that it was a sort of apple, and that is sufficient to justify a poet."[15] Newton thus attributes to Milton what Milton attributes to Satan.[16] The serpent is the only creature in *Paradise Lost* who refers to the forbidden fruit as an apple; unfallen creatures, divine beings, and the narrator invariably speak of "the fruit." It is true that *apple* may be a synonym for *fruit*; the *OED* comments that "from the earliest period" the term *apple* has been "used with the greatest latitude."[17] Nonetheless, there are clear indications in the text that the term *apple* Milton assigns to Satan is a deliberate invocation of *Malus*.

In the dream he induces in Eve, Satan (or his surrogate) gazes on the forbidden tree and calls it a "fair plant . . . with fruit surcharged" (*PL*, v.58), and then, having plucked and eaten, speaks of "fruit divine" (*PL*, v.67). But in the second, successful attempt on Eve's credulity, the serpent calls the fruit an apple. The renaming mischievously renders common and ordinary, and thus not to be feared, what God has designated as unique. In that sense it constitutes a lie.[18] The serpent also commits a sin of omission. Even as he misnames the fruit, observes John Leonard, he artfully withholds the name of the tree on which it grows, the Tree of Knowledge of Good and Evil. Leonard points out that the serpent waits for Eve to name the tree, and then, by seeming to understand everything about it when she does so, he makes her believe that eating its fruit has endowed him with "sudden apprehension" of its nature.[19] Whether Satan believes that the fruit actually has the power to bestow knowledge is something we cannot determine, Leonard states.[20] Upon returning to hell, the archfiend "sounds as if he has never had any illusions about the fruit," but this may be boasting after the fact.[21] Since we cannot know, Leonard suggests that we allow "the very impenetrability of Satan's mind" to serve as "an indication of his subtlety."[22] There may be another way to approach the problem. We remember that Satan first learns about the fruit when he overhears Adam reminding Eve of

God's prohibition. Adam dwells at some length on the fruit's ability to cause death:

> of all the trees
> In Paradise that bear delicious fruit
> So various, not to taste that only tree
> Of knowledge, planted by the tree of life,
> So near grows death to life, what e'er death is,
> Some dreadful thing no doubt; for well thou know'st
> God hath pronounced it death to taste that tree,
> The only sign of our obedience left
> Among so many signs of power and rule
> Conferred upon us   (*PL*, IV.421–30)

This overheard description of the fruit raises a more urgent question for Satan than whether the fruit can bestow knowledge. Is it, in fact, poisonous?

Unlike Adam and Eve, Satan knows what "dreadful thing" death is, for he has encountered Death at the gate of hell. He seizes upon the statement that "God hath pronounced it death to taste that tree" and, literal-minded and opportunistic, interprets it as offering a quick way to get rid of Adam and Eve. The reference to *mouths* is especially sinister under the circumstances, as Satan muses over what he has heard:

> Yet let me not forget what I have gained
> From their own mouths; all is not theirs it seems:
> One fatal tree there stands of knowledge called,
> Forbidden them to taste: knowledge forbidden?
> Suspicious, reasonless. Why should their Lord
> Envy them that? Can it be sin to know,
> Can it be death?
> *   *   *
>   Hence I will excite their minds
> With more desire to know, and to reject
> Envious commands, invented with design
> To keep them low whom knowledge might exalt
> Equal with gods; aspiring to be such,
> They taste and die: what likelier can ensue?   (*PL*, IV.512–18, 522–27)

As Fowler observes, Satan has begun here "to rough out the speech with which he *will excite* (line 522) Eve's mind" (*PL*, IV.515–22n). The themes that are going to figure in the temptation at the tree – forbidden knowledge, envy, equality with the gods – appear here. Here, too, appears the aim of all Satan's planning, expressed with monosyllabic brutality: "They taste and die." Believing that the fruit is poisonous, he therefore needs to represent it not merely as something Eve ought not to fear, but as something positively wholesome. So he calls it an apple.

Satan's misleading botanical usage betokens his scorn for the prohibition. But he is also contemptuous of the fruit, a fact which emerges when he returns to hell and announces to his fellows that he has seduced Adam and Eve, "the more to increase / Your wonder, with an apple" (*PL*, x.486–7). His contempt is quickly and appropriately punished when the fiends, newly transformed to monstrous serpents, are themselves made to consume "apples":

> greedily they plucked
> The fruitage fair to sight, like that which grew
> Near that bituminous lake where Sodom flamed;
> This more delusive, not the touch, but the taste
> Deceived; they fondly thinking to allay
> Their appetite with gust, instead of fruit
> Chewed bitter ashes, which the offended taste
> With spattering noise rejected: oft they assayed,
> Hunger and thirst constraining, drugged as oft,
> With hatefulest disrelish writhed their jaws
> With soot and cinders filled;   (*PL*, x.560–70)

What the infernal serpents chew is hell's prototype for "Sodom apples," or "apples of Asphaltus," widely reported to grow in the vicinity of the Dead Sea.[23] Though beautiful on the outside, they are but dust and ashes inside. Eating them, Satan and his crew immediately begin to fulfill God's curse on the serpent, "dust shalt thou eat all the days of thy life" (Genesis 3.14). Their punishment is also further evidence that the precision with which plants are named (or not named) expresses the poem's deep valuing of the natural world. "Sodom apples" are not, of course, apples, and the narrator of the poem refrains from so calling them.[24] They appear in the narrative only as "fruitage fair to sight," a phrase which conforms to experimental botanical decorum. Gerard and Parkinson do not admit "Sodom apples" to their herbals, even as "Exoticae et peregrinae planta," a fact which may suggest doubts about their existence or their usefulness. The poem translates the herbals' silence into a quiet withholding of the name. Satan, however, who has not scrupled to give a name to that which God has left unnamed, is punished precisely by the instrument with which he fashions Eve's downfall: by fruit which is misnamed "apple." In *Paradise Lost*, the penalty for misnaming and undervaluing the natural world is to be subject to the monstrous fictions told about it. As John Steadman notes, Milton has transplanted "the Dead Sea apples from Palestine to the soil of Hell."[25] They do not, that is, grow in the garden of Eden, for they lack the status of created things. Along with other lies, they are consigned to hell.

Unlike the general and deliberately unspecified "fruit" of the forbidden tree, the particular tree whose leaves cover Adam and Eve after the Fall is designated with great care.

> both together went
> Into the thickest wood, there soon they chose
> The fig-tree, not that kind for fruit renowned,
> But such as at this day to Indians known
> In Malabar or Decan spreads her arms
> Branching so broad and long, that in the ground
> The bended twigs take root, and daughters grow
> About the mother tree, a pillared shade
> High overarched, and echoing walks between;
> There oft the Indian herdsman shunning heat
> Shelters in cool, and tends his pasturing herds
> At loop-holes cut through thickest shade: those leaves
> They gathered, broad as Amazonian targe,
> And with what skill they had, together sewed,
> To gird their waist, vain covering if to hide
> Their guilt and dreaded shame; O how unlike
> To that first naked glory. Such of late
> Columbus found the American so girt
> With feathered cincture, naked else and wild
> Among the trees on isles and woody shores.
> Thus fenced, and as they thought, their shame in part
> Covered, but not at rest or ease of mind,
> They sat them down to weep   (*PL*, IX.1099–121)

The tree thus described is readily identifiable as the banyan (*Ficus bengalensis*), called in Milton's day the Indian fig tree. Because it is, apparently, uniquely particularized and uniquely exotic among the trees of paradise, the banyan tree has attracted more critical attention than any other botanical reference in *Paradise Lost*.

Many commentators cite Gerard's *Herball*, with its entry on "the arched Indian Fig tree" (fig. 11), as supplying Milton's description.[26] But as Patrick McHenry observes in "A Milton Herbal," Gerard makes no mention of the size or shape of the leaves. "A simpler explanation," McHenry concludes, "is that Milton lifted the metaphor straight out of Pliny," for Pliny specifically comments that the leaves are broad and shaped like an Amazon's shield.[27] Svendsen argues, however, that Milton

11 "The arched Indian Fig tree," from *The Herball* (1636) by John Gerard, edited by Thomas Johnson; "not that kind for fruit renowned."

might have borrowed the description from any number of writers who drew on the late medieval and early Renaissance encyclopedists, who themselves got the description from Pliny.[28] The question of Milton's source or sources for the banyan tree is unlikely to be resolved. One important point, however, needs to be made about Sir Walter Raleigh's discussion of the tree in his *Historie of the World*, another work cited as a possible source for the banyan tree and a work which Milton certainly knew. Raleigh is primarily concerned to refute the claim of Joannes Goropius Becanus that the Indian fig was the tree of knowledge. Becanus, claims Raleigh, has based his identification on a misapprehension.

For this *Indian* Fig-tree is not so rare a plant as *Becanus* conceiveth, who, because he found it no where else, would needes draw the garden of *Paradise* to the Tree, and set it by the river *Acesines*. But many parts of the world have them, and I my selfe have seene twentie thousand of them in one Valley, not farre from *Paria* in *America*.[29]

Raleigh may be referring here to a species of South American "strangler fig," which bears a superficial resemblance to the banyan as described by Pliny and Theophrastus.[30] Whatever Raleigh actually saw, his experience would have provided Milton with evidence that the Indian fig belongs not only to the East Indies and the world of the ancients, but *also* to the West Indies and hence the contemporary world. (This latter fact incidentally makes sense of the presence in the passage of both an Indian herdsman and an American native.) Without Raleigh's evidence, the arched Indian fig tree would probably have been banished from the garden of Eden, for only plants which belong geographically and historically to the whole world are represented in Milton's earthly paradise, a fact whose implications will be explored in the following chapters.

The debate about Milton's sources for the banyan tree has distracted attention from the forceful rejection with which the passage in book IX begins. This fig tree, declares the narrator, is "*not* that kind for fruit renowned" (emphasis added). This is a polemical statement, and we need to consider why the fig tree evokes it. The kind of fig tree that *is* renowned for its fruit is *Ficus carica*. It is also renowned for its association with human sexuality, an association which would seem to make it an appropriate choice for Adam and Eve. Thomas Browne elaborates in his "Observations upon Severall Plants mention'd in Scripture":[31]

13. What Fruit that was which our first Parents tasted in Paradise, from the disputes of learned men seems yet indeterminable. More clear it is that they

cover'd their nakedness or secret parts with Figg Leaves; which when I reade, I cannot but call to mind the several considerations which Antiquity had of the Figg Tree, in reference unto those parts, particularly how Figg Leaves by sundry Authours are described to have some resemblance unto the Genitals, and so were aptly formed for such contection of those parts; how also in that famous Statua of Praxiteles, concerning Alexander and Bucephalus, the Secret Parts are veil'd with Figg Leaves; how this Tree was sacred unto Priapus, and how the Diseases of the Secret Parts have derived their Name from Figgs.[32]

Unusually, Browne endorses a conventional view in this passage, as if, so apt is the symbolism, it does not occur to him that Genesis 3.7 could refer to anything but *Ficus carica*.[33]

It can be argued that this "apt" symbolism is precisely what Milton objects to. If so, his reasoning is distinctly more experimentalist than Browne's. The figurative sense of *fig-leaf*, meaning a cover for something shameful, reinforces the notion that the human body itself is shameful. This figurative sense, however, pertains only to the leaves of *Ficus carica*, and, although Genesis 3.7 designates as a fig the tree whose leaves provide clothing for Adam and Eve, it does not say what kind of fig. Milton is not therefore bound to use *Ficus carica*, with its inevitable implication that the body is a site of shame. But to counter the prevailing convention requires a polemical insistence. The point of the polemic is that the human body is not shameful in itself, even after the Fall. Adam and Eve's employment of their bodies for lustful purposes *is* shameful, but more shameful still is their attempt to transfer guilt at having disobeyed God to shame for their organs of generation. They are, in effect, blaming their bodies for the Fall – a transfer of blame which the symbolic entailments of *Ficus carica* seem to condone and which Milton's *Ficus bengalensis* resists.

Adam and Eve's is a misdirected use of cover. It is in the context of the passage's reflections on the use of cover that the Indian herdsman and the feather-cinctured American are mentioned. The herdsman "oft" uses the banyan tree as cover from the sun, not, as Adam and Eve use the bower, as cover during the brief "meridian heat" of the day (*PL*, v.369). Fowler's suggestion that the herdsman is "put in because he is primitive and pagan" therefore seems unlikely (*PL*, IX.1100–110n). Indeed, the "pillared shade" with its roof "high arched" and its "echoing walks" endows the herdsman, walking through his natural palace, with grace and nobility. The point is that he needs shelter from the sun; without it, his body will suffer. With the introduction of the American native, the passage considers another kind of cover, clothing. The

American "girt / With feathered cincture" has occasioned much critical comment. In his study of *Paradise Lost* and empire, David Quint associates both the American native and the Indian herdsman with Adam and Eve in their common colonial oppression: "Adam and Eve, who after their fall don fig leaves, which liken them both to the Indians of Malabar and to the Native Americans whom 'of late / Columbus found' (9.1099–1118), assume the roles of innocent natives victimized by their European conquerors."[34] Quint's use of *innocent* is puzzling here. The passage in book ix seems rather to imply that Adam and Eve are the victimizers. The American is "girt / With feathered cincture" because of Adam and Eve's sin. The phrase "naked else" of line 1117 implies not only that he is naked except for the feathered cincture, but also that he *would be* naked – in that state of naked glory that Adam and Eve once lived in – except for the Fall. Adam and Eve's history is written on the bodies of all their children. The American's feathered cincture and the Indian herdsman's tree-shelter do not point to the difference between natives and Europeans but to their common ancestry.

Yet the passage on the fig tree is not despairing. The polemical rejection of *Ficus carica* constitutes an insistence on the goodness of postlapsarian creation. Fallen humanity has not completely lost its resemblance to its Maker; the human face is still divine. Nor has the earth lost its original Edenic beauty. Far from it. A study of the ordinary plants of Adam and Eve's garden reveals how profoundly and how variously the poem proclaims value in the experience of the created world. Indeed, the poem reveals that the beauty in the garden of Eden is the same beauty (dimmed, but only slightly) that inheres in the world around us, in both hemispheres, in all eras.

CHAPTER 9

Botanical discretion

The verdurous wall that literally imparadises the garden of Eden in *Paradise Lost* is associated with a catalog of trees so brief and unadorned as to be almost invisible as a catalog.

> over head up grew
> Insuperable highth of loftiest shade,
> Cedar, and pine, and fir, and branching palm,
> A sylvan scene   (*PL*, IV.137–40)

The catalog *would* have been invisible, perhaps, had not C. S. Lewis commented upon it. These "are ladder-like or serial trees (cedar, pine, and fir)," states Lewis, "with one traditionally eastern and triumphal tree (the palm) thrown in."[1] Perhaps because the catalog has not otherwise attracted much critical interest, Lewis's comment is still influential. The notion of the "serial" tree has proved particularly attractive to scholars. It seems to be an objective correlative to Adam's understanding that "In contemplation of created things / *By steps* we may ascend to God" (*PL*, V.511–12; emphasis added). But the qualities that make the catalog easy to overlook, its brevity and spareness, are precisely those that ought to engage our attention. The virtual absence of modifiers and conventional tags is historically significant. This chapter will argue that the very bareness with which the trees of paradise are named is what allows them to be represented experimentally.

Lewis's most interesting perception may well lie in something he merely implies, which is that the palm does not really fit into the group of trees. Perhaps objecting to the breeziness of Lewis's "thrown in," Fowler suggests that the presence of the "unconventional" palm is due to Milton's recollection of Psalm 92.12: "The righteous shall flourish like the palm tree: he shall grow like a cedar in Lebanon" (*PL*, IV.138–43n). The grouping of trees in book IV is certainly biblical, but Fowler has not dealt with the disproportion Lewis points to. There are three "serial" trees and one non-serial tree. We need to consider the possibility that the palm tree is a deliberate imbalancer, that it is "thrown in" precisely to frustrate any neat symbolic scheme for the trees of paradise. One can construe several nearly satisfactory schemes. But the fact that there are several and that none is wholly satisfactory should not be ignored.

Most symbolizing schemes for plants and animals are based, however loosely, on physical properties, real or imagined. Hence the three-to-one imbalance between the conifers and the palm has implications for the way the *group* of trees signifies. The conifers (cedars, pines, and firs) are fragrant, resinous, and evergreen; the palm may or may not be, depending upon which seventeenth-century authority one consults. Ortelius claims in his atlas that the palm has a "pleasant and fragrant smell," but the herbalists do not mention any fragrance in their entries on the tree.[2] Nor do any of them classify the palm with resin- or gum-producing trees. They are clearly uncertain about whether to classify it as an evergreen. Parkinson claims the leaves "doe alwayes abide greene," but Gerard mentions "the falling away of the leaves" along the trunk.[3] On the basis of Parkinson's description, one could classify the palm as a sort of serial tree: the trunk has "knagges . . . sticking out round about the body, which give an easie footing like steps, to climbe or get up into the toppes of the trees to gather the fruite."[4] This detail does not appear in Gerard, however; and what Fowler calls the "climbing serialism" of the conifers does not appear to be generally associated with the palm.

The resistance of Milton's trees to easy schematizing is an important signal as to how to read them. To explain what is, symbolically, an uncomfortable grouping, Fowler calls attention to E. R. Curtius's identification of the literary "mixed forest" (*PL*, iv.138–43n). This form, Curtius notes, is "a subspecies of the 'catalogue.'"[5] He traces its origins to Virgil's eclogues. The two most distinctive features of the classical form, Curtius finds, are its remoteness from observable nature and the tendency for its constituent trees to proliferate as authors seek to outdo each other. Milton's catalog is guilty of neither excess. In its Renaissance manifestation, the mixed forest tends to be semi-moralized, its relationship to the natural world discernible but highly conventional. Du Bartas's description of the Third Day of Creation, for instance, emphasizes the practical uses trees have for humankind:

> No sooner spoken, but the loftie Pine
> Distilling pitch, the Larche yeeld-Turpentine,
> Th'ever-greene Boxe, and gummie Cedar sprout,
> And th'Airie Mountaines mantle round about:

The Mast-full Oake, the use-full Ashe, the Holme,
Coate-changing Corke, white Maple, shadie Elme,
Through Hill and Plaine ranged their plumed Ranks.
(*Divine Weeks*, 1.iii.545–51)

Spenser's catalog of trees in *The Faerie Queene* more explicitly fuses the
practical with the moral, beginning with the "sayling Pine" and ending
with "the Maple seeldom inward sound."[6] But the group of trees in
Paradise Lost is almost devoid of epithets: "Cedar, and pine, and fir, and
branching palm."[7] *Branching*, the sole epithet in the list, does not moralize the palm. Rather, the adjective is simultaneously naturalistic and self-
conscious of its representational status, for as a term in embroidery,
branching means decorating with foliage (or flowers).[8] Neither the classical nor the Renaissance "mixed forest," in short, is convincing as a
model for the catalog of trees in book IV.

The brevity and rhetorically unadorned nature of the catalog point
instead to a different model, to the Hebrew Bible, where trees are
grouped and listed in a distinctive way, as in this passage from Isaiah: "I
will plant in the wilderness the cedar, the shittah tree, and the myrtle,
and the oil tree: I will set in the desert the fir tree, *and* the pine, and the
box tree together" (Isaiah 41.19). In its absence of modifiers, the style of
the biblical naming of plants coincides with the rhetorical preferences
of the new naturalists of the seventeenth century. One looks in vain
through the works of Browne, Boyle, Evelyn, Parkinson, Johnson,
Hooke, and Ray for the conventional moralizing epithet characteristic
of Du Bartas's and Spenser's representation of trees and other plants.
The new philosophy did not so much call the old epithets in doubt as to
embrace a discourse in which such epithets were irrelevant. It is not,
however, only in the absence of rhetorical adornment that the Bible's
representation of trees would have corresponded for Milton with the
practices and assumptions of the new philosophy. English translators did
not agree about *which* trees were signified by the Hebrew names.
Compare the Geneva Bible's translation of Isaiah 41.19, for instance, to
that of the King James Version above: "I wil set in the wildernes the
cedre, the shittah tre, & the myrre tre & the pine tre, & I wil set in the
wildernes the fyrre tree, the elme and the boxe tree together." The biblical "mixed forest," in other words, is inherently unstable, for its constituent elements are changeable and even (as in the case of the shittah tree)
unknowable.

This instability suggests that it needs to be inserted into a symbolic
landscape with some care. Yet Thomas Browne, notable for his patient

unpicking of ill-founded conclusions, abandons caution in the case of biblical trees. Even as he admits that no one is quite certain what the shittah tree is, he suggests an overarching symbolic significance for the group of trees in Isaiah 41:[9] "Though some doubt may be made of the Shittah Tree, yet all these Trees here mentioned being such as are ever green, you will more emphatically apprehend the mercifull meaning of God in this mention of no fading, but always verdant Trees in dry and desart places."[10] Browne's willingness to say what the grouping of trees "means," given the presence both of the mysterious shittah tree and of a tree translated sometimes as "elm" and sometimes as "pine," is surprising for an experimentalist. It suggests that "haste to assertion without due and mature suspension of judgment" which Bacon warns against in *The Advancement of Learning*.[11] Bacon's own aphoristic collections of experimental data embody his determination to avoid the "methodizing" and the "haste to assertion" which he believes to be pernicious to natural philosophy. He knows the cost of that choice: some readers will regard his work as "an indigested heap of particulars," lacking "that lustre which books cast into methods have."[12] So writes his secretary, William Rawley, in the reader's address to *Sylva Sylvarum*, adding that Bacon

resolved to prefer the good of men, and that which might best secure it, before anything that might have relation to himself. And he knew well that there was no other way open to unloose men's minds, being bound and, as it were, maleficiate by the charms of deceiving notions and theories, and thereby made impotent for generation of works, but only nowhere to depart from the sense and clear experience; but to keep close to it.[13]

Bacon's belief in the power of the unconnected or free-standing particular to liberate thought lies behind the willingness of his self-styled disciples, the new philosophers, to admit, again and again, that they have "as yet" no theory to explain many of those particulars.

Milton's choice of a biblical mixed *sylva* for the garden of Eden is analogous in mode to Bacon's *Sylva sylvarum*, or, as Spedding translates it, a *"collection of collections*; that is, a variety of Sylvæ (or collections of facts relating to particular subjects) gathered together."[14] Like Bacon's collection of collections, and the Bible's collection of "places," Milton's collection of trees hinders and frustrates neat systematizing. This has a profound effect upon the symbolizing work of the trees of paradise. Because there is no obvious unifying symbolic link among the group, the emphasis of the passage tends to fall upon the individual trees, at least in the first instance. (Considering the trees as individuals eventually suggests new terms for ordering the whole list, but they tend to be terms by which one organizes a lack of cohesion, terms such as *discordance, tension,* and *contradiction.*)[15] The absence of conventional tags in Milton's catalog reinforces the need to pay attention to the nature of individual trees, not because they are strange or unique, but precisely because they are not. No matter how unsatisfactorily, an epithet justifies including an item in a catalog: a pine heads Du Bartas's list because it is "loftie"; the maple concludes Spenser's list because it is "seeldom inward sound." Without such tags to guide their thinking, readers must ask themselves why these particular trees grow in Milton's paradise. The answer lies in the intersection of the new naturalism with traditional symbolism.

The fact that Milton's catalog of paradisal trees begins with the cedar is significant. In most Renaissance natural histories, impressive size, usually coinciding with symbolic status, gives a creature pride of place. Thus, as we have seen, the lion or the elephant typically heads the section on "quadrupeds"; the whale, the section on "fishes." The cedar is first among the resinous trees in Gerard's *Herball* and Parkinson's *Theatrum Botanicum.* Gerard describes the cedar as "in his talnesse and largenesse farre surmounting all other trees," and Johnson offers no correction.[16] Parkinson declares, "This great Cedar groweth up with a great thicke upright body, taller then any other tree whatsoever stored with branches on all sides."[17] Whether Parkinson's "whatsoever" is absolute or refers only to trees with branches growing on all sides, his admiration for the cedar's height is clear. Thomas Browne observes in his tract on biblical plants that the titular name, "Cedars of Libanus," was bestowed on the trees "because they were of the noblest and largest kind of that Vegetable."[18]

But in fact Gerard, Johnson, Parkinson, and Browne had never seen a living, full-grown cedar.[19] Nor had John Evelyn, whose discussion of the cedar in *Sylva* we will return to. Nor, it seems plausible to suggest, had Milton.[20] They had perhaps seen a branch from the cedar tree or, at best, a sapling.[21] As Browne remarks, "Some are now so curious as to keep the Branches and Cones thereof among their rare Collections."[22] A picture of a branch is the sole illustration for both Gerard's and Parkinson's entries on the cedar (fig. 12), whereas the pine, fir, and pitch trees are illustrated with drawings of branches and whole trees. For the shape and size of the mature cedar, seventeenth-century readers of herbals have to rely largely on the verbal account, although they could see stylized depictions of the whole cedar on maps of the Holy Land. The map entitled "Libanus et eius vicinia" in Fuller's *Pisgah-sight of Palestine,* for instance,

12 Branch of "The Great Cedar tree of Libanus," from *The Herball* (1636) by John
Gerard, edited by Thomas Johnson. "Some are now so curious as to keep the
Branches and Cones thereof among their rare Collections."

shows a series of discrete, sharply mounded hills, on each of which are ten to fifteen "cedars."[23] Impossibly large in proportion to the represented landscape, the trees have long, straight, bare trunks, with a cone-shaped bush near the top. They are clearly conifers, and they are indeed lofty. But it seems likely that Fuller's cedars simply reflect the common opinion about the trees' height. What produced that opinion is undoubtedly the esteem in which the cedar was held by writers of the Bible. "The frequent and solemn allusions to the Cedar in Holy Writ, seem to give it something of a sacred character," remarks Jacob Strutt in his *Sylva Brittanica*.[24] Early modern readers translated that esteem into the tree's imagined height.

Given the almost universal assumption about the loftiness of the cedar, Evelyn's reticence on the subject is particularly impressive. He notes in the 1679 edition of *Sylva* that the "*New-England* [cedar], is a lofty grower," but he refrains from the usual superlatives.[25] Evelyn's eighteenth-century editor, Alexander Hunter, takes the occasion to scold Milton for not displaying a similar carefulness:

The epithet of *lofty* sometimes given to the Cedar is by no means just, since from the experience we have of these trees growing in England, as also from the testimony of travellers who have visited the few remaining ones on Mount Libanus, they are not inclined to be lofty, but, on the contrary, extend their branches very wide. The Psalmist makes a proper allusion to this tree in his description of the flourishing state of a people. "They shall spread abroad like a Cedar of Libanus." Had Milton been as good a Naturalist as he was a Poet, he would not have written,

... and over head upgrew
Insuperable height of loftiest shade
Cedar, and Pine, and Fir, and branching Palm.[26]

If nothing else, Hunter's irritation indicates that he reads the passage in book IV to mean that Milton has represented the cedars of paradise as the loftiest of trees. This reading of the passage's symbolic language, a reading which may be called conservative or traditional, is certainly available; the cedar's place in the catalog and the proximity of *cedar* to *loftiest* even encourage it.

Hunter is mistaken, however, to accuse Milton of bad botany. The description of paradisal trees in *Paradise Lost*, brief as it is, negotiates skillfully between old certainties partially discredited, and new uncertainties permitting (some) botanical license. A careful seventeenth-century reader is as capable as any other of noticing that the herbalists who claimed to describe the cedar's height had not, in fact, seen a cedar. A careful seventeenth-century reader might also have noted the absence of an illustration of the whole tree. Moreover, it is from Satan's perspective that trees (or walls) are regarded as "insuperable." A conservative reading of the passage's symbolism is forced, in other words, to endorse the extreme and absolute forms of comparison ("loftiest," "insuperable") typical of Satan's view of the world. A less conservative approach to the symbolic language of the passage can point out that the phrase "loftiest shade" does not have to mean that the *trees* casting shade are the loftiest, for *shade* is not necessarily a metonymy for *tree*. The shade *itself*, the passage suggests, is high and lofty – an effective way to describe what happens when one tries to see the top of a tree while looking into the sun.[27] One's eyes are dazzled. With the sun behind it, the tree appears to be only a tall dark mass, a lofty shade. Satan, looking up into the sun at the trees of paradise, perceives them as he perceives the throne of God: they are dark with exceeding light.

The passage simultaneously gives us, then, cedars which are the loftiest of trees and hence insuperable – cedars which are inscribed, that is, in a satanic discourse of hierarchy and old-fashioned botany – and cedars which are, simply, one kind of tree among several. It is the availability of both representational modes, for *all* the creatures of the garden of Eden, that marks Milton's depiction of the natural world as belonging to the beginning of modernity rather than the end of Renaissance. There is nothing "simple" about inserting the cedar in a catalog of kinds of trees, even when it is stripped of its title as "loftiest" among them.

Contradictory information about the cedar circulated freely in the seventeenth century. There is a sharp discrepancy, for instance, between Parkinson's *Theatrum Botanicum* and Evelyn's *Sylva* on the subject of the cedar's habitat. Parkinson is categorical:

This Cedar groweth on sundry mountaines in *Syria,* and the parts neere thereunto, and the coldest parts of them that are covered with snow as *Amanus, Taurus* and *Libanus,* and not in many places else that have beene observed;[28]

Evelyn is equally categorical, on the opposite point, praising the cedar,

which grows in all *extreams*; In the moist *Barbadoes,* the hot *Bermudas,* and the cold *New England*; even where the *Snow* lyes (as I am assur'd), almost half the year: Why then it should not thrive in *Old England,* I conceive is from our want of *industry*: It grows in the *Bogs of America,* and in the *Mountains* of *Asia:* It seems there is no place affrights it.[29]

Parkinson's relegation of the cedar to Syria – to a cold, remote region adjacent to the Holy Land – portrays it as an exotic tree. Evelyn's demand, "Why then it should not thrive in *Old England*," suggests that, on the contrary, the cedar is or could become a common domestic tree.[30] The implied suggestion may reflect Evelyn's reading of such New World historians as José de Acosta, who simply states: "Cedars in olde time so much esteemed, are there [in the West Indies] very common, both for buildings and shippes."[31]

Evelyn's comments on the cedar may also contain an oblique criticism of the fashion of putting cedar branches in curiosity cabinets. His interest is *not* in the tree as an exotic living relic of biblical times. Nor is it Milton's. One persistent critical approach to *Paradise Lost* maintains that "Milton was concerned . . . with dramatizing the *loss* of Eden; he wanted to overwhelm us with all that we might have had."[32] This approach characteristically finds that Milton depicts paradise as exotic, remote, distinct from ordinary reality, as if that which has never been available is analogous to that which has been lost. But a close reading of the natural world depicted in the poem will not sustain this notion of an exotic paradise. Exoticism, or strangeness, is a preoccupation of the old science. If the cedars in *Paradise Lost* were called "Cedars of Lebanon," or, indeed, if "loftiest" were more unambiguously applied to them, we would have to regard them as belonging to an "imagery of storied remoteness and oriental lushness with which," some critics maintain, "Milton saturates his Paradise."[33] But "cedar" in the poem is unmodified. It may refer to the cedar of Lebanon, but it may equally refer to the cedar of Bermuda, the Bahamas, or New England. The cedar of *Paradise Lost* belongs to the Holy Land and to the New World. It is worthy to serve as a gift for Solomon – and as a source of shingles for houses.

The garden of Eden is not, that is, a collector's paradise, where exotic plants are collected and preserved. Plants are not represented as commodities in the poem. As Simon Schama has shown, the seventeenth century relished accumulation and display, and plants could be treasures.[34] Whether desired for botanical gardens, herbariums, or the gardens of great estates, plants were subject to the incrementalizing and acquisitive impulse that propels all collecting. The rhetorical equivalent of collecting is the list, and indeed the plant list is a distinctive feature of seventeenth-century botanical literature.[35] But the catalog of trees in *Paradise Lost* is evocative rather than inclusive. Milton's garden of Eden is not, that is, a botanical garden in the sense that Andrew Cunningham has described it: "a sort of depot for the collection, storage and distribution of new plants . . . centres of correspondence and exchange networks . . . In this sense the gardens become living catalogues of plants, living catalogues of Creation."[36] Cunningham goes on to argue that early modern botanists used their collections to look for "the 'natural order' existing among plants."[37] This is an experimentally laudable end, but in the thirst to acquire new specimens, the botanist's passion is sometimes indistinguishable from the collector's. There is no place for this aspect of experimentalism in the garden of Eden of *Paradise Lost*.[38] The poem does not present us with an inventory of species, to use the modern terminology. Rather, the botanical decorum of Milton's paradise allows the species to be implied in the genus.

What is true of the cedar is true of the fir, pine, palm, and virtually every other tree the herbalists dealt with: there were inevitably several varieties of any kind one cared to name.[39] These were usually given descriptive titles, identifying them as "manured" and "tame" (i.e., cultivated) or wild, East Indian or West Indian, New World or Old, lesser or greater, bastard or true. Even the palm, that "traditionally triumphal and eastern tree . . . thrown in" among the paradisal trees, has its humble European cousin. In his entry on the palm tree, Parkinson includes three varieties, *Palma vulgaris*, *Palma chamaerops*, and, described below, *Palma humilis*:

The *Palmito* or low or wilde Date tree groweth in divers places of *Europe*, not to be above a yard high in the stocke or body, shooting out leaves from thence very like unto the former Date tree, but much lesser and shorter: this beareth a round head at the side of the leaves, composed of many foulds of skinnes, which breaking open, shew forth a number of white flowers, standing upon small thready stalkes: this head being cut off, before it open it selfe for flowers, is very delicate to eate like a Coleflower or Cabbage, and more pleasant then either Hartichoke, Chardon, or Tartoufli be, and are served to rich mens tables for a sallate of great delight.[40]

Indeed, at least one variety of any kind of tree was certain to be home-grown and common, given the practice of naming New World plants for their presumed resemblance to European plants, and European plants for their presumed resemblance to classical and biblical plants.

In the absence of qualifying, descriptive titles in the poem, "cedar," "pine," "fir," or "palm" can refer to any or all varieties. This referential latitude leads to one of the most distinctive features of *Paradise Lost*: the coexistence, indeed the coincidence, of the exotic and the everyday, which informs every aspect of the representation of the garden of Eden in the poem. What seems to be richly remote from our fallen reality is shown instead to be but an enriched version of what we have all around us, and what seems at first glance to be ordinary and everyday is shown to be imbued with the beauty of the rare and exotic. The garden of Eden is not a precious locked cabinet of curiosities. Its treasures are, on the contrary, animate, robust, and comfortably familiar. We assume the palms of book IV are date palms because they grow in paradise, but the poem does not say so. The palms of Eden and the palmitos of Europe may, after all, be "each to other like, more than on earth is thought."

The merging of paradisal and everyday reality in Milton's representation of the natural world renders untenable a nostalgic reading of the poem, a reading which claims that the poem dramatizes what has been lost. Milton's representation of the natural world dramatizes, instead, what our postlapsarian world and the prelapsarian paradise have in common. It is a representational mode which emphasizes human responsibility for preserving paradise, as a final look at the Edenic cedars will demonstrate. Lofty, evergreen, and fragrant, the great cedar is most notable, Gerard writes, for its wood:

> The timber is extreame hard, and rotteth not, nor waxeth old; there is no wormes nor rottennesse can hurt or take the hard matter or heart of this wood, which is very odoriferous, and somwhat red. *Solomon* King of the Jewes did therefore build Gods Temple in Jerusalem of Cedarwood. The Gentiles were wont to make their Divels or Images of this kinde of wood, that they might last the longer.[41]

Parkinson makes a related case for the rosin of the cedar of Libanus, which "preserveth the dead bodies from rotting, and therefore was called the life of the dead."[42]

Inevitably, cedars are symbolically associated with immortality, an association which seems at first glance to be explanation enough for their presence in the garden of Eden.[43] But Milton's representation of natural creatures needs, as always, to be considered in light of experimentalist findings, and Browne, Parkinson and Gerard all express concern that the cedars of Mount Libanus are disappearing. Browne laments:

> And, though much Cedar Wood be now brought from America, yet 'tis time to take notice of the true Cedar of Libanus, imployed in the Temple of Solomon; for they have been much destroyed and neglected, and become at last but thin. Bellonius could reckon but twenty eight, Rowolfius and Radzevil but twenty four, and Bidulphus the same number. And a later account of some English Travellers saith, that they are now but in one place, and in a small compass, in Libanus.[44]

Evelyn, too, laments the disappearance of the cedar, noting that "we might have of the very *best* kind in the *World* from the *Summer Islands*, though now almost utterly exhausted there also, and so the most incomparable of that *sacred* wood like to be quite *destroy'd* by our *Negligence*, which is by nature almost *eternal*."[45] That which for earlier generations had seemed to be a symbol of eternal life could itself, as the seventeenth century saw, become "exhausted." Milton's naming of the cedar among the paradisal trees becomes more interesting and complex in light of this perception. It is not sufficient to say that the cedar belongs in Milton's paradise because it symbolizes eternal life, although the poem does not repress that symbolic possibility. Overlaying it, however, is an implicit reminder that salvation does not inhere in venerable objects. The cedar may symbolize preservation even unto eternal life, but it also signifies the human responsibility to preserve that which preserves.

CHAPTER 10

Flourishing colors

There are no flower beds in *Paradise Lost.*[1] The term *beds* itself appears only in the context of an explicit rejection:

> Flowers worthy of Paradise which not nice art
> In beds and curious knots, but nature boon
> Poured forth profuse on hill and dale and plain.   (*PL*, IV.241–43)

Fowler observes of knots that "such formal, artificial arrangements could already seem insipid" by the mid-seventeenth century (*PL*, IV.242n).[2] The new style in flower bed design was the *parterre de broderie* (fig. 13), popularized by the francophile Stuart monarchs.[3] The difference between a knot and a *parterre de broderie* is the difference between strict, often geometrical, precision and freer, abstract floral forms. The symbolizing modes of the knot and the *parterre* are thus of different orders. While the knot points beyond itself (to moral or political virtues, a family name, or an owner's credo), the *parterre* points to the flowers out of which it is composed. It symbolizes, if at all, reflexively.[4]

The flowers in Milton's paradise, though not confined to beds, suggest in their way of growing the fluid design of the *parterre de broderie*. When Satan approaches Eve in book IX, "now hid, now seen," he makes his way

> Among thick-woven arborets and flowers
> Embordered on each bank, the hand of Eve: (*PL*, IX.437–38)

Alastair Fowler sees in *Embordered* a fusion with the heraldic term *Imbordured* (*PL*, IX.438n). Yet as he states in the same note, "the hand of Eve" means "handiwork; as one might say with respect to a painting – or an embroidery." It thus seems likely that *embordered* also refers to the practice of putting ornamental work of embroidery or lace around the edge of a garment.[5] (Such ornamental work may well have had a floral pattern, a sign of the impact of floral-printed cotton imports from India upon English embroidery in the sixteenth and seventeenth centuries.[6])

13 Design for *parterre de broderie*, from *Wilton Garden* (1645) by Isaac de Caus, showing the abstract floral design that replaced the knot in popularity.

The reference to embroidered flowers is more explicit in the description of the bower in book IV:

> the roof
> Of thickest covert was inwoven shade
> Laurel and myrtle, and what higher grew
> Of firm and fragrant leaf; on either side
> Acanthus, and each odorous bushy shrub
> Fenced up the verdant wall; each beauteous flower,
> Iris all hues, roses, and jessamine
> Reared high their flourished heads between, and wrought
> Mosaic; underfoot the violet,
> Crocus, and hyacinth with rich inlay

>   Broidered the ground, more coloured than with stone
>   Of costliest emblem: (*PL*, IV.692–703)

Conspicuously missing here is a key for interpreting the fluid designs of
the embroidered ground or the bordered bank, or indeed the bower's
"mosaic" and "the soft downy bank damasked with flowers" (*PL*, IV.334)
on which Adam and Eve have their supper. Like the script of insects
whose creeping turns the earth into an illuminated manuscript, the
embroidered earth wrought by Eden's flowers cannot be translated into
a fixed meaning. As Thomas Browne might say, indeterminacy is to be
valued where "there is no determination in the Text" (*PE*, 537). Floral
creation has been so represented in *Paradise Lost* that we can read it as
Milton believed we should read the Bible: as a god-given collection of
fragments and "places" to be ceaselessly "conferred." Hence the flowers
of the garden of Eden are not bedded; their meanings are not embedded in convention.

At the opposite extreme from the symbolizing mode of the flowers of
Paradise Lost is the emblematic garden of Henry Hawkins's *Partheneia
Sacra* (1633), with its explicitly interpreted "Flowers of al Vertues."

The Lillie of spotles and immaculate Chastitie, the Rose of Shamfastnes and
bashful Modestie, the Violet of Humilitie, the Gilloflower of Patience, the
Marygold of Charitie, the Hiacinth of Hope, the Sun-flower of
Contemplatio[n], the Tulip of Beautie and gracefulnes.[7]

The reader's experience of Milton's garden of Eden has little or nothing
to do with such emblematizing. The sole use of *emblem* in *Paradise Lost*, in
the description of the bower quoted above, removes the term from the
realm of the allegorized picture and restores it to its etymological sense,
meaning "inlaid work"[8]:

>   underfoot the violet,
>   Crocus, and hyacinth with rich inlay
>   Broidered the ground, more coloured than with stone
>   Of costliest emblem: (*PL*, IV.700–03)

A passage in *Eikonoklastes* better known for its allusion to "some Twelf-
nights entertainment" places "quaint Emblems" in the company of
"devices begg'd from the old Pageantry" of the masque.[9] The implication is that emblems are an outmoded art form, an implication not
refuted in *Paradise Lost* or elsewhere in Milton's works.[10] "Milton," as
Walpole astutely remarked, "was forced to wait until the world had done
admiring Quarles."[11]

Milton's editors have occasionally attempted to re-inscribe the poem in this older symbolic mode. After noting that *emblem* means an inlaid ornament in book IV, Fowler goes on to argue that the passage also, inevitably, invokes the term's more common meaning: "it is difficult to think that the other sense of *emblem* (pictorial symbol) is not also meant to operate here, and to draw attention to the emblematic properties of the flowers" (*PL*, IV.700–03n). Fowler proceeds to do so, pointing to "the humility of the *violet*, prudence of the *hyacinth*, amiability of the *jessamin*, etc." (*PL*, IV.700–03n). So applied, however, an emblematic reading is static. It wishes to fix the meaning of Edenic flowers and so precludes the pleasure to be had from continual interpretive activity. Reading the garden's flowers as emblems pushes *Paradise Lost*, in its symbolizing mode, back towards *The Faerie Queene* rather than allowing it to remain where it belongs, a contemporary of Sprat's *History of the Royal Society* (1667), Boyle's *Usefulness of Experimental Natural Philosophy* (1663), and Browne's *Pseudodoxia Epidemica* (the sixth edition of which was published in 1672). We thereby render ourselves unable to perceive what is historically distinctive about the poem's representation of floral nature. That distinctiveness is most apparent in Milton's treatment of the rose, the subject of the rest of the chapter and of all flowers the most deeply embedded in conventional readings.

In *Paradise Lost*, book IX, Satan finds Eve, alone, tending her flowers:

> Eve separate he spies,
> Veiled in a cloud of fragrance, where she stood,
> Half spied, so thick the roses bushing round
> About her glowed, oft stooping to support
> Each flower of slender stalk, whose head though gay
> Carnation, purple, azure, or specked with gold,
> Hung drooping unsustained, them she upstays
> Gently with myrtle band, mindless the while,
> Her self, though fairest unsupported flower,
> From her best prop so far, and storm so nigh.   (*PL*, IX.424–33)

Eve's appearance among her roses has long been a site of critical interest to Milton scholars. Earlier discussion tended to center on Eve and the sensuality of the scene, Christopher Ricks memorably observing that line 425 suggests, momentarily, that "the scent was so thick that it almost hid her."[12] More recently, scholars have been concerned with Satan's voyeurism and Eve's placement as the object of his gaze.

The natural history of the passage has not seemed problematic, or even suggestive, to most critics of *Paradise Lost*. Yet the roses merit our attention, for the passage hints at the possibility that they are azure (and carnation, purple, and gold). Fowler, with his usual careful attention to detail, has commented on these colors, but in terms of their symbolism rather than their significance for natural history. They are, he observes, "the colours of Minerva, the virgin goddess" (*PL*, IX.426–31n). His chief concern is not in any case with the colors of the rose but with its emblematic significance. Citing Valeriano's *Hieroglyphica* (1613) and Ripa's *Iconologia* (1603), he notes:

The rose, particularly when the focus is on the head as distinct from the leaves, as here, was a symbol of human frailty and of the mutability of mortal happiness . . . Thus Eve's supporting the rose with myrtle should be read as an emblem of the dependence of unfallen bliss upon conjugal virtue. (*PL*, IX.426–31n)

His preoccupation with the emblem tradition prevents Fowler from seeing that the passage raises scientific issues of great interest to Milton's contemporaries. It is not that Eve's roses are not symbolic; they are. But their mode of symbolizing does not look back to the emblem tradition. It is a mode of symbolizing renovated and reshaped by its contact with the scientific concerns of the mid-seventeenth century.

A conventional reading of Eve's flowers and their colors is certainly available, however. We might begin by putting the case *against* the possibility that Eve is tending azure roses in the garden of Eden. The referent of "whose head" (*PL*, IX.428) is clearly *flower* in the same line; that is, Eve, obscured by rose bushes, supports the heads of each of the drooping ground flowers around her. These are gaily colored, "Carnation, purple, azure, or specked with gold." One might even argue that *Carnation* is a substantive, and that it is the gay carnations around Eve which are "purple, azure, or specked with gold." This last possibility, however, leaves us with azure carnations (as problematic, in their way, as azure roses). Moreover, although *Carnation* can be a substantive in the seventeenth century, it would be unusual to describe only the "head" of the flower as a carnation. It is much more likely that *Carnation* is adjectival – along with "purple," "azure," and "specked with gold." To return to the possibility that Eve is engaged in supporting various and variously colored flowers, lines 425–26 state only that she is *standing* among roses. She in fact had proposed earlier that she go to garden "[i]n yonder spring of roses intermixed / With myrtle" (*PL*, IX.218–19).

Working against this relatively subdued, conventional reading of the passage, however, is the fact that roses are the only flowers that Eve explicitly mentions in her proposal ("yonder spring of roses") and the only flowers explicitly mentioned by the narrator when Satan comes upon Eve. It is, moreover, common seventeenth-century usage to speak of the "flower" of the rose as distinguished from the plant. Thus *flower*, the referent of "whose head" (*PL*, ix.428), can mean the flower of the rose plant. *Stalk*, in the same line, can be a synonym for *stem*; it therefore does not have to imply flowers growing individually from the ground, but can also refer to flowers growing on a bush.[13] This allows for the possibility that Eve is supporting roses whose heads are large and heavy, roses which are "Carnation, purple, azure, or specked with gold." The unconventional interpretive option, which the reader just glimpses in the verse as Satan just spies Eve in her roses, releases an extraordinary re-creative energy into the symbolizing mode of the poem. In the spirit of what Catherine Wilson calls the "charm" of the experimental philosophy, "its similarity to child's play," let us play with the possibility that there are azure roses in Eden.[14]

A "spring" of roses suggests an exuberant bursting forth of roses in a vernal world, and we need to consider the possibility that Eve's azure roses are intended to suggest that the colors of the prelapsarian garden are richer, more vivid, and more rainbow-like than the colors of our postlapsarian world.[15] Some support for this theory can be found in the fate of the garland of roses that Adam intends to give Eve when she returns from gardening alone. As Eve tells her story,

> in her cheek distemper flushing glowed.
> On the other side, Adam, soon as he heard
> The fatal trespass done by Eve, amazed,
> Astonied stood and blank, while horror chill
> Ran through his veins, and all his joints relaxed;
> From his slack hand the garland wreathed for Eve
> Down dropped, and all the *faded* roses shed:
> (*PL*, ix.887–93; emphasis added)

In this context, however, *faded* does not signify primarily a loss of color, but rather means what we today signify by the word *wilted*.[16] The phenomenon of wilting was not understood in Milton's day, and the term was not introduced into general usage until the eighteenth century.[17] *Faded* or *withered* were the terms used until then to describe plants drooping or becoming limp.

Perhaps, then, the unorthodox colors of Eve's roses are intended to suggest an Eden which is exotic, remote, and Other. If so, the roses of paradise would suggest what the trees of paradise do not. As the previous chapter showed, the use of general, unmodified names (cedar, pine, and fir) allows the poem simultaneously to evoke "exotic" and domestic varieties of trees. This works _against_ a representation of the garden as radically Other. Paradisal roses, however, seem to have two characteristics that point toward the exotic: not only are their colors unusual; the roses are also thornless. After the Fall, there are "faded roses"; before the Fall, there are "Flowers of all hue, and without thorn the rose" (_PL_, IX.256). But thornless roses are in fact commonplace features of sixteenth- and seventeenth-century depictions of prelapsarian life, epitomizing the desire for a world void of obnoxious qualities.[18] By themselves, they would not suffice to render Milton's paradise exotic. Moreover, thornless roses were known and cultivated in England. Gerard depicts "The Rose without prickles" in the first edition of his _Herball_ (fig.14). John Parkinson mentions in _Paradisi in Sole_ the "Rosa sine spinis simplex et multiplex," or "the rose without thornes single and double." This rose, he explains, "hath divers greene smooth shootes, rising from the root, without any pricke or thorne at all upon them, eyther young or old."[19] What is true of a single kind of rose in the present world (and is a quality so rare that the rose is named for it) is true of every rose in paradise. The thornlessness of the Edenic rose thus suggests simultaneously the strangeness and the familiarity of paradise.

Flowers of "all hue" are also commonplace in depictions of paradise, but not when _all_ is uncircumscribed by everyday experience.[20] In "Lycidas," the springing up of "flowrets of a thousand hues" (135) signifies the return of normality when the "dread voice is past" (132). Line 144 of the poem, "The white pink, and the pansy freaked with jet," plays with the naming of colors, but the colors themselves are the ordinary ones for pinks and pansies. In _Paradise Lost_, however, there is an initial hint in the description of Adam and Eve's bower that the colors of the paradisal flowers may well be extraordinary. Creating a mosaic for the bower are "Iris all hues, roses, and jessamine" (_PL_, IV.698). Iris's bow, the prism, _does_ contain "all hues." Is there a suggestion that in paradise the flower named for her does, too? Prismatic colors and color in general, a traditional concern of philosophers, became increasingly the concern of natural philosophers in the seventeenth century. If Aristotle in his _Problems_ was the first to ask why creatures have the colors they do, the seventeenth century put the question to new polemical uses.[21]

In the preface to his _Historie of the World_, Walter Raleigh uses a version of the Aristotelian question to criticize Aristotle:

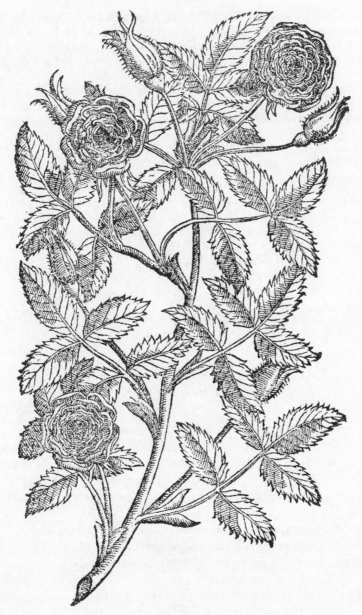

14 "The Rose without prickles," from *The Herball* (1597) by John Gerard, which could be found growing in the garden of Eden and the gardens of England.

I shall never be persuaded that God hath shut up all light of Learning within the lanthorne of Aristotles brains . . . *The Cheese-wife knoweth it as well as the Philosopher, that sowre Runnet doth coagulate her milke into a curde. But if wee ask a reason of this cause, why the sowrenesse doth it? whereby it doth it? and the manner how? I thinke that there is nothing to bee found in vulgar Philosophie, to satisfie this and many other like vulgar questions. But man, to cover his ignorance in the least things, who cannot give a true reason for the Grasse under his feete, why it should bee greene rather than red, or of any other colour . . . will disable Gods power to make a world, without matter to make it of.*[22]

John Donne "triumphantly" incorporates the same question in *The Second Anniversary*, along with several other fundamental and unanswered questions.

> Knowst thou but how the stone doth enter in
> The bladders Cave, and never breake the skin?
> Knowst thou how blood, which to the hart doth flow,
> Doth from one ventricle to th'other go?
> And for the putrid stuffe, which thou dost spit,
> Knowst thou how thy lungs have attracted it?
>
> *   *   *
>
> What hope have we to know our selves, when wee
> Know not the least things, which for our use bee?
>
> *   *   *
>
> Why grasse is greene, or why our blood is red,
> Are mysteries which none have reach'd unto.
>
> (*Second Anniversary* 269–74, 279–80, 288–89)[23]

Triumphantly is John Carey's adverb. He observes that Donne "takes the present inconclusive state of knowledge as proof that knowledge will always be inconclusive," whereas "to a Baconian Donne's list would constitute a programme for future research."[24] Indeed Bacon himself appropriates the problem of color for a reformed natural philosophy.

In *Sylva Sylvarum*, Bacon raises the problem of color in several forms, most of them echoing the questions raised in the *Problems*. He notes, for instance, that birds are more brightly colored than beasts, remarking: "no beast hath any fine azure, or carnation, or green hair."[25] Although he does not believe that the color of birds is due to their being "more in the beams of the sun than beasts,"[26] he repeats Aristotle's claim, "The heat of the sun maketh men black in some countries, as in Æthiopia and Ginny."[27] Bacon later suggests as an experiment the removal of the first growth of feathers and fur from chicks and whelps to see if the second growth is white. He cites the common opinion that lack of moisture and nourishment drains color and produces whiteness:

And therefore in birds, it is very likely that the feathers that come first will be many times of divers colours, according to the nature of the bird; for that the skin is more porous; but when the skin is more shut and close, the feathers will come white.[28]

Believing that flowers derive their colors from the "juice" of the soil, he urges, as an experiment, sowing the seeds of one kind of gillyflower and noting the results:[29]

there will come up gilly-flowers, some of one colour, and some of another, casually, as the seed meeteth with nourishment in the earth; so that the gardeners find that they may have two or three roots amongst an hundred that are rare and of great price; as purple, carnation of several stripes: the cause is (no doubt) that in earth, though it be contiguous and in one bed, there are very several juices; and as the seed doth casually meet with them, so it cometh forth.[30]

In *New Atlantis*, the preoccupation with experiments to change color manifests itself among the works of Salomon's House. "And we make (by art)," says one of the Fathers of the House,

in the same orchards and gardens, trees and flowers to come earlier or later than their seasons; and to come up and bear more speedily than by their natural course they do. We make them also by art greater much than their nature; and their fruit greater and sweeter and of differing taste, smell, colour, and figure, from their nature.[31]

For Bacon, the ability to change the colors of fruit, flowers, fur, and feathers means that humankind has achieved that control over nature which he equates with the advancement of learning.

The gillyflowers that Bacon singles out above as being "rare and of great price" are purple and carnation, which are among the colors of Eve's roses. Given the fact that all names for colors are relative, purple and carnation have a particularly wide range of meanings. *Purple* may signify anything from crimson to violet.[32] In Donne's "The Flea," the question, "hast thou since / Purpled thy naile, in blood of innocence?" (19–20), implies that purple is the color of blood – unless Donne is being so precise as to indicate the slightly different color that blood has when one sees it through the filter of a fingernail.[33] Blood in any case is not a uniform color: arterial blood is brighter red than venous blood. *Carnation*, as the name suggests, means "flesh-colored." Flesh tones are notoriously varied; in the eighteenth century, the term *carnations* refers to the particular and characteristic color a given painter uses for representing human

skin. For Bacon and Milton, *carnation* could denote various shades of rosy
pink, including even deep crimson.[34] It is thus impossible to say precisely
what shade of pink Eve's carnation roses are, or precisely what is the proportion of blue to red in her purple ones. We will return later in the
chapter to the mixed nature of these colors.

Those who followed where Bacon led quickly realized that the
problem of color was not in fact a single problem, but a complex of
problems. Thomas Browne repeatedly considers the nature of color in
Pseudodoxia Epidemica, introducing the topic in book VI, chapter 10:

Thus of colours in generall, under whose glosse and vernish all things are seen,
few or none have yet beheld the true nature, or positively set downe their incon-
troulable causes; which while some ascribe unto the mixture of the Elements,
others to the graduality of opacity and light; they have left our endeavours to
grope them out by twilight, and by darknesse almost to discover that whose existence is evidenced by light. (*PE*, 507)

No one, that is, understands the nature of color. Furthermore, Browne
admits, even if we could explain it, how could we explain why a given
creature is a particular color?

Thus although a man understood the generall nature of coloures, yet were it no
easie probleme to resolve, Why grasse is green? Why Garlick, Molyes, and
Porrets have white roots, deep green leaves, and blacke seeds? Why severall
docks, and sorts of Rhubarb with yellow roots, send forth purple flowers? Why
also from Lactary or milky plants which have a white and lacteous juice dis-
persed through every part, there arise flowers blue and yellow? Moreover beside
the specificall and first digressions ordained from the Creation, which might bee
urged to salve the variety in every species; why shall the marvaile of Peru
produce its flowers of different colours, and that not once, or constantly, but
every day and variously? Why Tulips of one colour produce some of another,
and running through almost all, should still escape a blew? And lastly, why some
men, yea and they a mighty and considerable part of mankinde, should first
acquire and still retaine the glosse and tincture of blacknesse? (*PE*, 507–08)

Although Bacon's concerns shape the development of this passage, and
Raleigh's query ("Why grasse is green?") heads its list of questions,
Browne's treatment of color is not as conventional here as might at first
appear. He gives it an experimental twist when he mentions the tulip's
"escape" from blue. Alone among all his examples, this one is couched
in the negative. It is here that Browne's speculations have particular relevance for Eve's azure roses.

Because the study of plants in the sixteenth and seventeenth centuries
belongs to natural *history* rather than natural *philosophy*, and thus takes the

form of encyclopedic collections of observations and experiments, Browne's tulip example is highly problematic. If one's knowledge is not systematic but empirical (a collection of sense data, in this case), then one cannot prove a negative. Browne discusses this problem in the first book of *Pseudodoxia Epidemica* when he considers the question of authority in historical matters. He observes:

a Testimony in points historicall, and where it is of unavoydable use, is of no illation [that is, one cannot draw a conclusion from it] in the negative, nor is it of consequence that Herodotus writing nothing of Rome, there was therefore no such city in his time; or because Dioscorides hath made no mention of Unicornes horne, there is therefore no such thing in Nature. (*PE*, 43)

We can apply this point to roses. The vaunted method of the new philosophy – which was just beginning to differentiate between *experience* and *experiment* – cannot say that azure roses do not exist; it can only say that no one has yet seen an azure rose. Roses without thorns exist. Why not azure roses, growing in some part of the world remote from Europe?[35] In the distance between what the new experimentalism wants to say and what it can say about color, there is enough room for the creative imagination to paint "flowers of *all* hue." Are blue roses, then, an exception to the rule that there are no plants in paradise which exist (or may exist) *only* in distant and exotic places?

Even as the new natural history was removing restraints upon the poetic imagination, the new optics was positively encouraging the assignment of new colors to natural creatures.[36] As Browne indicates with his punning introduction to the chapter on color ("they have left our endeavours . . . by darknesse almost to discover that whose existence is evidenced by light"), the relationship between color and light was increasingly attracting the attention of experimental philosophers. Robert Boyle published *The Experimental History of Colours* in 1664, though the ideas in the treatise were in circulation some years before its publication.[37] It has been ranked in importance with the *Spring and Weight of the Air* and *The Usefulness of Experimental Philosophy*, and Newton adopted several of its generalizations for his work on optics. Boyle asserts in the treatise that color is not "an inherent quality of the object," but rather that "light itself produces the sensation of a colour."[38]

I incline to take colour to be a modification of light . . . this be at present the hypothesis I præfer, yet I propose it but in a general sense, teaching only, that the beams of light, modified by the bodies whence they are sent (reflected or refracted) to the eye, produce there that kind of sensation men commonly call colour.[39]

Boyle explains the qualification, "but in a general sense," by acknowl-
edging that he does not know why "the skin of a ripe cherry, should
exhibit a red, and not a green, and the leaf of the same tree should
exhibit a green rather than a red."[40] He admits, as it were, that he cannot
answer Raleigh's question. But he is certain that color does not result
from gross differences in bodies, as "the schools" and "some modern
Atomists" declare, but rather from the way an object reflects or refracts
light, which is then received by the eye.[41]

The prime importance of light in Boyle's theory shifts the problem of
color toward perception, and that shift creates further space for a poetic
re-imagining of paradise. Understanding color as a function of perception, that is, opens the possibility that Milton is representing not a qual-
itative difference in the roses of paradise, but a quantitative difference in
the way Adam and Eve can *see* the roses. The convention that prelapsarian Adam and Eve had acuter vision than their fallen progeny is one to
which Milton gives silent assent in *Paradise Lost*.[42] Adam is able to see fruit
growing on the trees when the "shape divine" leads him through the air
to paradise, and his discussion about the heavens in book VIII reveals him
to be a gifted astronomical observer. Only after the Fall does he require
aid for his vision, as Michael removes from his eyes "the film" produced
by the forbidden fruit. Moreover, the earth is represented as enjoying
perpetual spring before the Fall, so there are no winds, dense precipita-
tion, and shimmering heat to lessen or trouble visibility. In other words,
Milton may be representing as a normal feature of prelapsarian life the
sensitivity to color displayed in the postlapsarian world only by a gifted
observer under carefully controlled conditions.

Boyle demonstrates such sensitivity in the tenth of the "promiscuous"
experiments in his *History of Colours*. The experiment calls for making an
infusion of *lignum nephriticum*, which was commonly available in drug-
gists' shops and much valued as a remedy for kidney stones.[43]

Decant this impregnated water into a clear glass phial; and if you hold it directly
between the light and your eye, you shall see it wholly tincted . . . with an almost
golden colour . . . But if you hold this phial from the light, so that your eye be
placed betwixt the window and the phial, the liquor will appear of a deep and
lovely ceruleous colour . . . If you so hold the phial over against your eyes, that
it may have a window on one side of it, and a dark part of the room both before
it and on the other side, you shall see the liquor partly of a bluish and partly of
a golden colour. If turning your back to the window, you pour out some of the
liquor towards the light and towards your eyes, it will seem at the coming out of
the glass to be perfectly ceruleous; but when it is fallen down a little way, the
drops may seem parti-coloured, according as the beams of light do more or less

fully penetrate and illustrate them . . . If you pour a little of this tincture upon a sheet of white paper, so as the liquor may remain of some depth upon it, you may perceive the neighbouring drops to be partly of one colour, and partly of the other, according to the position of your eye in reference to the light when it looks upon them; but if you pour off the liquor, the paper will seem dyed of an almost yellow colour.[44]

If an infusion made from common *lignum nephriticum* flashes from golden to cerulean as the light strikes it differently, then surely Eve's roses can sparkle gold and azure in the unclouded light of paradise. If, that is, color is not an inherent quality of the object, we do not have to construe the poem as meaning that Edenic roses are azure and gold. Rather, Adam and Eve can perceive fully what we perceive only dimly, the subtle and changeable beauties of color belonging – *still* belonging – to all created things.

Not only the famous tenth experiment, but many other experiments that Boyle describes in the tract are based on his work with tinctures. His bibliographer, John Fulton, points out that "Boyle was the first to record that certain vegetable extracts . . . change colour when the solution is made acid or changed from acid to alkali."[45] The significance of this fact, for chemistry, is that in so doing, Boyle "gave to the world the first account of . . . chemical 'indicators.' "[46] The significance of the fact for poetry is that it grants color a certain independence from the body in which it apparently resides. Boyle cites the "Marvel of Peru," the plant whose ability to "produce its flowers of different colours . . . every day and variously" provokes Browne's wonder.[47] For Boyle, the plant's ability demonstrates that "a considerable diversity of colours" does *not* "argue an equal diversity of nature."[48] Color does not result from gross differences in bodies, that is, but from "alterations in the disposition of parts of bodies."[49] By the latter, Boyle means something like differences in chemical composition or the internal nature of a thing, differences which are not obvious to the eye but which are demonstrable "in the extraction of tinctures" of different colors.[50] The fact that these tinctures themselves can be changed is further proof that color is not inherent and hence not a fixed and stable quality.

Boyle's Experiment 20 demonstrates the remarkable fluidity of color by adding, first, acidic, and then, alkaline substances to a "good syrup of violets, impregnated with the tincture of the flowers":

drop a little of it upon a white paper . . . and on this liquor let fall two or three drops of spirit either of salt or vinegar, or almost any other eminently acid liquor, and upon the mixture of these you shall find the syrup immediately turned red . . . But to improve the experiment, let me add what has not (that I know of) been hitherto observed . . . namely, that if instead of spirit of salt, or that of vinegar, you drop upon the syrup of violets a little oil of tartar *per deliquium*, or the like quantity of solution of pot-ashes, and rub them together with your finger, you shall find the blue colour of the syrup turned in a moment into a perfect green; and the like may be performed by divers other liquors.[51]

Though in a way his predecessor would not have imagined, Boyle realizes in this experiment Bacon's old dream of changing the "normal" colors of natural creatures. By releasing color (or the notion of color) from the body in which it seems to inhere, Boyle perceives that color is endlessly changeable. Most of the experiments in his tract have to do with the transformation or metamorphosis of one color into another. Thus there is a particular emphasis upon colors "tinged," blended, mixed, and compounded. This emphasis leads Boyle to one of his chief arguments: that the colors of "changeable taffaties, the blue and golden necks of pigeons, and divers water-fowl, rainbows natural and artificial, and other bodies, whose colours the philosophers have been pleased to call not real, but apparent and fantastical"[52] – these iridescent and prismatical colors are indeed "real" because they can be compounded.

What is most noticeable about the colors of Eve's roses is that two are compounded and two are iridescent colors. Purple and carnation, as we noted above, make no claim *not* to be blended (unlike red, blue, or yellow). They have, moreover, a particularly wide range of reference. Azure and gold raise different issues of reference, as both are products of an identifiable precious substance. It is true that "Specked with gold" may mean streaked or flecked with some shade of yellow. *Golden* and *yellow* are both used, for instance, to denote the many different tones of blond hair. But because the color derives from the metal (sometimes literally), it is also fair to assume that "specked with gold" can also imply the flash or sparkle associated with metallic sheens. The name *azure* – and indeed azure pigment – is derived from lapis lazuli, capable of being highly polished. Azure and gold, moreover, are the colors associated from antiquity with the iridescence of birds' feathers.[53] Boyle himself mentions the "blue and golden necks of pigeons" and the phosphorescent "ceruleous" and "golden" tincture of *lignum nephriticum*. Azure and gold, in short, connote not "flat" colors, but colors that shimmer in the play of light. Eve's roses, "carnation, purple, azure, or specked with gold," are as changeable as Boyle's "taffaties." They refuse fixity. They are *not* conventional roses, either in color or in symbolic status.

There is another way to say this. Though roses are mentioned repeatedly in connection with the garden of Eden in *Paradise Lost*, they are never red nor white. Indeed, except in the passage in book IX, they are not given colors at all. In the single reference to "rosie red" in book VIII, describing Raphael's blush, "rosie" is already an adjective. Yet red and white roses fill the poems of Milton's predecessors; they celebrate Petrarchan mistresses and Tudor sovereigns, and both of those in the person of Elizabeth I. Roy Strong has observed of Queen Elizabeth that she was "always the Tudor Rose, the union of the white rose of York and the red of Lancaster. Through that rudimentary equation, she was ever present in any garden in the kingdom."[54] Milton does not try to rehabilitate the red and the white rose: Eve, who is not a virgin but is chaste, who is not a monarch but is queenly, needs greater symbolic range and subtlety. With its emphasis upon perception and light and its admissions of uncertainty, the new experimental philosophy makes it possible for representation to play with the colors of the natural world – in the fully serious way that verbal playfulness, in the seventeenth century, was used to liberate thought.

The new philosophy, in short, suggests a new palette for Eve's roses. Purple is associated with the most expensive dye of the ancient world, Tyrian purple, derived from shellfish; gold and azure, with the costliest pigments; carnation, with the painterly representation of flesh. These are self-conscious colors, as it were, colors that call attention to their role in depiction. They flourish their ability to symbolize. It is thus more useful to ask *how* rather than *what* an azure rose symbolizes – or a gold, purple, or carnation rose. The colors are so richly symbolic that they flash before the reader a succession of possibilities: Eve as the embodiment of true queenliness; Eve as the matronly Virgin; Eve as Laura, reified not in diamonds, gold, and topazes, but incarnate in gold, azure, and purple roses; Eve as the illuminator of the border of God's other book; Eve as Iris with a prism of roses. Such symbolic possibilities, as luminous and as fleeting as the pattern held momentarily in a kaleidoscope, are far removed from the allegorical rigidity which Fowler ascribes to the colors in book IX. Rather, in the flashing play of the colors we find the equivalent, at the level of symbols, of Milton's syntactical suspensions, his ability to allow meaning to hover between two or more resolutions. It is a reformed symbolic mode released for Milton by the liberating diffuseness of the new experimental philosophy – a diffuseness born of its tentative theories and its admitted limitations, by what it thinks it knows and what it knows it does not. In that space, Milton finds room for poetic re-creation.

CHAPTER 11

The balm of life

Long before *Paradise Lost* represents it to our sight, we are aware that
there is balm in Eden. Beelzebub metaphorically wafts it under the nose
of the fallen angels at the conclusion of the great consult in hell.
Gratified that they have voted for his satanic plan – to "possess / All as
our own" the new created world (*PL*, 11.365–66) – Beelzebub hints at the
benefits to be derived from being on earth. Either he and his cohorts will
be able to re-enter heaven from there, he suggests,

> or else in some mild zone
> Dwell not unvisited of heaven's fair light
> Secure, and at the brightening orient beam
> Purge off this gloom; the soft delicious air,
> To heal the scar of these corrosive fires
> Shall breathe her balm. (*PL*, 11.397–402)

Beelzebub's prediction is accurate in one respect at least. The air of paradise is indeed fragrant with balm. Thomas Greene associates that balmy
air with the "oriental lushness" of Milton's paradise: "The scented air
and tangled flowers are not calculated to permit hard work much relevance . . . the fragrance seems an invitation to indolence."[1] But Greene's
reading of paradise, which overlooks natural history, misunderstands the
function of balm. So, too, does Beelzebub's.

What Beelzebub imagines – balm as the precious, restorative product
of a distant country – would inevitably have conjured up for Milton's
readers what the seventeenth century called the "true" balm, the balm
of the ancients, mentioned repeatedly in the Scriptures and in the
natural histories of classical antiquity.[2] Early herbalists attribute to it the
virtues of a panacea. Parkinson's list of what the true balm will cure
occupies most of a folio page in *Theatrum Botanicum*. A few sentences will
illustrate its range:

The liquour or *Opobalsamum*, is of great good use against all poysons and infections, both Vipers, Serpents and Scorpions, the pestilence and spotted fevers,

and all other putride and intermissive agues that rise from obstructions, and crude cold humours . . . and is very effectuall in all cold griefes and diseases of the head or stomacke, helping the swimmings and turnings of the braine, weake memories, and the falling sicknesse: it cleareth the eyes of filmes or skinnes, overgrowing the sight, and easeth the paine in the eares, and their deafenesse and other diseases . . . it clenseth also the reines and kidneyes, and freeth them from the generation of stones in them, and expelleth the gravell or stones in them: it is singular good against the palsie, crampe, tremblings, convulsions or shrinking of sinewes, and for greene wounds, the most speedy operatour of any: from the singular effect whereof all other medicines made for the health of the body or to heale wounds were called *Balsamum*, Balme. The women in *Egypt*, herewith as *Alpinus* sheweth, preserve their beauty, and young forme for a long time.[3]

In thus suggesting that Eden's balm will restore the bodies and minds of the fallen angels, Beelzebub anticipates Satan's role as quacksalver and charlatan at the Tree of Knowledge. *Balm* in fact becomes a synonym for quack medicine in the early modern period.[4] Unlike Parkinson, Gerard declines in his *Herball* to specify "[t]he marvelous effects [balm] worketh in new and green wounds," as physicians already know them, "and as for the beggerly Quacksalvers, Runnagates, and knavish Mountibankes, we are not willing to instruct them in things so far above their reach, capacitie, and worthinesse."[5] The desire for a panacea is, in *Paradise Lost*, a deep-rooted one. The metaphor becomes literal in the garden of Eden, where Satan's apple and Beelzebub's balm are both the (misapprehended) fruit of deep-rooted trees.

Beelzebub's hint that paradisal balm will cure all the ills of the fallen angels is of course a lie. This fact becomes clear as soon as Satan approaches Eden and smells its air. Fragrance and hope undulate towards him as he draws close to the garden:

> of pure now purer air
> Meets his approach, and to the heart inspires
> Vernal delight and joy, able to drive
> All sadness but despair: (*PL*, IV.153–56)

But Satan's sadness *is* despair. The balmy air of Eden cannot drive away what in theological terms is the unforgivable sin. To despair is to lose faith in God's omnipotence, which is to misunderstand his deity, which is to fail to know that God is God. There can be no balm for despair, even in paradise; Satan, in despair, is always in hell.

It is significant, therefore, that Beelzebub and his fellows affect to believe that balm will cure them.[6] Their collective pretense can be read historically. By the time Milton wrote *Paradise Lost*, the reputation of the legendary balm had suffered a serious decline. This is apparent even in Parkinson's herbal, with its daunting list of balm's virtues. At the outset of his account, Parkinson offers a paean to the true balm, which, however, is followed immediately by a remarkable admission. First Parkinson protests that he is unworthy to write of

> so rare, so excellent a subject, being heretofore accounted as one of the greatest jewels, and richest endowments of the earth, and as a parcell of the treasure of great Kings, and Princes, and it is thought by many that the greatest and worthyest present that the Queene of *Sheba* did or could bring and give unto King *Salomon*, was some Balsame trees, which she brought out of her Country, that *Salomon* might plant them in his: and it was also one of the greatest Jewels the first *Ptolomoy* could bring away from thence into *Egypt*, as Authours doe record it:[7]

Then follows the admission: "but now the times are so changed, that I thinke I shall scarce gaine credit, that the same true *Balsamum* is extant in *rerum natura*."[8] Just as Robert Burton asks, "What extraordinary vertues are ascribed unto plants?" and exhaustively answers, so Parkinson, it seems, feels obligated to record what is said about the virtues of balm.[9] But his own skepticism is apparent.

In showing the fallen angels readily falling in with Beelzebub's optimistic prediction about Eden, Milton paints a picture of intellectual bad faith. The fallen angels participate, that is, in upholding what they know to be a fiction about balm, in part because disputing it means challenging a potent authority. This is a portrait of minds which have ceased to believe in an old knowledge, an old science, but which do not have the courage and independence necessary to forge a new one. Against such intellectual defeatism, the poem proposes for balm something altogether more interesting and more experimental than the old-fashioned botany which the fallen angels cling to and which Svendsen ascribes to Milton. Beelzebub is not entirely wrong about Eden's balm, though he is mistaken about the way it functions. It cannot heal the spiritual scars of the fallen angels. Its supposed effectiveness "against all poysons and infections, both Vipers, Serpents and Scorpions" cannot offer any protection against the serpent to Adam and Eve. Nor can balm endow them with youthfulness and perfect health. These they already possess, and when they lose them, balm cannot restore them. The balm which fills the garden of Eden is not a panacea – and yet it *does* promote their health. How it does so is the subject of this chapter.

A discussion of balm in the garden of Eden might begin with a basic question. What does balm look like? In "A Milton Herbal," James McHenry notes that *balm* in the seventeenth century could refer to "either the resin of various *balsamodendron* trees (Balm of Gilead), or a domestically grown perennial (one to two feet high with heart-shaped leaves) now called lemon balm or bee balm, *Melissa officinalis*, which is related to mint. Milton uses the word in both senses."[10] In Milton's representation of the garden of Eden, McHenry concludes, *balm* invariably signifies the resin or the resin-bearing tree rather than the perennial.[11] But is it necessary or even desirable to choose between them in every instance? The seventeenth century was not confused about the difference between tree balm and herb balm and repeatedly emphasizes what they have in common. Of the Latin name for chervil, Gerard remarks, "*Myrrhis* is also called *Myrrha*, taken from his pleasant savor of Myrrh."[12] Parkinson comments on bee balm in *Paradisi in Sole*: "I verily thinke, that our forefathers hearing of the healing and comfortable properties of the true naturall Baulme, and finding this herbe to be so effectuall, gave it the name of Baulme, in imitation of his properties and vertues."[13] We need to be alert to the possibility that *Paradise Lost* declines the botanical precision that a modern scientific attitude assumes, and that its interest lies in establishing similarities between two outwardly different orders of plants. Indeed, while some usages of *balm* in the poem clearly refer to the tree, others are ambiguous. When Satan gives directions to the fruit tree from which he claims to have eaten, for instance, he explains to Eve that the tree stands

> Beyond a row of myrtles, on a flat,
> Fast by a fountain, one small thicket past
> Of blowing myrrh and balm;   *(PL,* IX.627–29)[14]

The tiny ambiguity lodged in *thicket* troubles rather than clarifies the distinction McHenry wishes to make, for a thicket of balm may mean shrubs or small trees. According to Parkinson, the "Balme tree, never groweth very great."[15] As for myrrh, he reports, "I have not heard or read, that any now adayes hath seene the tree that beareth it," but he thinks it may be like an acacia, as Dioscorides claims.[16] What is relevant for a thicket, as the name implies, is density, not height.

If we let *thicket* remain ambiguous, thus allowing *balm* and *myrrh* to signify either (or both) herbs and trees, we can see that the representation of balm follows the pattern now familiar from Milton's representation of paradisal trees, fruits, and roses. The passage in book ix, that is, signifies both the balm which is a priceless luxury and the sweet cicely and lemon balm found in every English garden.[17] In this merging of the exotic and the everyday lies the potential to counteract Satan's entire temptation strategy, which is to belittle the wondrous beauty of the familiar while magnifying the desirability of the strange. Yet the fact that the poem declines to make a uniformly clearcut distinction between balm as an exotic tree and balm as a domestic herb should not be allowed to mask the fact that it also declines to distinguish among – or to hierarchize – kinds of balm trees. This is the most important feature of the poem's representation of balm, from the perspective of natural history. Limiting *balm* to a choice between the resinous tree or the perennial does not do justice to the complex botanical and economic functioning of the term in *Paradise Lost*. There *is* confusion and disagreement about the identity of balm in the seventeenth century. But it concerns the relationship between the balms of the New World and the "true" balm of the ancient.

In his *Naturall and Morall History of the East and West Indies* (translated into English in 1604), José de Acosta declares that New World balms or resins are not identical to the balm of the ancient world, although they have much in common:

> The Balme which comes from the West *Indies*, is not of the same kind of right Balme which they bring from *Alexandria* or *Caire*, and in old time was in *Judea* . . . The reason why I say the liquor of the one and the other are not of one kinde, is for that the trees from which it comes are very different: for the balme tree of *Palestine* was small, and fashioned like to a Vine . . . At the *Indies* I have seene the tree from whence they draw the Balme, which is as bigge as a poungarnet tree, and some thing neere the fashion; and if my memory failes me not, it hath nothing common with the vine . . . But in their accidents and operations, their liquors are alike, as likewise they be in their admirable smells, and in the cure and healing of wounds, in colour and substance[18]

Acosta's enthusiasm for distinctions fails him when, in a discussion of New World "ambers" (resins which he describes as being slightly thicker than balms) and other resinous products, he ends rather abruptly: "There are at the *Indies* infinite numbers of other aromatical woodes, gummes, oyles, and drugges, so as it is not possible to name them all, neither doth it now much import."[19]

What begins as a careful attempt to designate and describe different types of balms flounders in the face of the abundance of the New World. A similar sense of being overwhelmed by that abundance pervades Gerard's entries on balm.

There be divers sorts of trees from which do flow Balsams, very different one from another, not only in form, but also in fruit, liquor, and place of growing; the which to distinguish would require more time and travell than either our small time will afford, or riches for our maintenance to discover the same in their natural countries.[20]

Johnson makes two main contributions to Gerard's discussion of balm. He adds a paragraph on Prosper Alpini's work on the balm of the ancients, and he replaces Gerard's illustrations. In the 1597 edition of *The Herball*, Gerard had provided three illustrations, two of the fruit and one of the wood, the latter consisting of four sticks (fig. 15).[21] Johnson improves the rendering of the fruit and, to illustrate the wood, borrows from Alpini's depiction of the tree (fig. 16).[22] But he allows Gerard's conclusion to stand: "There be divers sorts more, which might be omitted because of tediousnesse."[23] Without a system of classification for trees and other plants, the descriptive vocabulary of early modern naturalists proves to be wholly inadequate for the botanical treasures of the New World. These must be omitted, they explain, because of sheer numbers, or tediousness, or lack of time.

This is the discursive equivalent of that trade in material goods which devalues whatever is too plentiful. Indeed, Parkinson's entry on balm in *Theatrum Botanicum* displays some recognition of the perils of overproduction. As the passage cited above demonstrates, he faithfully records what is usually said about the "true balm," even though he doubts its existence and efficacy. His treatment of balms from the New World is notably less detailed. This is not surprising, since he clearly has not seen these "West Indian *Balsamums*," or at most has seen their "fruite." This fruit, a kind of pod, is the sole illustration for the entry (fig. 17).[24] More surprising, however, is the disillusioned note that creeps into the entry:

Of the true *Balsamum* I have entreated in the last foregoing Classis or Tribe, but there have beene divers other sorts of liquours called *Balsamum* for their excellent vertues, brought out of the West Indies, every one of which for a time, after their first bringing were of great account with all men, and bought at great prices, but as greater store was brought, so did the prices diminish, and the use decay, when as it was the same thing and of the same vertue it formerly was, such is the inconstant course of the world in all things.[25]

One of the authorities whom Parkinson cites on the question of West Indian balm, Nicholas Monardes, simply remarks, "they brought so much and such great quantity, that it is nowe of small value: this commeth of the abundance of thinges."[26]

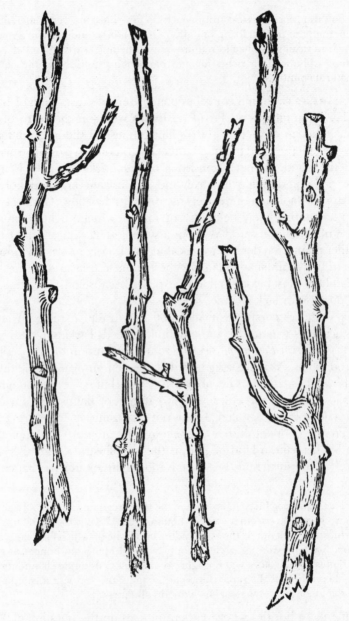

15 "The wood of the Balsame tree," from *The Herball* (1597) by John Gerard; "a small
description may serve for a dry sticke."

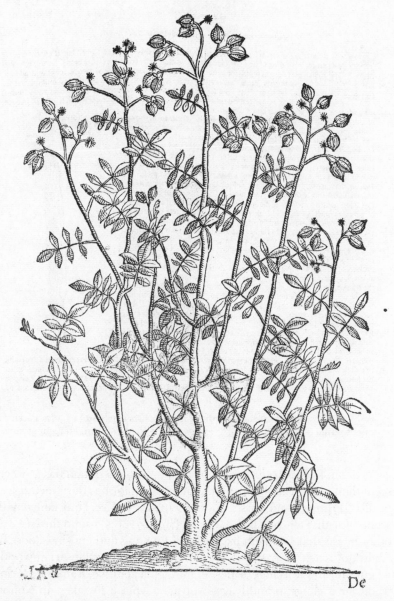

16 The balm of the ancients, from *De plantis aegypti liber* (1592) by Prosper Alpini. Old
and New World balms are alike "in their admirable smells, and in the cure and healing
of wounds, in colour and substance."

CHAP. IX.

Balſamum Peruvianum, The Weſt Indian *Balſamums.*

F the true *Balſamum* I have entreated in the laſt foregoing Claſſis or Tribe, but there have beene divers other ſorts of liquours called *Balſamum* for their excellent vertues, brought out of the Weſt Indies, every one of which for a time, after their firſt bringing were of great account with all men, and bought at great prices, but as greater ſtore was brought, ſo did the prices diminiſh, and the uſe decay, when as it was the ſame thing and of the ſame vertue it formerly was, ſuch is the inconſtant courſe of the world in all things. One ſort of *Balſamum* which is of moſt frequent uſe with us, is called blacke or browne Balſamum, becauſe the colour is blackiſh, and tending to browne being dropped forth, which as *Monardus* ſaith is gathered from a tree, ſomewhat bigger then a Pomegarnet tree, (whoſe fruite or long pod I here ſhew you, as I received it, with a very browne almoſt blacke colour, and ſmelt ſo like this *Balſamum* or *Benzoin,* that I am certainely perſwaded it was gathered from this tree) not by in-ciſion, as the juyces, liquours, and gummes of other trees (which yet this tree doth alſo in ſmall quantity, yet being white, and ſo precious with the Indians, that they will not part with any of it) but made after the manner that the Indians uſe to draw forth the juyces and liquours out of all their o-ther trees, which is by cutting the branches, and the bodies alſo ſometimes of trees into ſmall peeces, which after the boyling in a great quantity of water, the oyle ſwimming on the toppe, after it is cold is ſcummed of by them and reſerved. This is of a thicke, yet running conſiſtence, and of a ſharpe and ſomewhat bitter taſte, but of an excellent fine ſent, comming neereſt unto *Benzoin,* but will not long endure, being rubbed on any thing that is kept in the ayre, but never loſeth it ſent being kept cloſe in a glaſſe or the like. This is uſed inwardly and outwardly for divers good uſes, and although in ſome it cauſeth a kinde of loathing to the ſtomacke, if it touch the tongue, in drinking foure or five droppes in wine faſting, yet it helpe-eth the weakeneſſe of the ſtomacke, the Tiſſicke, and ſhortneſſe of breath, thoſe that are purſie and the paines and difficulty in making water, it mo-veth alſo womens courſes, and cauſeth a good colour, and a ſweete breath, rectificth the evill diſpoſition of the liver, openeth obſtructions, and pre-ſerveth youthfullneſſe even in aged perſons that have much uſed it, and hel-peth the barrenneſſe in women : being outwardly uſed, it is ſingular good to heale any freſh or greene wound, and old ulcers, and ſores alſo : it eaſeth paines in the head or necke, and ſwelling in any part of the body, the places thereof being annoynted therewith, or a cloth wet therein and applyed : it helpeth digeſtion, ſtrengtheneth the ſtomacke, diſſolveth winde, eaſeth the ſpleene, and the Sciatica, the ſtrangury and ſtone, and diſcuſſeth all nodes and hardneſſe of tumours, being ap-plyed warme to the places pained : it warmeth and comforteth the ſinewes, and keepeth them from ſhrinking.

Fructus ſive theca Balſami Occiden-talis arboris. The fruite of the Weſt Indie Balſame tree,

17   Pod from West Indian *Balsamum,* from *Theatrum Botanicum* (1640) by John Parkinson; "after their first bringing were of great account with all men, and bought at great prices."

As Satan knows, fruit that is rare and difficult to obtain has a sweeter scent than other fruit, but fruit that others long for has the sweetest scent of all. "[H]unger and thirst," the serpent says to Eve, "quickened at the scent / Of that alluring fruit" (*PL*, IX.586, 587–88); "round the tree / All other beasts that saw, with like desire / Longing and envying stood, but could not reach" (*PL*, IX.591–93). Fragrance in a postlapsarian world is a figure for the workings of desire: intangible, elusive, it makes precious whatever it clings to and leaves worthless what it forsakes. In Milton's garden of Eden, fragrance does not dissipate; it cannot be exhausted. It defines the very air as "balmy," which means that the breath of life and "[t]he balm of life" (*PL*, XI.546) are one. What matters about paradisal balm is not whether one can identify it as a plant or a tree, a New World or an Old World gum-resin. What matters is that *all* varieties of paradisal balm are sweet-smelling.

Drawing ever finer distinctions among plants and animals and searching for a basis upon which to classify them are only part of the agenda of the new natural history. The experience it constantly extols *also* includes adding the New World, with its vast treasury of flora and fauna, to the empire of knowledge. To identify as the one "true" balm the (now unidentifiable) balm of the ancient world, and to view all other balms as necessarily inferior to it, is nostalgic and superstitious, the attitude of the old science. To include – even if only implicitly, by not excluding – the balms of the New World in a representation of the garden of Eden, as Milton does, is an attitude that belongs to the beginning of modernity. *Cedar, pine, fir,* and *palm* also appear as generic terms in the poem and thus also participate in bridging the sea of difference between new and ancient worlds, the scriptural era and the seventeenth century. But balm is inscribed in an altogether richer cultural history than the other trees, and its treatment in *Paradise Lost* is correspondingly more complex. It is by filling paradise with the fragrant balms of all the world that the poem makes one of its most penetrating criticisms of the desire for material possession fueling colonial expansion in the early modern period.

David Quint has argued that colonization, defined as merchant-adventuring, provides Milton with an underlying metaphoric context for Satan's entry into paradise. Quint thus puts Satan's Odyssean journey into dynamic and suggestive relationship with the early modern trade in spices and drugs.[27] Quint's concern lies mainly with the implications of the rise of the mercantile class for epic's portrayal of heroic adventure. There is more to be said, however, about Milton's representation of the commodity itself:

> now gentle gales
> Fanning their odoriferous wings dispense
> Native perfumes, and whisper whence they stole
> Those balmy spoils. As when to them who sail
> Beyond the Cape of Hope, and now are past
> Mozambic, off at sea north-east winds blow
> Sabean odours from the spicy shore
> Of Arabie the blest, with such delay
> Well pleased they slack their course, and many a league
> Cheered with the grateful smell old Ocean smiles.
>
> (*PL*, IV.156–65)

Alastair Fowler notes that this passage echoes the description of *Arabia felix* in the account of Diodorus Siculus (*PL,* IV.159–66n). Martin Evans, in contrast, argues that "[c]ontemporary representations of America" shape Milton's garden of Eden. Evans asserts that the passage echoes "the experience of innumerable European explorers" who smelled the fragrant plants of the New World long before they landed.[28] The resemblances between Milton's description and the accounts of sixteenth- and seventeenth-century explorers, he notes in passing, may "have a common source in the long-standing *topos* of the earthly paradise," but he does not pursue the matter.[29] Evans thus provides, without resolving, two quite different explanations for the passage above: either it embodies the actual experiences of New World explorers, or it repeats a convention. The representation of other features of Milton's paradisal natural world, however, make it clear that we need to look for a reconciliation between these two positions. The spicy forests of Eden, that is, belong to both the New World and the world of the ancients. Both worlds are subject to material desire's predatory raids, for if, as Fowler maintains, "[t]he idea of perfumes stolen by the wind was a commonplace" (*PL,* IV.156–58n), the phrase "balmy *spoils*" is not. It unexpectedly juxtaposes the sweet and the spoiled, for in seventeenth-century usage, the latter term could refer to instances of damaging or injuring.[30] The phrase implies the futility of trying to turn the fragrance produced by a forest of trees into commercial profit. The effort will end by spoiling the forest – and hence the sweet air. This is not necessarily to condemn trade but to suggest, forcefully, that not everything which contributes to "the sweet of life" (*PL,* VIII.184) can be commodified.[31]

At the most pragmatic level, the fragrance inhaled by those "who sail / Beyond the Cape of Hope" cannot be conveyed to Europe for sale, because it is impossible to export a forest of living trees. The distance between what ancient writers and modern herbalists describe and the reality of what Europeans can actually possess elicits from Gerard a rare glint of humour: "The wood we have dry brought unto us from the Indies for our use in physicke (a small description may serve for a dry sticke)."[32] In seventeenth-century England, the balsam tree was so rare that the location of individual trees was recorded. When John Aubrey searched for the remains of the Tradescants' garden in South Lambeth, he concluded that most of the rare plants had disappeared.[33] He comments regretfully that Tradescant

had a Garden stor'd with choice Plants; amongst others he had the *Balm of Gilead Tree; Edm. Wyld,* Esq; had some Layers of it, which grew very well at *Houghton-*

Conquest in *Bedfordshire*, 'till in the hard Winter the Mice kill'd it. I do not hear of any other now in *England*.[34]

Bringing back to Europe even a living balsam, much less its berries or twigs, cannot duplicate the effect of a "spicy forest" (*PL*, v.298).

This fact sheds a different light on the theme of New World overabundance that Martin Evans finds "cannot be explained by the paradisal tradition."[35] But in fact the theme of overabundance pervades classical descriptions of foreign countries, whose strangeness was seen to include their inability to name and control a burgeoning natural world. The passage from Diodorus's *History* immediately preceding the one echoed in *Paradise Lost* iv.156–65 contains this description of Sheba in Arabia Felix:

In the *Mediterranean* parts thereof are many goodly Forrests, full of Trees bearing Frankincense, and Myrrhe; therein grow also Palme-trees, Canes, Cinamon, and other such like odoriferous things, whereof it is not possible to recount all the severall sorts in particular, so abundantly hath Nature assembled them there together; so that the odours, which come to our sences from those Trees, seeme to be somewhat that is truly Divine, and which cannot well be exprest.[36]

Evan's argument that the overabundance, or excessive fertility, of Milton's garden refers solely and straightforwardly to a peculiar quality of the American continent is thus unconvincing. So, too, is his designation of paradisal overabundance as "ominous."[37] Perhaps from the perspective of mercantile capitalism, overabundance is sinister. From another perspective, however, overabundance is symbolic of a richness that cannot be inscribed in an economy of ownership. Associated with the soul, the breath of life, bodily spirits, and the incense of praise and sacrifice, fragrant air is a sign of spiritual wealth. Foul air signals its loss.

Hence the significance of the reference to Asmodeus and the "fishy fume" in the lines immediately following the description of Arabia Felix in *Paradise Lost*.

> So entertained those odorous sweets the fiend
> Who came their bane, though with them better pleased
> Than Asmodeus with the fishy fume,
> That drove him, though enamoured, from the spouse
> Of Tobit's son, and with a vengeance sent
> From Media post to Aegypt, there fast bound.   (*PL*, iv.166–71)

The "strained" reference to Tobit and Asmodeus, which elicits C. S. Lewis's displeasure, in fact highlights a contrast that runs through the poem: that between foul, infernal smoke and the pure, sweet air of

paradise.[38] Like Asmodeus, Satan is responsible for generating the foul-
ness that ultimately repels him. In his greed to possess the garden, he
ends up poisoning the garden's balmy air, one of its chief attractions for
the infernal spirits.

The poisoning is literal as well as figurative. One of the consequences
of the Fall is the building of the Tower of Babel, which Adam witnesses
in book XII. Its construction involves the manufacture of brick, with
"slime," or bitumin, as mortar (*PL*, XII.41–44). The stench of its building, though not the tower itself, certainly reaches heaven. The materials
with which it is built, moreover, link the Tower of Babel with Pandaemonium. Both are enveloped in a dense, smoky atmosphere. From the
roof of Pandaemonium,

> Pendent by subtle magic many a row
> Of starry lamps and blazing cressets fed
> With naphtha and asphaltus yielded light
> As from a sky.   (*PL*, 1.727–30)

The irony in "light / As from a sky" has to do not only with the fact that
the light produced from the cressets would be dim at best. Burning
"naphtha and asphaltus," or paraffin and pitch, would emit a very dis-
agreeable odor, combining the heavy and tarry with the penetrating and
acrid. The whole effect is very unlike the purifying effect of sunlight, and
how to obtain pure air was of profound concern to the seventeenth
century. Thomas Browne calls the belief "[t]hat there is power in
Bitumen, pitch or brimstone, to purifie the aire from his uncleannesse"
(*PE*, 63) a delusion fostered by the devil himself.[39]

John Evelyn is equally passionate about the value of pure air. In his
essay *Fumifugium, or The Inconveniencie of the Aer and Smoak of London
Dissipated* (published in 1661), he inveighs against what we would now call
the air pollution of London, inverting the topos of the perfumed countryside to claim that "the weary *Traveller*, at many Miles distance, sooner
smells, then sees the City to which he repairs."[40] Evelyn blames London's
foul air on the use of "sea coal" for dyeing, lime-burning, soap-boiling,
brewing, and brick-making. In a version of the greed of Satan-
Asmodeus, which spoils the very sweetness that attracts him, Evelyn
maintains that the industrialized quest for gold is destroying one of
London's chief riches, its healthful situation.[41] Industry is wrapping the
city in a "Hellish and dismall Cloud," "an impure and thick Mist accompanied with a fuliginous and filthy vapour."[42] The smuttiness of the air
besmirches everything, from linen drying on hedges to possessions closed

up "in our very secret *Cabinets*, and most precious *Repositories*."[43] But its most pernicious effects are on living creatures, Evelyn insists. It kills birds and bees, and it blights the budding and fruiting of plants, "imparting a bitter and ungrateful Tast to those few wretched *Fruits*, which never arriving to their desired maturity, seem, like the *Apples* of *Sodome*, to fall even to dust, when they are but touched."[44] It is in describing the evil effects on human health, however, that Evelyn is most vividly indignant. No congregation in London is free of "*Coughing* and *Snuffing* . . . Barking and . . . Spitting"; our very expectorations, he declares, quoting Kenelm Digby, are "of a blackish and fuliginous Colour."[45] Worst of all is the prevalence of respiratory disease: "this acrimonious Soot . . . rendring the people obnoxious to Inflammations . . . comes (in time) to exulcerate the *Lungs*, which is a mischief so incurable, that it carries away multitudes by Languishing and deep *Consumptions* . . . almost one half of them who perish in *London*, dye of *Phthisical* and *pulmonic* distempers."[46] No wonder that "the City of *London* resembles . . . the Suburbs of *Hell*."[47]

Indeed, by the "*infernal Smoake*" of London, Evelyn seems to mean something rather more specific than smoke that is merely noisome.[48] A clear symbolic association exists between the infernal and the subterranean in Evelyn's work, and also in Milton's. Fowler warns that the hell of *Paradise Lost* "is not under the earth" (*PL*, XII.41–44n). Nonetheless, the materials for all ungodly works in the poem (Pandaemonium in hell, the Tower of Babel on earth, gunpowder in heaven) are subterranean. Evelyn remarks that "all *subterrany* Fuell hath a kind of *virulent* or *Arsenical* vapour rising from it; which, as it speedily destroys those who dig it in the *Mines*; so does it by little and little, those who use it *here* above them."[49] In a late essay on "The Insalubrity and Salubrity of the Air," Robert Boyle directs his abiding interest in the properties and nature of air to the question of these "subterraneaneal steams."[50] The phenomenon of what Boyle calls "the Averni" had long been recognized and described. Boyle wishes to argue that certain "endemical diseases" – among them, "the consumption . . . in *England*, whence foreign physicians call it the *Tabes Anglica*" – can be attributed to the poisonous effluvia of mines and other underground caverns.[51] He provides experimental evidence for what Evelyn clearly believes, that diseases affecting one's breathing derive from breathing bad air. "But how frequently do we hear men say," asks Evelyn, "(speaking of some deceased Neighbour or Friend) *He went up to* London, *and took a great Cold, &c. which he could never afterwards claw off again*."[52]

To dissipate the smoke of London, Evelyn proposes two expedients.

The first is to move smoke-producing and other foul-smelling industries out of London. The second is to surround London with a huge, aromatic "plantation," which is to be

> elegantly planted, diligently kept and supply'd, with such *Shrubs*, as yield the most fragrant and odoriferous *Flowers*, and are aptest to tinge the *Aer* upon every gentle emission at a great distance: Such as are . . . the *Sweet-brier*, all the *Periclymena's* and *Woodbinds*; the Common *white* and *yellow Jessamine*, both the *Syringa's* or *Pipe trees*; the *Guelder-Rose*, the *Musk*, and all other *Roses*; *Genista Hispanica*: To these may be added the *Rubus odoratus, Bayes, Juniper, Lignum-vitæ, Lavander*: but above all, *Rosemary*.[53]

With the mention of rosemary, he re-inverts the topos of the fragrant countryside: "but above all, *Rosemary*, the *Flowers* whereof are credibly reported to give their sent above thirty Leagues off at Sea, upon the coasts of *Spain*."[54] The assumptions behind Evelyn's plan for a vast, "odoriferous" hedge around London are similar to those behind Milton's representation of the garden of Eden. Just as foul air produces disease, so clean air promotes good health.

Pure, sweet air is the "true" balm of paradise. It is not necessary to attribute to it the power of a panacea. Balm's legendary, quasi-magical properties and its associations with the wonders of the New and the Old Worlds are invoked by the poem – and then reformed. Eden's balmy air is, above all, balmy in its fragrance and purity, and that is sufficient to make a paradise. "There is a virtue in the *Aer*," notes Evelyn, "to penetrate, alter, nourish, yea and to multiply Plants and Fruits, without which no vegetable could possibly thrive."[55] As for its effects on human beings, "the Lucid and noble *Aer*, clarifies the Blood, subtilizes and excites it, cheering the Spirits and promoting digestion," and for "the very Rational faculties" of human beings, "the purer *Aer* does so far illuminate, as to have rendred some Men healthy and wise even to Miracle."[56]

In an essay marking the beginning of a poststructuralist critique of Milton's poetry, Geoffrey Hartman "wonders about the decorum of introducing" a conceit on the evaporation of sweat "at a point which is the inaugural moment of human consciousness."[57] He refers to the passage in which Adam describes for Raphael his first moments of life:

> As new waked from soundest sleep
> Soft on the flowery herb I found me laid
> In balmy sweat, which with his beams the sun
> Soon dried, and on the reeking moisture fed.   (*PL*, VIII.253–56)

Hartman raises and then dismisses without comment the possibility that *reeking* here is a neutral term meaning "that rises as a vapour."[58] He is more concerned that the sun is represented as feeding on Adam's perspiration, a representation which Hartman calls "startling" and "extreme."[59] Moving over the course of the essay from *reeking* to *balmy*, he concludes that "balmy sweat" is "an oxymoron that brings language close to a limit of expression."[60] He then asks rhetorically, "Does not 'Balmy Sweat', in this context of a birth scene, mingle proleptically the balm of fruitfulness and the sweat of the curse, the labor to come and the regeneration to come from that?"[61] One must answer, yes, of course, "balmy sweat" is proleptic. But the surest way to lose paradise is to trample its landscape in search of proleptic signs. Christopher Ricks might well point out that "balmy sweat" is an oxymoron only in a fallen world. We need to ask what it is in a prelapsarian world. What is balmy sweat, that is, when it is neither proleptic nor oxymoronic?

Is it a preservative? In Adam's balmy sweat, Milton may be glancing at the concept of the radical balsam, the preservative fluid said by the alchemists to reside in all organic bodies.[62] The role of balm in the process of embalming, moreover, is linguistically self-evident. One might argue that the ubiquitous presence of balm in the garden of Eden, including Adam's balmy sweat, symbolizes the absence of mortality in paradise. This traditional symbolic reading is not denied by the poem. It is, however, shown to be inadequate. In *Religio Medici*, Browne points out that those who "found themselves on the radicall balsome or vitall sulphur of the parts, determine not why *Abel* liv'd not so long as *Adam*."[63] The archangel Michael says to Adam that "a melancholy damp of cold and dry" will at last "consume / The balm of life" (*PL*, XI.544–46). A preservative that acts differentially and that fails in the face of death is not a very powerful symbol of eternal life. There is an analogy here with the cedars of paradise, which traditionally symbolize eternal life but were feared in Milton's day to be in danger of extinction. We would do better to assign to Adam's balmy sweat a figurative sense that takes into account the literal, or naturalistic, one. Adam's balmy sweat is, simply, sweet-scented sweat. It is analogous to the tears of balm wept by the paradisal trees. We are used to regarding sweating and weeping as signs of human suffering. In paradise, their fragrance transforms what they signify. All living creatures in the poem ooze and drip, sweat and weep, and their fluids are fragrant offerings to their Creator. As the trees weep, so Adam sweats balm, and that balm perfumes the air of paradise. Adam and Eve's morning hymn at *PL*, v.153–208 is based on the premise that each creature praises God by doing what is proper to it. Thus birds praise him by flying; plants, by swaying in the breeze; water, by gurgling as it flows; the very mists and exhalations, by rising and falling. Adam's sweat, dripping and reeking, also praises God. Human beings still sweat and weep, admittedly not as fragrantly. But the difference is in degree rather than kind, which suggests that the experiences of the animal or vegetable body so valued in the prelapsarian world of Milton's imagining have not for him lost their value in the fallen world.

Conclusion

On the first morning of their postlapsarian life, Adam and Eve try to carry on their sweet prelapsarian routine, though change is all around them:

> Mean while
> To resalute the world with sacred light
> Leucothea waked, and with fresh dews embalmed
> The earth, when Adam and first matron Eve
> Had ended now their orisons, and found
> Strength added from above, new hope to spring
> Out of despair, joy, but with fear yet linked;   (*PL*, XI.133–39)

Joy is now mixed with fear; hope and strength are now necessary for daily life; despair, never known before, must now be overcome. The light is different (and most likely the temperature).[1] The narrator's description of the dew as having "embalmed / The earth" now carries, notes Alastair Fowler, "a sinister overtone" (*PL*, XI.134–35n). His reading of *embalmed* reflects Christopher Ricks's argument that "[w]ith the Fall of Man, language falls too."[2] Words, whether the narrator's or the characters', become infected after the Fall and are liable to take on grim meanings to which they were previously immune.

But in our haste to discover the fallen sense of *embalmed*, we must not forget that the innocent sense, too, still resides in the word. It is easy to underestimate the degree of continuity between Adam and Eve's pre- and postlapsarian life. Everything changes at the Fall – but not completely, not beyond recognition. In the passage above, Adam and Eve succeed in continuing at least part of their prelapsarian routine: they complete their orisons, just as they do in book v. Their joy is now linked to fear, yet it is nonetheless joy. They need hope and strength for their daily life, but they also needed hope and strength before the Fall, even though the need was not perhaps as great nor perhaps as fully recognized.[3] The earth's orientation to the sun has changed, but the light dawning on their world remains "sacred." The dews which embalm the earth continue to be "fresh," and *embalmed* still has *balm* at its root.

It is not surprising, then, that reading the fallen natural world in the poem is not represented as being qualitatively different from reading the unfallen natural world. Just as the new-created Adam learns *in time* to read the sun and the fair earth, so time (albeit more of it) is required for him to learn to read fallen creatures. The difference in reading is of degree rather than of kind: indeterminacy assumes a larger role in post-lapsarian interpretation, and the work of interpretation itself is more laborious and proceeds amidst a more general obscurity of understanding. Whereas Adam's prelapsarian reading of Creation leads him quickly and clearly to articulate praise of the Creator, his postlapsarian reading leads him to confront the consequences of his sin and hence to recognize his need for the Creator. That postlapsarian reading practices resemble prelapsarian practices is made clear on the two occasions when, after the Fall, Adam is shown explicitly reading the animal world.

The first reading serves as a preface to Adam's long, self-pitying soliloquy in book x:

> Beast now with beast gan war, and fowl with fowl,
> And fish with fish; to graze the herb all leaving,
> Devoured each other; nor stood much in awe
> Of man, but fled him, or with countenance grim
> Glared on him passing: these were from without
> The growing miseries, which Adam saw
> Already in part, though hid in gloomiest shade,
> To sorrow abandoned, but worse felt within,
> And in a troubled sea of passion tossed,
> Thus to disburden sought with sad complaint.   (*PL*, x.710–19)

The phrase "hid in gloomiest shade" describes both Adam's literal hiding place and the truth that he sees "[a]lready" but merely "in part." He perceives among beasts, fowl, and fish only hostile pairings, the terribly intimate relationship of devourer to devoured. The grammatical form which these pairings take – "Beast now *with* beast gan war, and fowl *with* fowl/ And fish *with* fish" – is a distorted image of what Adam had once praised: the fact that animals belong with their kind:

> they rejoice
> Each with their kind, lion with lioness;
> So fitly them in pairs thou hast combined;
> Much less can bird with beast, or fish with fowl
> So well converse, nor with the ox the ape;
> Worse then can man with beast, and least of all. (*PL*, viii.392–97)

The hostile pairings that Adam perceives in book x distort this earlier perception, but in "beast *with* beast" there is at least a potential for harmonious pairing, a potential that Adam cannot yet see, abandoned as he is to sorrow and gloomiest shade.

By the time of his second reading, which occurs in book xi, Adam's ability to interpret the fallen world has developed:

> nature first gave signs, impressed
> On bird, beast, air, air suddenly eclipsed
> After short blush of morn; nigh in her sight
> The bird of Jove, stooped from his airy tower,
> Two birds of gayest plume before him drove;
> Down from a hill the beast that reigns in woods,
> First hunter then, pursued a gentle brace,
> Goodliest of all the forest, hart and hind;
> Direct to the eastern gate was bent their flight.
> Adam observed, and with his eye the chase
> Pursuing, not unmoved to Eve thus spake.
>   O Eve, some further change awaits us nigh,
> Which heaven by these mute signs in nature shows
> Forerunners of his purposes, or to warn
> Us haply too secure of our discharge
> From penalty, because from death released
> Some days; how long, and what till then our life,
> Who knows, or more than this, that we are dust,
> And thither must return and be no more.
> Why else this double object in our sight
> Of flight pursued in the air and o'er the ground
> One way the self-same hour?   (*PL*, xi.182–203)

Perhaps the most notable feature of this reading is its diffidence. Whereas earlier he had seized upon the darkest interpretation for "beast with beast," Adam now declines to say precisely what the signs mean, except in the general sense that they indicate further change. The fact that he calls the creatures "forerunners" (rather than "foretellers") of God's purposes not only underlines his diffidence; it suggests that observing the creatures' bodies and actions is part of a mode of understanding *how* (rather than *what*) they signify for humanity. Indeed, the meanings Adam proposes for these "mute signs" are actually intelligent extrapolations from animal to human behavior. Significantly, he provides alternative readings. The actions of the creatures may be warning us, he tells Eve, not to assume that we know the future length and course of our lives; they may even be reminding us that we are but dust and will return to dust. The fact that Adam offers alternative readings constitutes an acknowledgment that he is engaging in an act of interpretation. Consciously to interpret is to accept the possibility of misinterpreting. Diffidence and its concomitant acceptance of indeterminacy may well be the chief qualities that Adam and Eve need for reading a fallen world. They are also the qualities that "fit readers" need for reading the *products* of a fallen world, one of which is *Paradise Lost.*

By the end of the 1650s, Nicholas von Maltzahn has recently argued, the rhetoric of republican humanism – with its ideal of disinterestedness and its valuing of a complexly coherent, or totalizing, discourse – was no longer to the taste of the English public.[4] Milton's prose (especially *The Readie and Easie Way*) was widely seen to epitomize the outmoded style of republican humanism and was so attacked by opponents.[5] The new commercial culture of the coffee-house scoffed at a stance of disinterestedness. For it, a complex, totalizing discourse smacked of the fanatical and the fantastical; it preferred the demotic, self-interested discourse of the pamphleteers. Milton would have felt nothing but repugnance for the new style of pamphleteering. But the new "scientific" discourse which emerged between 1645 and 1665 – and which thus accompanied and arguably participated in the eroding of the totalizing discourse of republican humanism – *was* valued by him, if not for his prose, then certainly for his poetry. The new experimentalists associated a totalizing natural philosophy with Aristotle and the "schoolmen," and as Bacon had urged, they tried to avoid "the charms of deceiving notions and theories" in order to "unloose" their minds. The style they proposed to achieve this unloosing was the "anti-magisterial" style pioneered by *Pseudodoxia Epidemica*, precursor of the "wary and diffident" style that Boyle proposed a decade later. The experimentalists proposed a style of writing, that is, which corresponded to a new way of reading the natural world, a way which encouraged each reader to engage in a continuing process of interpretation – exactly as Milton by then understood the Bible to encourage its readers to do.

That *Paradise Lost* is based on the Bible is self-evident. I have argued in the preceding chapters, however, that Milton has employed the biblical model in a way that has not previously been recognized. In its representation of the natural world (whether pre- or postlapsarian), *Paradise Lost* is written so that it responds to an experimental reading, precisely, so Milton believed, as the Bible was written to do. The mode in which the poem inscribes the natural world encourages the reader's engagement in continual "musing, searching, revolving new notions." It is a mode which values re-creative acts of construing new meaning by "conferring places"; it discourages declarations of absolute interpretive certainty; and it leads the reader to value the fragments out of which the whole is composed. By fusing this experimental mode, borrowed from Protestant devotional practices, with the experimental mode of the new philosophy, Milton creates a new, "modern," representational mode for depicting the natural world. Even as his prose style was being derided by the new men of the Restoration as the antiquated remnant of a past age (a misapprehension repeated by some modern critics), Milton was fashioning a poetic representation of the natural world that was responsive to the latest intellectual and stylistic currents of the day. Milton's Adam and Eve are not nostalgic. Nor was their author.

Notes

INTRODUCTION

1 All quotations from Milton's poems are from *The Poems of John Milton*, ed. John Carey and Alastair Fowler (London: Longman, 1968). Book and line numbers for *Paradise Lost* (hereafter cited *PL*) will be given parenthetically in the text, as will references to the editorial notes of Alastair Fowler, editor of *Paradise Lost*.

2 Michel Foucault, *The Order of Things: an Archaeology of the Human Sciences*, trans. A. Sheridan (London: Tavistock, 1970). More precisely, Foucault's interest lies in defamiliarizing the scientific, that is, in ascertaining the cultural nature of the discourse which was constructed in the seventeenth century and then labeled "Scientific."

3 Pierre Bourdieu, *Distinction: a Social Critique of the Judgement of Taste*, trans. R. Nice (Cambridge, MA: Harvard University Press, 1984), 157–59; Roger Chartier, *Cultural History: Between Practices and Representations*, trans. L. Cochrane (London: Polity, 1988), 133.

4 Kester Svendsen, *Milton and Science* (Cambridge, MA: Harvard University Press, 1956).

5 Svendsen, *Milton and Science*, 3.

6 Don M. Wolfe, "Introduction," *Complete Prose Works of John Milton*, gen. ed. Don M. Wolfe, 8 vols. in 10 (New Haven: Yale University Press, 1953–82), I, 1.

7 William Parker, *Milton: a Biography*, 2nd edn., ed. Gordon Campbell, 2 vols. (Oxford: Clarendon Press, 1996), I, 641.

8 Avoiding the anachronistic term *science* for the seventeenth century is sometimes impossible and perhaps undesirable, as long as one remains wary (and scrupulous; see chapter 1, note 12). Milton and his contemporaries speak of "natural philosophy" and hence, for the new science, the "new philosophy" (or the "real," "mechanical," or "experimental philosophy"). I will generally follow their example. However, while using the term *science* may lead to overestimating the similarities between present and seventeenth-century practice, *never* using it may lead to underestimating them. A sparing use of the term seems most reasonable.

9 Stephen Fallon, *Milton among the Philosophers: Poetry and Materialism in Seventeenth-Century England* (Ithaca: Cornell University Press, 1991).

10 Fallon, *Milton among the Philosophers*, 18.
11 John Rogers, *The Matter of Revolution: Science, Poetry, and Politics in the Age of Milton* (Ithaca: Cornell University Press, 1996), xi.
12 Harinder S. Marjara, *Contemplation of Created Things: Science in "Paradise Lost"* (University of Toronto Press, 1992).
13 Phillip R. Sloan, "Natural History, 1670–1802," R. C. Olby et al., eds., *Companion to the History of Modern Science* (London: Routledge, 1990), 295–96.
14 The term *botany* appears at the very end of the seventeenth century. (See *OED*, botany, sense 1.) The modern meaning of *zoology* developed in the eighteenth century; in the seventeenth century, the term, occurring in translations of Greek works, denoted the study of medicines made from animals. (See *OED*, zoology.)
15 Svendsen, however, takes issue with this view, as is obvious from the quotation above. (See *Milton and Science*, 43–85.)
16 Carlo Ginzburg, "The High and the Low: the Theme of Forbidden Knowledge in the Sixteenth and Seventeenth Centuries," *Myths, Emblems, Clues*, trans. John and Anne Tedeschi (London: Hutchinson Radius, 1990), 62–63.
17 Two exceptions are Rebecca Smith, "The Source of Milton's Pandemonium," *MP* 29 (1931), 187–98, and Majorie Nicolson, "Milton and the Telescope," *ELH* 2 (1935), 1–32 (rpt. in Marjorie Nicolson, *Science and Imagination* [Ithaca: Great Seal–Cornell University Press, 1956], 30–57).
18 Thomas Stearns Eliot, "Milton I," *On Poetry and Poets* (London: Farrar, Straus, Giroux – Noonday, 1957), 162.
19 Christopher Hill, *Milton and the English Revolution* (New York: Viking, 1977), 5.
20 Roland Mushat Frye, *Milton's Imagery and the Visual Arts: Iconographic Tradition in the Epic Poems* (Princeton University Press, 1978).
21 Frye, *Milton's Imagery*, 4.
22 Diane McColley, *A Gust for Paradise: Milton's Eden and the Visual Arts* (Urbana: University of Illinois Press, 1993), 13n8.
23 McColley, *A Gust for Paradise*, xii.
24 Robert Hooke, *Micrographia* (London, 1665).
25 Thomas Browne, *Pseudodoxia Epidemica*, ed. Robin Robbins, 2 vols. (Oxford: Clarendon Press, 1981), I, 367. Unless otherwise noted, all quotations from *Pseudodoxia Epidemica* (hereafter cited *PE*) are from the first volume of this edition; page numbers will be given parenthetically in the text.
26 Hooke, *Micrographia*, a2^v.
27 Ibid., g2^v.
28 Ibid., b2^v.

1 CORRUPTING EXPERIENCE: SATAN AND EVE

1 Stanley Fish, *Surprised by Sin: the Reader in "Paradise Lost"* (1967; Berkeley: University of California Press, 1971), 249.
2 Fish, *Surprised by Sin*, 249.

3 Georgia B. Christopher, *Milton and the Science of the Saints* (Princeton University Press, 1982), 158.

4 Linda Gregerson, *The Reformation of the Subject: Spenser, Milton, and the English Protestant Epic* (Cambridge University Press, 1995), 188.

5 Christopher, *Milton and the Science*, 160.

6 Ibid., 7. We will return to the importance for Milton of experimental reading and the reading of experience in chapter 3.

7 Gregerson, *The Reformation of the Subject*, 6.

8 In terms of formalistic studies, Keith Stavely in *The Politics of Milton's Prose Style* (New Haven: Yale University Press, 1975) is unusual in claiming that Milton's use of rhetorical skills *fails* to answer to his experience of politics. My point still holds, however; Stavely's argument relies upon a notion of experience.

9 Robert Boyle, *The Works of the Honourable Robert Boyle*, ed. Thomas Birch, 6 vols. (London, 1772), V, 513 [*The Christian Virtuoso*]. Unless otherwise noted, all quotations from Boyle's works are from this edition, hereafter cited as *Works*.

10 Fish, *Surprised by Sin*, 250. Jonathan Sawday, in *The Body Emblazoned: Dissection and the Human Body in Renaissance Culture* (London: Routledge, 1995), 246–48, has recently followed Fish in positing a scientific Satan, though Sawday is more interested in what he sees as the archfiend's scientific voyage of discovery than in the empiricist temptation of Eve claimed by Fish.

11 Fish, *Surprised by Sin*, 250.

12 Ibid., 251. In the seventeenth century, *science* is a general term for knowledge or knowing, Satan's meaning here. (*OED*, science, senses 1, 2, and 3.) In his parenthetical glance at the term, Fish seems to imply that Satan cunningly exploits modern connotations of *science* in order to deceive Eve.

13 For the phrase, "To make, take (an) experiment," see *OED*, experiment, sb., sense 1a. The formulation is useful for purposes of historical analysis. Because the article is optional, the phrase conveys the seventeenth-century fluidity of the term *experiment*. Using the modern formulation ("perform, conduct an experiment") for the early modern context too easily suggests an equivalence between what are in fact very different notions of "experiment." To explore that historical difference is one of the aims of this chapter.

14 Peter Dear, "Jesuit Mathematical Science and the Reconstitution of Experience in the Early Seventeenth Century," *Studies in the History and Philosophy of Science* 18 (1987), 141.

15 Dear, "Jesuit Mathematical Science," 134.

16 Charles B. Schmitt, "Experience and Experiment: a Comparison of Zabarella's View with Galileo's in *De Motu*," *Studies in the Renaissance* 16 (1969), 86.

17 Schmitt, "Experience and Experiment," 86. For Agrippa, see also Charles G. Nauert, *Agrippa and the Crisis of Renaissance Thought*, Illinois Studies in the Social Sciences, Number 55 (Urbana: University of Illinois Press, 1965), 214–15.

18 *OED*, occult, a. (sb.), sense 2.

19 *OED*, occult, a. (sb.), sense 3.a. and c. For the new philosophers, occult causation (causation they cannot explain) represents a problem to be investigated. For Eve, it is not a problem. She does, however, invent a little fable to explain *why* the fruit is "Of virtue to make wise" (*PL*, IX.778). Heavenly beings drink nectar, she knows from Raphael, oblivious in her fallen state to the fact that the very rivers of paradise "Ran nectar" (*PL*, IV.240). She surmises that the indwelling power has infused heavenly nectar (or a nectar-derivative) into the tree, thus producing "sciential sap" for tree and fruit. The phrase, with the latinate *sciential* and the bathetic *sap*, gently mocks Eve's natural theologizing.

20 *OED*, strange, a., senses 1, 2, 8, and 10.

21 The notion of a trial or test is especially apparent in early modern usage of *taste*. (*OED*, taste, sb.[1], sense 1.2; and taste, v., senses 1, 6.d., and 12.a.)

22 *OED*, experiment, sb., senses 1, 2, 5, and 6; experiment, v., senses 1 and 2; experimental, a. and sb., senses 1 and 2; experience, sb., senses 3, 4, 6, 7, and 8; experience, v., sense 2.

23 *OED*, experience, sb., senses 1 and 2; experience, v., sense 1; experiment, sb., senses 3 and 4; experiment, v., senses 3 and 4.

24 *Experience* occurs five times in the poem; *experienced*, once.

25 *OED*, sad, a. and adv., sense A.5.f. The "winds" she dismisses so confidently return with a vengeance in the form of exhaled "vapour" and "unkindly fumes" (*PL*, IX.1047, 1050) and the fricatives of *PL*, IX.1046 ("Soon as the force of that fallacious fruit").

26 Stuart Clark, *Thinking with Demons: the Idea of Witchcraft in Early Modern Europe* (Oxford: Clarendon Press, 1997), 231.

27 Francis Bacon, *The Works of Francis Bacon*, ed. James Spedding, R. L. Ellis, and D. D. Heath, 14 vols. (1857–74; Stuttgart-Bad Cannstatt: Friedrich Frommann Verlag, 1962–63), IV, 366–67. All quotations from Bacon's works are from this edition. On Bacon and natural magic, see Paolo Rossi, *Francis Bacon: from Magic to Science*, trans. Sacha Rabinovitch (London: Routledge & Kegan Paul, 1968), 11–35.

28 A number of important studies treat the new philosophy's attitude toward occult causation, an issue which, Clark notes, "is still being worked out by historians" (*Thinking with Demons*, 304). See also Keith Hutchison, "What Happened to Occult Qualities in the Scientific Revolution?", *Isis* 73 (1982), 233–53; G. MacDonald Ross, "Occultism and Philosophy in the Seventeenth Century," *Philosophy, its History and Historiography*, ed. A. J. Holland, Royal Institute of Philosophy Conference, 1983 (Dordrecht: D. Reidel, 1985), 95–115; John Henry, "Occult Qualities and the Experimental Philosophy: Active Principles in Pre-Newtonian Matter Theory," *History of Science* 24 (1986), 358–66. For a discussion of "the natural" as a changing category, see Stuart Clark, "The Scientific Status of Demonology," *Occult and Scientific Mentalities in the Renaissance*, ed. Brian Vickers (Cambridge University Press, 1984), 361–63.

29 Rossi, *Francis Bacon*, 19; Clark, *Thinking with Demons*, 220.
30 Daniel Sennert, *Thirteen Books of Natural Philosophy* [1632] [trans. N. Culpepper and A. Cole] (London, 1661), 431, 435.
31 See Clark, *Thinking with Demons*, 217–20, and Nauert, *Agrippa and the Crisis*, 222–91.
32 Clark, *Thinking with Demons*, 218.
33 *Mimetic* refers to the production of *natural* operations. Thus Clark defines magic as "simply the art of producing wonderful natural effects outside the usual course of things and above the common understanding of men" ("The Scientific Status of Demonology," 351).
34 Bacon, *Works*, IV, 367.
35 Ibid., IV, 296.
36 James VI and I, *Daemonologie* (Edinburgh, 1597), 44.
37 Ibid.
38 Clark, "The Scientific Status of Demonology," 360.
39 Ibid., 359.
40 Boyle, *Works*, V, 532.
41 These explanations appear frequently in Renaissance commentaries on Genesis. See Arnold Williams, *The Common Expositor: an Account of the Commentaries on Genesis 1527–1633* (Chapel Hill: University of North Carolina Press, 1948), 116–17.
42 The sense of *organic* as belonging to a bodily organ developed in the early eighteenth century (*OED*, organic, a. and sb., sense 3).
43 *OED*, organic, a. and sb., senses A.2.b. and 7.a.
44 Fowler notes the pun on *impulse*, which means both "thrust, motion" and "under the strong suggestion of a spirit" (*PL*, IX.530n).
45 James VI and I, *Daemonologie*, 46–47.
46 Fowler, *PL*, IX.670–76n.
47 *OED*, secret, a. and sb., sense B.4.a. and b.
48 William Eamon, *Science and the Secrets of Nature: Books of Secrets in Medieval and Early Modern Culture* (Princeton University Press, 1994), 269.
49 The popular collections functioned, notes Eamon, as "self-help manuals in medicine, the crafts, and the domestic arts" (*Science and the Secrets of Nature*, 234).
50 Ben Jonson, *Volpone or, The Fox*, ed. R. B. Parker, The Revels Plays (Manchester University Press, 1983), II.ii.139, 146–48.
51 Jonson, *Volpone*, II.ii.9–19.
52 Thomas Coryate, *Coryats Crudities* [1611] (London: Scolar, 1978), 273–74.
53 William Shakespeare, *Twelfth Night, or What You Will*, *The Complete Works*, rev. edn., gen. ed. Alfred Harbage (Baltimore, MD: Penguin, 1969), I.v.196–97. All quotations from Shakespeare's plays are from this edition.
54 Jonson, *Volpone*, II.ii.5–6.
55 See, for instance, Lucinda Beier's description of the "medical marketplace" in *Sufferers and Healers: the Experience of Illness in Seventeenth-Century England* (London: Routledge & Kegan Paul, 1987), 8–50.

56 John Henry argues that "a large proportion of Paracelsianism can be seen to have derived from magical traditions" ("Doctors and Healers: Popular Culture and the Medical Profession," Stephen Pumfrey, Paolo Rossi, and Maurice Slawinski, eds. *Science, Culture and Popular Belief in Renaissance Europe* [Manchester University Press, 1991], 218). On natural magic in Paracelsian medicine, see Clark, *Thinking with Demons*, 220–21; Henry, "Doctors and Healers," 217–18; and Charles Webster, *From Paracelsus to Newton: Magic and the Making of Modern Science* (Cambridge University Press, 1982), 56–58. (See also Webster's *The Great Instauration: Science, Medicine, and Reform 1626–1660* [London: Duckworth, 1975], 273–82.) For a fascinating account of Robert Boyle's attitude toward natural magic and medicine, see Michael Hunter, "Alchemy, Magic and Moralism in the Thought of Robert Boyle," *BJHS* 23 (1990), 387–410.

57 Beier, *Sufferers and Healers*, 32.

58 Henry, "Doctors and Healers," 218. Lucinda Beier, however, cautions against underestimating the importance of the humors even in Paracelsian medicine: "Virtually everyone in seventeenth-century England had a humoral view of the human body, health and illness . . . [including] those espousing relatively new schools of medical thought, such as Paracelsians, Van Helmontians, iatro-chemists and iatro-mechanists" (*Sufferers and Healers*, 163).

59 On magical practitioners, see Beier, *Sufferers and Healers*, 23–25.

60 Jonson, *Volpone*, II.ii.108–12.

61 Fish, *Surprised by Sin*, 251n1.

62 Joan Bennett argues that the spirit of the law against marriage to Gentiles was to preserve God's people from subjecting themselves to heathen influences. In Samson's case, marriage to a Philistine woman (a violation of the letter of the law) could have ended the Israelites' political subjection to the Philistines (thus fulfilling the spirit of the law), had the Hebrew people not betrayed Samson to their oppressors (*Reviving Liberty: Radical Christian Humanism in Milton's Great Poems* [Cambridge, MA: Harvard University Press, 1989], 129–31).

63 Bennett, *Reviving Liberty*, 130.

64 *Complete Prose Works of John Milton*, gen. ed. Don M. Wolfe, 8 vols. in 10 (New Haven: Yale University Press, 1953–82), VI, 341 and 342. Unless otherwise noted, all quotations from Milton's prose are from this edition, hereafter cited *CPW*.

65 *CPW*, VI, 340–41.

66 Ibid., VI, 130–31.

67 Ibid., VI, 131.

68 Fish, *Surprised by Sin*, 249.

69 Boyle, *Works*, II, 193.

70 *OED*, empiric, a. and sb., sense B.1. and 2.a. and b.

71 Boyle, *Works*, II, 162.

72 The term "old women" probably refers in this context to "wise women," women with knowledge of herbal and other remedies. Rose-Mary Sargent

notes that Boyle's pragmatic open-mindedness frequently led him to cite "women's testimony about the course of their own illnesses and the successful use they made of remedies to cure illness in others" (*The Diffident Naturalist: Robert Boyle and the Philosophy of Experiment* [University of Chicago Press, 1995], 152). This amounts to a public validation of women's experience.

73 Sargent, *The Diffident Naturalist*, 288n98.

74 Boyle's complex attitude toward Paracelsian and Helmontian chemistry is laid out in *The Sceptical Chymist* (1661). For discussion of Boyle's criticisms of contemporary chemistry, see Antonio Clericuzio, "Carneades and the Chemists: a Study of *The Sceptical Chymist* and its Impact on Seventeenth-Century Chemistry," Michael Hunter, ed., *Robert Boyle Reconsidered* (Cambridge University Press, 1994), 79–90.

75 Boyle, *Works*, II, 196.

76 Until recently, studies of Boyle have been characterized by what Michael Hunter classifies as "intellectualist" and "contextualizing" approaches. The former focus on the rise of the scientific method, disregarding whatever appears to be non-progressive and non-revolutionary in Boyle's thought; the latter focus on the context (political, ideological, or philosophical) against which Boyle's ideas developed. For his discussion of the terms and an overview of the development of Boyle studies, see Hunter, "Introduction," Hunter, ed., *Robert Boyle Reconsidered*, 1–18. For approaches concentrating on Boyle's contributions to the general ethos of the scientific revolution, see especially Marie Boas Hall, *Robert Boyle and Seventeenth-Century Chemistry* (Cambridge University Press, 1958), and Richard S. Westfall, *The Construction of Modern Science: Mechanisms and Mechanics* (1971; Cambridge University Press, 1977). For contextualizing approaches, see especially J. R. Jacob, *Robert Boyle and the English Revolution: a Study in Social and Intellectual Change* (New York: Burt Franklin, 1977); Steven Shapin and Simon Schaffer, *Leviathan and the Air-Pump: Hobbes, Boyle, and the Experimental Life* (Princeton University Press, 1985); and Webster, *Great Instauration*. For criticism of Jacob, see Hunter, "Introduction," 3–6; for criticism of Shapin and Schaffer, see Sargent, *The Diffident Naturalist*, *passim*; for criticism of Sargent's criticism of Shapin and Schaffer, see Peter Dear, "Narratives, Anecdotes, and Experiments: Turning Experience into Science in the Seventeenth Century," Peter Dear, ed., *The Literary Structure of Scientific Argument: Historical Studies* (Philadelphia: University of Pennsylvania Press, 1991), 161–62.

77 Shapin and Schaffer, *Leviathan and the Air-Pump*, 225.

78 Sargent, *The Diffident Naturalist*, 131.

79 Ibid., 137. Sargent sees experiment and observation as being very closely linked for Boyle, though experiment tends to follow observation and involves the researcher in a more active role. For Sargent's full discussion of Boyle's experimental method, see especially chapters 6 and 7.

80 It is noticeable that the account of the mercurial powder stresses the professional competence and high social status of the witnesses to the cure. Shapin

and Schaffer memorably declare that "[i]n Boyle's community, inanimate bodies and privileged witnesses had the most authority in experiments" (*Leviathan and the Air-Pump*, 218). Sargent contests at least the second part of this claim, arguing that Boyle did not set "prior conditions . . . to indicate a specific class of people that would qualify as witnesses. Rather, each person was to be assessed for credibility based upon individual experience and competence" (*The Diffident Naturalist*, 152). Sargent perhaps overstates the case for Boyle's freedom from class bias; there is no reason to believe that he doubted that those with high social status rightfully possessed authority. Nonetheless, though he may have overvalued a high title, he is careful never to undervalue the contribution of someone who lacks a title. A number of scholars have noted that Boyle seems to have incorporated into his experimental method the ancient law of the two witnesses. See, for instance, Shapin and Schaffer, *Leviathan and the Air-Pump*, 327, who relate the requirement for two witnesses to Restoration law; and Sargent, *The Diffident Naturalist*, 242n50, who relates it to biblical injunction and medieval and continental practice.

81 Sargent, *The Diffident Naturalist*, 148–49.
82 Ibid., 153.
83 Renaissance commentators on Genesis were much exercised by Eve's modifications to God's command. See Williams, *Common Expositor*, 121.
84 Boyle, *Works*, II, 196.
85 Ibid., II, 197 [*The Usefulness of Experimental Natural Philosophy*].
86 Thomas Browne, *"Religio Medici" and Other Works*, ed. L. C. Martin (Oxford: Clarendon Press, 1964), 68.
87 Maureen Quilligan, *Milton's Spenser: the Politics of Reading* (Ithaca: Cornell University Press, 1983), 126.
88 Boyle, *The Usefulness of Experimental Natural Philosophy* (Oxford, 1664), pt.1, 51–52. (These pages are missing from the 1772 edition of Boyle's works.)
89 *CPW*, VI, 120.

2 EXPERIMENTALISTS AND THE BOOK OF THE WORLD

1 See Williams, *Common Expositor*, 116.
2 See, for instance, the depiction of "Serpens Americanus" in Ulisse Aldrovandi, *Serpentum, et draconum historia* (Bologna, 1640), 308. A sketch of a raised cobra appears in Peter Mundy's journal of his travels in India (Peter Mundy, *The Travels of Peter Mundy in Europe and Asia, 1608–1667*, ed. Richard Carnac Temple, 5 vols. in 6, Hakluyt Society second series 17, 35, 45–46, 55, 78 [London: Hakluyt Society, 1907–36], II, 308).
3 Unless otherwise noted, quotations from the Bible are from the Authorized Version. Kitty W. Scoular collects and discusses conventional instances of praise for "insect or worm" in classical, medieval, and early modern literature in *Natural Magic: Studies in the Presentation of Nature in English Poetry from Spenser to Marvell* (Oxford: Clarendon Press, 1965), 38–117.

4 Catherine Wilson, *The Invisible World: Early Modern Philosophy and the Invention of the Microscope* (Princeton University Press, 1995), 183.

5 *Theatrum Insectorum* (1634) is Mouffet's revision of the work of Thomas Penny, the latter regarded by Charles Raven as a true entomologist. The treatise was translated in 1658 and, with the title, *The Theater of Insects*, appeared as the third volume of Topsell's *History of Four-Footed Beasts*. For Penny, Mouffet, and the significance of *The Theater of Insects*, see Charles Raven, *English Naturalists from Neckam to Ray: a Study of the Making of the Modern World* (1947; New York: Kraus Reprint, 1968), 153–91. For the debate about spontaneous generation, see Wilson, *Invisible World*, 196–202. For the earliest microscopical observation of insects, see Wilson, *Invisible World*, 75–76; and Ernst Mayr, *The Growth of Biological Thought: Diversity, Evolution, and Inheritance* (Cambridge, MA: Harvard University Press, 1982), 138. W. D. P. Wightman points out that "the first 'scientific' monograph on insects," that of Francisco Stelluti (Rome, 1625), deals with the mouth parts and limbs of the bee (*The Growth of Scientific Ideas* [New Haven: Yale University Press, 1951], 203).

6 Guillaume de Saluste, Sieur Du Bartas, *The Divine Weeks and Works*, trans. Josuah Sylvester, ed. Susan Snyder, 2 vols. (Oxford: Clarendon Press, 1979), I.v.897, 900. Unless otherwise noted, all quotations from *The Divine Weeks and Works* are to this edition and hereafter will be parenthetically cited in the text. The citation refers to week, day, and line number.

7 *OED*, minim, a. and sb., senses 2 and 4.

8 Scoular has noted that fine craftsmanship in the sixteenth and seventeenth centuries was particularly associated with the miniature, "in both nature and art" (*Natural Magic*, 85). In his 1729 edition of *Paradise Lost*, Thomas Newton associates "minims" with Proverbs 30.24 and notes that "[t]he word was in use before for an order of friars, *Mini, minimi*, so called from affected humility" (*PL*, VII.482n). Milton's minims are truly humble – and hence truly exalted by their Maker.

9 Wilson, *Invisible World*, 27.

10 Wilson includes among the standard histories Charles Coulton Gillispie, *The Edge of Objectivity: an Essay in the History of Scientific Ideas* (Princeton University Press, 1960); Alexandre Koyré, *From the Closed World to the Infinite Universe* (Baltimore: Johns Hopkins University Press, 1953); and Westfall, *The Construction of Modern Science*.

11 Wilson, *Invisible World*, 10–13.

12 Among recent studies which assume a wider notion of science in the early modern period see, for natural history, Nicholas Jardine, J. A. Secord, and E. C. Spary, eds., *Cultures of Natural History* (Cambridge University Press, 1996), especially the essay by William Ashworth, "Emblematic Natural History of the Renaissance," 17–37, 461–62; for chemistry, Hunter, ed., *Robert Boyle Reconsidered*; for medicine, Roger French and Andrew Wear, eds., *The Medical Revolution of the Seventeenth Century* (Cambridge University Press, 1989); for biology, Wilson, *Invisible World*.

13 Peter Bowler, *The Fontana History of the Environmental Sciences*, Fontana History of Science (London: HarperCollins–Fontana, 1992), 68.

14 Harold J. Cook, "The New Philosophy and Medicine in Seventeenth-Century England," David Lindberg and Robert Westman, eds., *Reappraisals of the Scientific Revolution* (Cambridge University Press, 1990), 400.

15 Joseph M. Levine, "Natural History and the History of the Scientific Revolution," Clio 13 (1983), 68–69; emphasis added.

16 Levine, "Natural History," 69.

17 Ibid., 65.

18 Wilson, *Invisible World*, 10.

19 Ibid., 34.

20 What constitutes a fact is itself a vexed question for the new philosophers and therefore for historians of the scientific revolution. See especially Lorraine Daston, "Baconian Facts, Academic Civility, and the Prehistory of Objectivity," *Annals of Scholarship* 8 (1992), 337–63, and "Marvelous Facts and Miraculous Evidence in Early Modern Europe," *Critical Inquiry* 18 (1991), 93–124. See also the disputes between Rose-Mary Sargent in *Diffident Naturalist* and Shapin and Schaffer in *Leviathan and the Air Pump*, on the nature of Robert Boyle's "matters of fact."

21 The *locus criticus* for the trope is Ernst Robert Curtius, *European Literature and the Latin Middle Ages*, trans. Willard R. Trask (1953; New York: Harper and Row–Harper Torchbooks, 1963), 319–26.

22 Foucault, *Order of Things*, 32.

23 Dear, "Narratives, Anecdotes, and Experiments," 135.

24 Anne Ferry has shown that the verb *to read* did not primarily signify a linguistic act in the sixteenth century; hence it was possible to speak non-metaphorically of reading objects or speech (*The Art of Naming* [University of Chicago Press, 1988], 23–39). While the notion of "reading the book of nature" is obviously metaphorical, it is probable that older, non-metaphorical senses of the verb are encompassed by the trope. (See *OED*, read, v., sense 2.a.)

25 By W. H. Greenleaf, among others, in *Order, Empiricism and Politics: Two Traditions of English Political Thought 1500–1700* (London: Oxford University Press for Hull University Press, 1964), 10.

26 Raven, *English Naturalists*, 349–50.

27 W. G. Sebald, *The Rings of Saturn*, trans. Michael Hulse (London: Harvill, 1998), 9. Sebald's work may itself be described as a Browneian meditation.

28 It is quite possible that Milton knew Robert Boyle. He certainly knew of him and his work, either through Boyle's sister, Lady Katherine Ranelagh, or through mutual acquaintances in the Hartlib circle. See Parker, *Milton: a Biography*, I, 572; II, 923n118 and 1046n149.

29 Christopher Ricks, *Milton's Grand Style* (Oxford: Clarendon Press, 1963), 78.

30 Browne, *"Religio Medici,"* 15.

31 Henry Power, *Experimental Philosophy in Three Books: Containing New Experiments Microscopical, Mercurial, Magnetical* (London, 1664), b3ᵛ–b4ʳ. Gordon Keith

Chalmers notes that Power imitates Browne throughout *Experimental Philosophy* and suggests that in some instances imitation shades into plagiarism ("Sir Thomas Browne, True Scientist," *Osiris* 2 [1936], 29n7).

32 See Du Bartas, *Divine Weeks*, I.vi.885–906. Regiomontanus, named for his birthplace, Königsberg, is Johann Müller (1436–76), astronomer and mathematician.

33 Half a century ago, Gordon Chalmers and Robert Merton argued that Browne was a true scientist, Chalmers ignoring the question of Browne's style altogether and Merton, though concerned with Browne's "prose art," failing to connect the way Browne wrote to the way he practiced natural philosophy. (See Chalmers, "Sir Thomas Browne," and Merton, *Science and Imagination in Sir Thomas Browne* [1949; New York: Octagon, 1969], 124–26.) Scholars interested in Browne's status as a literary artist now far outnumber those interested in his status as a scientist. The latter typically regard the "literary" style as an irrelevance or a veneer. Marie Boas Hall, arguing that Browne should be regarded as "a naturalist, a pure natural historian, a serious collector of every sort of fact," insists that "it is necessary to look *beneath his style*" to understand his contributions to the scientific thought of his day ("Thomas Browne Naturalist," C. A. Patrides, ed., *Approaches to Sir Thomas Browne: the Ann Arbor Tercentenary Lectures and Essays* [Columbia, MO: University of Missouri Press, 1982], 179, 180; emphasis added). Frank L. Huntley cautiously notes that whether we consider Browne a scientist "depends on what we mean by science"; he sees the wordplay and wit of *Pseudodoxia Epidemica* as proof simply of Browne's "intellectual detachment" (*Sir Thomas Browne: a Biographical and Critical Study* [Ann Arbor: University of Michigan Press, 1962], 89, 169). In his major study of Browne, Leonard Nathanson reserves only a few pages for *Pseudodoxia Epidemica*, asserting that it reveals Browne to be a "serious scientist" but taking no account of its style (*The Strategy of Truth: a Study of Sir Thomas Browne* [University of Chicago Press, 1967], 156). Jonathan Post concludes that Browne's "scientific pursuits were shaped by . . . a humanist's respect for antiquity and the written word"; accordingly, he argues that the style of *Pseudodoxia Epidemica* derives from the tradition of textual criticism rather than scientific observation (*Sir Thomas Browne* [Boston: Twayne–G. K. Hall, 1987], 38). Michael Hunter goes against the prevailing trend and argues that Browne's literary style cannot be divorced from the question of his status as a "true scientist." He implies, however, that the more literary the style, the less scientific the thought. Thus, Hunter finds that Browne's later work on urns, "Concerning some Urnes found in *Brampton-Field*, in *Norfolk*, Ann. 1667," is properly archaeological because it is "quite free from [the] metaphors, literary parallels, and philosophical speculations" of *Hydriotaphia* (*Science and the Shape of Orthodoxy: Intellectual Change in Late Seventeenth-Century Britain* [Woodbridge: Boydell, 1995], 194).

34 Wilson, *Invisible World*, 5.

35 For contemporary references to Browne's standing as a new philosopher, see Robin Robbins, "Introduction," *Pseudodoxia Epidemica*, I, xxxix–xlix; Joan

Bennett, *Sir Thomas Browne* (Cambridge University Press, 1962), 163–77; and Chalmers, "Sir Thomas Browne," 28–32.

36 Browne, *"Religio Medici,"* 12.

37 The doctrine of signatures is founded on the assumption that God has provided signs to aid humanity in discovering the curative or protective virtues of plants. Keith Thomas defines the doctrine as "the belief that every plant had some human use, and that its colour, shape and texture were designed to give some external indication of that use, so that, for example, spotted herbs cured spots, yellow ones healed jaundice, and adder's tongue was good for snake-bites" (*Man and the Natural World: a History of the Modern Sensibility* [New York: Pantheon, 1983], 84).

38 Browne, *"Religio Medici,"* 13.

39 *OED*, speculate, v., senses 1 and 2. *Religio Medici* is probably too early for *magnifie* to refer to microscopic observation. Later in the century, physico-theology, one might say, attempted to demonstrate that one could magnify the Creator by magnifying the creatures under a microscope.

40 See Gordon Keith Chalmers, "Hieroglyphs and Sir Thomas Browne," *Virginia Quarterly Review* 11 (1935), 547–60, for a view of how Browne and his contemporaries understood Egyptian hieroglyphs.

41 Browne, *"Religio Medici,"* 15.

42 Revised and expanded editions of *Pseudodoxia Epidemica* were published in Browne's lifetime in 1650, 1658, 1669, and 1672. For details of its publishing history, see Robbins, "Introduction," *Pseudodoxia Epidemica*, I, xlix–liii.

43 Rosalie L. Colie, "Dean Wren's Marginalia and Early Science at Oxford," *Bodleian Library Record* 6 (1960), 542.

44 Dean Wren's copy is at the Bodleian Library (shelfmark O 2.26 Art.Seld); most of his annotations have been incorporated into the footnotes of Simon Wilkin's edition of *Pseudodoxia Epidemica* in vol. II of *Sir Thomas Browne's Works*, 4 vols. (London, 1826–35).

45 Browne, *Pseudodoxia Epidemica* (1646; Menston, England: Scolar, 1972), a6^r–a6^v.

46 Wilkin, ed., *Sir Thomas Browne's Works*, II, 182n6.

47 *OED*, desiderate, v.; desire, v., sense 1.

48 Browne, *Pseudodoxia Epidemica* (1646), a3^v.

49 See chapter 6, pp. 122–24.

50 The various chapters of *Pseudodoxia Epidemica*, Robbins says, merely "synthesize ancient and modern opinions, performing that intermediate task desiderated by Bacon of clearing the path for subsequent investigators" ("Introduction," *Pseudodoxia Epidemica*, I, xxxvii). He overlooks the importance of Browne's style for the developing new philosophy, but Robbins's borrowing of *desiderated* suggests that he has nonetheless been affected by it.

51 Wilson, *Invisible World*, 23–24.

52 Ibid., 13.

53 Ibid., 13.

54 Barbara J. Shapiro, *Probability and Certainty in Seventeenth-Century England: a Study of the Relationships between Natural Science, Religion, History, Law, and Literature* (Princeton University Press, 1983), 232.

55 Steven Shapin, "Pump and Circumstance: Robert Boyle's Literary Technology," *Social Studies in Science* 14 (1984), 493–97. Boyle's most sustained discussion of writing styles appropriate for scientific inquiry occurs in the "Proëmial Essay" of *Certain Physiological Essays*, published in 1661 (*Works*, I, 299–318).

56 Boyle, *Works*, I, 304–05.

57 Ibid., I, 307.

58 Ibid.

59 See Brian Vickers, "The Royal Society and English Prose Style: a Reassessment," Brian Vickers and Nancy S. Struever, eds., *Rhetoric and the Pursuit of Truth: Language Change in the Seventeenth and Eighteenth Centuries* (Los Angeles: William Andrews Clark Memorial Library, 1985), 3–76.

60 Shapin, "Pump and Circumstance," 515–16n29, drawing on Lisa Jardine, *Francis Bacon: Discovery and the Art of Discourse* (Cambridge University Press, 1974), 174–78. Bacon makes the distinction between "magistral" and "initiative" for methods of discourse in *De Augmentis* (*Works*, IV, 449).

61 Boyle, *Works*, I, 306.

62 I am indebted to Martin Dzelzainis for this observation.

63 Robbins cites others who adopted Browne's "coinages and phraseology": Walter Charleton in his translation of Helmont's *Ternary of Paradoxes* (1650); Noah Biggs in *The Vanity of the Craft of Physick* (1651); Agricola Carpenter in *Pseuchographia Anthropomagica: or, A Magicall Description of the Soul* (1652); and John Bulwer in *Anthropometamorphosis* (1653). (See Robbins, "Introduction," *Pseudodoxia Epidemica*, I, xliii and xliii nn.1–3.) By 1665, when he published the second edition of his work, Glanvill had reformed his writing to suit what he took to be the Royal Society's preferred style.

64 John Harwood, "Science Writing and Writing Science: Boyle and Rhetorical Theory," Michael Hunter, ed., *Robert Boyle Reconsidered* (Cambridge University Press, 1994), 50.

65 Sargent, *The Diffident Naturalist*, 101.

66 Ibid.

67 Boyle, *Works*, II, 6.

68 Boyle's formulation is ambiguous. He may mean that the truths remain "abstruse and veiled" only until they are found out, but his continuing meditation on the trope implies that they *remain* abstruse.

69 Boyle, *Works*, II, 20.

70 It is possible that Boyle picked up the term *indagation* from Browne, who speaks of Satan the natural magician exploiting discoveries made by "humane indagation" (*PE*, 63, quoted in chapter 1).

71 Boyle, *Works*, II, 7.

72 Boyle, *Works*, II, 12 [*The Usefulness of Experimental Philosophy*].

73 Samuel Hartlib, *Ephemerides, The Hartlib Papers*, CD-ROM (Ann Arbor, MI: UMI, 1995), 30/4/54A.
74 The essay was first published in 1686, but Boyle says in the preface that it was actually written two decades earlier.
75 Boyle, *Works*, V, 252.
76 Ibid., II, 24.
77 Ibid., II, 22.

3 THE PLACE OF EXPERIMENTAL READING

1 The apparent "lack of reply" to his questions has been taken to demonstrate the "inadequacy of natural theology" (Christopher, *Science of the Saints*, 147). The fact that there is a reply, though not the one looked for, problematizes this claim. In any case, natural theology is not equivalent to a theology of nature, to use a distinction drawn by George Huntston Williams, "Christian Attitudes toward Nature," *Christian Scholar's Review* 2, nos. 1–2 (1979), 112–19, and it is the latter that concerns me here.
2 Dayton Haskin, *Milton's Burden of Interpretation* (Philadelphia: University of Pennsylvania Press, 1994), 211, 205; emphasis added.
3 Haskin, *Milton's Burden*, 214.
4 Ibid., 216.
5 Peter Harrison, *The Bible, Protestantism, and the Rise of Natural Science* (Cambridge University Press, 1998), 4.
6 Catherine Wilson notes that by the eighteenth century, physico-theology had "assumed increasing momentum and even developed into a standard format for the presentation of natural history" (*Invisible World*, 176). By the nineteenth century, it had metamorphosed into " 'scientific' physiognomy," in which form it "finally loses its empiricist pretensions altogether" (*Invisible World*, 63).
7 According to the *OED*, the term first appears in the title of William Derham's *Physico-Theology: or, a Demonstration of the Being and Attributes of God from His Works of Creation* (1712). Boyle uses the adjectival form, *physico-theological*, in an essay of 1675. Derham's work was heavily influenced by John Ray's *The Wisdom of God Manifested in the Works of the Creation* (1691), perhaps the period's most eminent work of physico-theology.
8 Harrison, *Bible, Protestantism*, 193.
9 Wilson, *Invisible World*, 176.
10 This paragraph and the two following are largely indebted to Dayton Haskin's study, whose richness can only be hinted at here.
11 Haskin, *Milton's Burden*, 15–16.
12 Ibid., 181.
13 Ibid., 145.
14 Ibid., 109, 117.
15 The most memorable demonstration is his rereading of Sonnet 19, "When I consider . . ." (See Haskin, *Milton's Burden*, 29–53, 91–109, 165–73.) The

parable of the talents (Matthew 25.14–30) is the paradigmatic biblical place for Milton.

16 Haskin, *Milton's Burden*, 137.

17 Ibid., 77, 181.

18 Ibid., 226.

19 Haskin observes that although experimental reading of the Bible endured in England only as long as the "literature of afflicted consciences . . . was popular, that is, through the middle decades of the seventeenth century," it was practiced in New England until at least the Great Awakening of the eighteenth century (*Milton's Burden*, 15, 246n27).

20 Levine, "Natural History," 64.

21 See Williams, *Common Expositor*, 80–82. "Hexameral tradition had long accepted the naming of the animals as a sign of man's domination over them and as a proof of his wisdom," notes Williams (*Common Expositor*, 81), but there was much disagreement over the extent and nature of Adam's knowledge about the natural world.

22 Barbara K. Lewalski, "Innocence and Experience in Milton's Eden," *New Essays on "Paradise Lost,"* ed. Thomas Kranidas (Berkeley: University of California Press, 1971), 100.

23 John Leonard, *Naming in Paradise: Milton and the Language of Adam and Eve* (Oxford: Clarendon Press, 1990), especially the introduction (1–22) and chapter 1, "Naming Names" (23–85).

24 Leonard, *Naming in Paradise*, 27, 32.

25 Foucault, *Order of Things*, 128–32. Svetlana Alpers's *The Art of Describing: Dutch Art in the Seventeenth Century* (University of Chicago Press, 1983) takes Foucault's distinction between a discourse of hermeneutics and a discourse of description as the theoretical basis for a consideration of Dutch art and natural science in the seventeenth century. By insisting too rigidly upon the distinction, however, she weakens an otherwise useful study. Her scheme leaves her with no way to address the "descriptive" depiction of oddities or monsters. If the aim of description is to lead solely to classification (as it does in Foucault's analysis), what is the point of drawing a vegetable or animal "accident," a unique particular, with meticulous accuracy? To "expand knowledge of God's creation" is Alpers's inadequate but perhaps inevitable conclusion.

26 Foucault, *Order of Things*, 129. The first volume of Jonston's *Historia naturalis* was in fact published in 1650; 1657 is the date of the second printing. William Ashworth has observed that Foucault's insistence upon 1657 might give "ammunition to those who question the depth of Foucault's scholarship," remarking that "if we are going to use a date at all, it might as well be the right one, that is, 1650" ("Natural History and the Emblematic World View," *Reappraisals of the Scientific Revolution*, ed. David Lindberg and Robert Westman [Cambridge University Press, 1990], 330n41). Foucault admits, however, that 1657 is "not definitive" but is meant "to symbolize a land-mark" and mark "the apparent enigma of an event" (*Order of Things*,

128–29). The choice of 1657 seems to me to demonstrate Foucault's acute sense of how symbols function: 1650 has the disadvantage of being at once historically accurate and symbolically trite – and therefore unmemorable. (It is also too early, just as 1700 is too late.) My objection in any case is to using Jonston's work as the exemplar of a new approach to animals.

27 John Ray, *The Ornithology of Francis Willughby* (London, 1678), A3ᵛ.
28 For a detailed account of the animal encyclopedias, see Paul Delaunay, *La zoologie au seizième siècle*, Histoire de la Pensée 7 (Paris: Hermann, 1962) and Raven, *English Naturalists*. There are good, brief introductions in Allen Debus, *Man and Nature in the Renaissance*, Cambridge History of Science Series (Cambridge University Press, 1978), and F. D. Hoeniger and J. F. M. Hoeniger, *The Growth of Natural History in Stuart England from Gerard to the Royal Society*, Folger Booklets on Tudor and Stuart Civilization ([Charlottesville, VA:] University Press of Virginia for the Folger Library, 1969).
29 "Pandects" is the usual term. (See Raven, *English Naturalists*, 39.) The term "humanist encyclopedia" is William Ashworth's. He attributes the length of the animal histories to their ambition to include "*hieroglyphic, antiquarian, Aesopic, mythological, adagial,* and *emblematic* traditions" ("Natural History," 307).
30 Debus terms "monographic studies" the work of Belon and Rondelet on fish, Piso on the natural history of South America, and Bondt on that of the East Indies (*Man and Nature*, 37–38). *Monographic*, however, needs to be understood fairly widely. Under "fish," for instance, Belon and Rondelet consider any animal having something to do with water.
31 Ray, *The Ornithology*, A4ʳ. Ashworth discusses each of these categories in "Natural History."
32 For this reason, the specialized natural histories of Belon, Rondelet, Bondt, and Piso, which mainly treat "new" animals, seem more modern than the pandects.
33 Joan Barclay Lloyd's *African Animals in Renaissance Literature and Art*, Oxford Studies in the History of Art and Architecture (Oxford: Clarendon Press, 1971), provides a lively account of these encounters. In another category of exceptions are those animals such as the bird of paradise which were among the earliest "new" creatures brought back to Europe. Some of these were made the subject of emblems. (See Wolfgang Harms, "On Natural History and Emblematics in the 16th Century," *The Natural Sciences and the Arts: Aspects of Interaction from the Renaissance to the 20th Century*, ed. Allan Ellenius, Acta Universitatis Upsaliensis, Figura Nova, no. 22 [Stockholm: Almqvist & Wiksell, 1985], 67–83; and Ashworth, "Emblematic Natural History.")
34 These have been analyzed in fascinating detail by William Ashworth. See especially "The Persistent Beast: Recurring Images in Early Zoological Illustration," *The Natural Sciences*, ed. Ellenius, 46–66.
35 Foucault, *Order of Things*, 129.
36 For further comment on Jonston's illustrations, see S. Peter Dance, *The Art of Natural History: Animal Illustrators and their Work* (Woodstock, NY: Overlook, 1978), 35.

37 So, too, in fact, does Jonston's text. Foucault admits that Jonston does not provide new information in his natural history (*Order of Things*, 129). John Ray has a harsher judgment. In a letter to John Aubrey in 1677, he declares of Jonston: "I find him a meer plagiary & compiler of other mens labours" (*Further Correspondence of John Ray*, ed. Robert W. T. Gunther [London: The Ray Society, 1928], 160). What matters to Foucault is that Jonston omits the "animal semantics" that Aldrovandi includes. But Jonston does not entirely omit them; he discusses, for instance, an animal's "sympathies and antipathies," as Foucault mentions in passing (*Order of Things*, 129).

38 Dance, *Art of Natural History*, 25, 34.

39 F. J. Cole, "The History of Albrecht Dürer's Rhinoceros in Zoological Literature," *Science Medicine and History: Essays on the Evolution of Scientific Thought and Medical Practice Written in Honour of Charles Singer*, ed. E. Ashworth Underwood, 2 vols. (London: Oxford University Press, 1953), I, 50.

40 James S. Ackerman, "Early Renaissance 'Naturalism' and Scientific Illustration," *The Natural Sciences*, ed. Ellenius, 15–16.

41 Ashworth, "The Persistent Beast," 50.

42 Elizabeth L. Eisenstein, *The Printing Press as an Agent of Change: Communications and Cultural Transformations in Early-Modern Europe*, 2 vols. (Cambridge University Press, 1979), II, 487.

43 David Murray, *Museums: Their History and Their Use*, 3 vols. (Glasgow: James MacLehose, 1904), I, 206. Giuseppe Olmi, "Science–Honour–Metaphor: Italian Cabinets of the Sixteenth and Seventeenth Centuries," Oliver Impey and Arthur MacGregor, eds., *The Origins of Museums: the Cabinet of Curiosities in Sixteenth- and Seventeenth-Century Europe* (Oxford: Clarendon Press, 1985), 5–16, and Paula Findlen, *Possessing Nature: Museums, Collecting, and Scientific Culture in Early Modern Italy* (Berkeley: University of California Press, 1994), 153–287, argue for the scientific nature of at least some of the Italian collections.

44 Mundy, *Travels*, III, pt. 1, 2–3. For the curiosity collections of the period, see Arthur MacGregor, "Collectors and Collections of Rarities in the Sixteenth and Seventeenth Centuries," Arthur MacGregor, ed., *Tradescant's Rarities: Essays on the Foundation of the Ashmolean Museum 1683 with a Catalogue of the Surviving Early Collections* (Oxford: Clarendon Press, 1983), 70–97.

45 Mundy, *Travels*, III, pt.1, 1.

46 For the history of European zoos and menageries, see Gustave Loisel, *Histoire des ménageries de l'antiquité à nos jours*, 3 vols. (Paris: Octave Doin et Fils and Henri Laurens, 1912).

47 Parker, *Milton: a Biography*, I, 170. If he did, the fruit of his visit seems to be a resistance to the kind of exhibition favored by Grand Duke Ferdinand II, as I will argue in chapter 6.

48 Ray, *The Ornithology*, 151.

49 Raven, *English Naturalists*, 145.

50 Agnes Arber, *Herbals: Their Origin and Evolution. A Chapter in the History of Botany 1470–1670* [1912; 1938], 3rd edn., ed. William Stearn (Cambridge

University Press, 1986), 142. For a useful history of the origin of the *hortus siccus*, or herbarium, see 138–43.

51 Karen Reeds, "Renaissance Humanism and Botany," *Annals of Science* 33 (1976), 528.

52 Reeds's essay, "Renaissance Humanism and Botany," provides an excellent, brief introduction to the subject. See her *Botany in Medieval and Renaissance Universities* (New York: Garland, 1991) for the academic study of plants in the period. On the relationship between the botany of classical antiquity and that of the sixteenth century, see Edward Lee Greene, *Landmarks of Botanical History*, ed. Frank Egerton, 2 vols. (Stanford University Press, 1983).

53 Blanche Henrey, *British Botanical and Horticultural Literature before 1800*, 3 vols. (London: Oxford University Press, 1975), I, 77. The first volume provides a useful introduction and bibliography for the herbals, "scientific and floristic" books, and works on gardening and cultivation in the period. The first volume of *The Catalogue of Botanical Books in the Collection of Rachel McMasters Miller Hunt*, 3 vols. (Pittsburgh: Hunt Botanical Library, 1958–61), is a standard bibliographical work for sixteenth- and seventeenth-century botanical works. Robert T. Gunther, *Early British Botanists and their Gardens: Based on Unpublished Writings of Goodyer, Tradescant, and Others* (Oxford University Press, 1922), Hoeniger and Hoeniger, *The Growth of Natural History*, and Raven, *English Naturalists*, treat botany along with other sixteenth- and seventeenth-century natural sciences.

54 Unless otherwise noted, references to Gerard are to Johnson's revised edition of 1636.

55 James E. Smith, "Parkinson, John," *The Cyclopædia; or, Universal Dictionary*, ed. Abraham Rees, 45 vols. [London: Longman, Hurst, et al., 1819–20], XXVI, n.p.; cited in Henrey, *British Botanical*, I, 79. For Gerard and Johnson, see Henrey, *British Botanical*, I, 36–54, and Raven, *English Naturalists*, 204–17, 273–97; for Parkinson, see Henrey, *British Botanical*, I, 79–82, and Raven, *English Naturalists* 248–73.

56 Raven, *English Naturalists*, 248.

57 Ibid.

58 For the continental herbals, see Arber, *Herbals*, chapter 4; Reeds, *Botany in Medieval*, 111–33 (on the Bauhins); Raven, *English Naturalists*, 235–38 (esp. on L'Obel); and Henrey, *British Botanical*, I, 5–11.

59 Jack Goody, *The Culture of Flowers* (Cambridge University Press, 1993), provides a particularly valuable and lively account of the commercialization of flowers.

60 See Arthur MacGregor, "The Tradescants Gardeners and Botanists," and "The Tradescants as Collectors of Rarities," MacGregor, ed., *Tradescant's Rarities*, 3–16, 17–23, and Raven, *English Naturalists*, 243–44.

61 Claus Nissen, *Die botanische Buchillustration, ihre Geschichte und Bibliographie*, 2 vols. (Stuttgart: Hiersemann, 1951), is the standard bibliographical work on botanical illustration. For discussion of the subject, see, in addition to

Nissen's historical account, Ackerman, "Early Renaissance 'Naturalism'";
Arber, *Herbals*, 185–246, 315–17; Wilfrid Blunt, *The Art of Botanical Illustration*,
3rd edn., ed. William Stearn (London: Collins, 1955); and Harms, "On
Natural History."

62 For the doctrine of signatures in relation to botany of the period, see Arber,
Herbals, 247–63; Foucault, *Order of Things*, 25–30; Henrey, *British Botanical*, I,
82–92; and Thomas, *Man and the Natural World*, 84–85.

63 Donald Worster, *Nature's Economy: a History of Ecological Ideas*, 2nd edn.
(Cambridge University Press, 1994), 32.

64 See Svendsen, *Milton and Science*, 35; Barbara K. Lewalski, *"Paradise Lost" and
the Rhetoric of Literary Forms* (Princeton University Press, 1985), 45; George
Coffin Taylor, *Milton's Use of Du Bartas* (Cambridge, MA: Harvard
University Press, 1934), xvi; and Williams, *Common Expositor*, 57.

65 Walter Raleigh, *Historie of the World* (London, 1614), 1.1.3.6. Citation is to
part, book, chapter, and section number.

66 For summaries of the controversy, see Joseph E. Duncan, *Milton's Earthly
Paradise: a Historical Study of Eden* (Minneapolis: University of Minnesota
Press, 1972), 202–12; and Williams, *Common Expositor*, 95–101.

67 Hooke, *Micrographia*, f2ᵛ.

4   MILTON'S COMPLICATED SERPENTS

1 Neil Forsyth's *The Old Enemy: Satan and the Combat Myth* (Princeton University
Press, 1987), however, shows how profoundly complex the "commonplace"
satanic dragon actually is.

2 See, for instance, Job 20.14, 16, Isaiah 11.8, and Romans 3.13 for the asp; 1
Kings 12.11, 14, Ezekiel 2.6, Luke 10.19, and Revelation 9.3, 10 for the scorpion.

3 Michael Lieb, *The Dialectics of Creation: Patterns of Birth and Regeneration in
"Paradise Lost"* (Boston: University of Massachusetts Press, 1970), 179–81.

4 Merritt Y. Hughes, ed., *John Milton: Complete Poems and Major Prose* (New York:
Odyssey, 1957), *PL*, x.524n.

5 Svendsen, *Milton and Science*, 144.

6 Ibid., 3.

7 "[M]ost of the classical names are still used in serious herpetology, though
they do not always relate nowadays to their original proprietors," remarks
T. H. White, ed. and trans., *The Book of Beasts, Being a Translation from a Latin
Bestiary of the Twelfth Century* (London: Jonathan Cape, 1954), 185n1.

8 *OED*, amphisbæna, sense 2. Druce found *Amphisbaena alba* and *Amphisbaena
fuliginosa* displayed at the Natural History Museum, London ("The
Amphisbaena and its Connexions in Ecclesiastical Art and Architecture,"
Archaeological Journal 67 [1910], 302–03).

9 Ulisse Aldrovandi, *Serpentum, et draconum historia* (Bologna, 1640), 237–39. See
Druce, "The Amphisbaena," 295–300, for a translation of Aldrovandi's
entry.

10 Isabel MacCaffrey, *"Paradise Lost" as "Myth"* (Cambridge, MA: Harvard University Press, 1959), 169.

11 Alexander Grosart, ed., *The Divine Weeks and Works*, by Guillaume Du Bartas, trans. Joshuah Sylvester, vol. 1 of *Joshuah Sylvester: The Complete Works*, 2 vols. (1880; Hildesheim: George Olms, 1969), marginal gloss at *Divine Weeks* I.vi.194.

12 Mundy, *Travels*, II, 308.

13 Ibid., II, 309.

14 Ibid., II, 308n4; emphasis added.

15 Typically, and undoubtedly because Browne questions it, Alexander Ross defends the existence of the amphisbaena in *Arcana Microcosmi: or, the Hid Secrets of Man's Body Discovered* (London, 1652), 147.

16 He notes that it is "the practise of Christians" to baptize "these geminous births, and double connascencies with severall names, as conceiving in them a distinction of soules" (*PE*, 218). See Katharine Park and Lorraine Daston, "Unnatural Conceptions: the Study of Monsters in Sixteenth- and Seventeenth-Century France and England," *Past and Present* 92 (1981), 20–54, for a discussion of the "Two Inseparable Brothers," Lazarus and John Coloredo, who toured England and Scotland between 1637 and 1642.

17 Park and Daston, *"Unnatural Conceptions,"* 23.

18 Ibid., 35, 45.

19 Ibid., 53.

20 I say "extraordinary" because of the date at which Browne was writing. Park and Daston imply that the medicalization of monstrosity occurs in the *late* seventeenth century, but the first edition of *Pseudodoxia Epidemica* was published in 1646.

21 *OED*, monster, sb. and a., sense 2.a. Browne's equation of monstrosity with birth defects may arise from his study of Ulisse Aldrovandi's *Monstrorum historia* (Bologna, 1642).

22 Richard Bentley, ed., *Paradise Lost* [1732] (New York: AMS, 1974), *PL*, X.524n.

23 Edward Topsell, *The History of Four-Footed Beasts and Serpents and Insects*, 3 vols. (1658; New York: Da Capo, 1967), II, 746.

24 P. Ansell Robin, *Animal Lore in English Literature* (London: John Murray, 1932), 84. See also Robin's discussion of the vexed semantic relationship between the basilisk and the cockatrice at pages 84–95.

25 Robin, *Animal Lore*, 84–92, 181–84; and T. H. White, *Book of Beasts*, 168–69.

26 John Evelyn, *The Diary of John Evelyn*, ed. E. S. de Beer, 6 vols. (Oxford: Clarendon Press, 1955), III, 200.

27 Robert Hubert, *A Catalogue of Many Natural Rarities* (London, 1664), 29.

28 Hughes, ed., *John Milton: Complete Poems*, *PL*, X.524n, X.525n, and X.526n.

29 Ibid., *PL*, X.525n.

30 *OED*, ellops.

31 Robin, *Animal Lore*, 150.

32 Ricks, *Milton's Grand Style*, 14.

33 Browne cites the contradictory opinions of various authorities: "So Bonaventure and Comestor affirme it was a Dragon, Eugubinus a Basiliske, Delrio a viper, and others a common snake" (*PE*, 539). Browne spends much of his discussion of the basilisk on the problem of naming. He declares, reflecting on Isaiah 59.5: "what kind of serpents are meant [is] not easie to be determined, for translations are very different: Tremellius rendring the Asp Hæmorrhous, and the Regulus or Basilisk a Viper, and our translation for the Aspe, sets down a Cockatrice in the text, and an Adder in the margine" (*PE*, 185). The difficulty, Browne implies, is that there is no way to move from the "translations" to the serpent.

34 Bacon, *Works*, III, 267.

35 This is due to a longstanding confusion between *hydrus* (water snake) and *enhydris* (otter). Robin disentangles the confusion (*Animal Lore*, 149–50, 184–85).

36 *CPW*, II, 224.

37 For commentary on Spenser's dragons, see "dragons" in *The Spenser Encyclopedia*, ed. A. C. Hamilton et al. (University of Toronto Press, 1990), 223–24.

38 The union also occurs, differently elaborated, in *Of Reformation*: "I recall to mind at last, after so many darke Ages, wherein the huge overshadowing traine of *Error* had almost swept all the Starres out of the Firmament of the *Church*; how the bright and blissful *Reformation* (by Divine Power) strook through the black and settled Night of *Ignorance* and *Antichristian Tyranny*" (*CPW*, I, 524).

39 *CPW*, II, 223.

40 Ibid., I, 524–25.

41 Ibid., I, 535.

42 Ibid., VI, 118.

43 Study and application have a greater role in the Latin original than the Yale edition's "puzzle out" implies: "et quod mearum erat partium non omisso, ex ipsa Dei scriptura quam diligentissime perlecta atque perpensa, unumquodque habere mihimet ipsi, meaque ipsius opera exploratum atque cognitum" (*The Works of John Milton*, gen. ed. F. A. Patterson, 18 vols. [New York: Columbia University Press, 1931–38], XIV, 4). The Columbia editors translate the passage: "and . . . having neglected nothing which depended on my own industry, I thought fit to scrutinize and ascertain for myself the several points of my religious belief, by the most careful perusal and meditation of the Holy Scriptures themselves" (XIV, 5).

44 We recall the brass serpent of Moses, which Hezekiah later "brake in pieces" because it had become an idol and "the children of Israel did burn incense to it" (2 Kings 18.4).

45 *CPW*, I, 522.

46 For discussion of the "apple," see chapter 8, pp. 144–49.

47 *CPW*, VI, 133.

48 See *CPW*, VI, 135n15, and, for commentary on Milton's doctrine of accommodation, Hugh R. MacCallum, "Milton and the Figurative

Interpretation of the Bible," *UTQ* 31 (1961–62), 397–415.

49 *CPW*, VI, 133.

50 James Grantham Turner, *One Flesh: Paradisal Marriage and Sexual Relations in the Age of Milton* (Oxford: Clarendon Press, 1987), 228.

5 NEW USES FOR MONSTROUS LORE

1 Nine of the first dozen entries under "Fourfooted Beasts" in John Tradescant's *Musæum Tradescantianum: or, A Collection of Rarities Preserved at South-Lambeth neer London* (London, 1656), for instance, are explicitly listed as parts of animals: "Lions head and teeth. Lynxe's head. Beares head, clawes, and skin. Wolfes teeth. Parde, Leopard's teeth. Tygers head. Gulo's legge. Hippopotamus. Ai, Ignavus, Sloath . . . Fox, from *Virginia*. Munkyes skeleton. Brocks skin" (5).

2 Tradescant, *Musæum Tradescantianum*, 1.

3 Quoted in MacGregor, "Tradescants as Collectors," 19–20.

4 See Wilma George, "Alive or Dead: Zoological Collections in the Seventeenth Century," Impey and MacGregor, eds., *The Origins of Museums*, 184.

5 Olmi, "Science–Honour–Metaphor," 9–10.

6 Svendsen, *Milton and Science*, 226.

7 Hamon L'Estrange, "Observations on *Pseudodoxia Epidemica*," British Museum Sloan MS 1839, 53.

8 Ross, *Arcana Microcosmi*, 199.

9 John Wilkins, *An Essay Towards a Real Character, and a Philosophical Language* (1668; Menston: Scolar, 1968), 121.

10 H. Stanford London explains that griffin claws "were really rhinoceros horns, or the horn of an antelope or bull," while "griffin eggs" were actually ostrich eggs *(Royal Beasts* [East Knoyle: The Heraldry Society, 1956], 17n5). Griffin claws and eggs were highly prized: they "were commonly mounted as drinking vessels . . . because they were supposed to change colour on contact with poison" *(Royal Beasts*, 18). This trait undoubtedly accounts for their frequent presence in inventories of royal treasures. David Murray notes that King Aaron of Persia presented the claw of a griffin to Charlemagne in 807 *(Museums*, I, 12). The association of griffins with the Holy Land explains why their eggs and claws were displayed as relics in medieval churches. Murray states that "the horn of an antelope, which Duke Henry the Lion (1129–1195) brought back from Palestine as being the claw of a griffin," was exhibited in the Cathedral of Brunswick; "in the church of St. Michael, in Hildesheim, another griffin's claw was exhibited, which was in reality a goat's horn" *(Museums*, I, 8–9).

11 Browne, for instance, argues that "Gryps" in the Bible or in classical literature "signifies some kinde of Eagle or Vulture" *(PE*, 199), but it is difficult to tell how widespread this reading was. As one of the most distinctive features of a griffin's head is the presence of very lion-like ears, it is difficult to

know how collectors managed to show an eagle's head (if they did) and call it a "griffin."

12 Bacon, *Works*, III, 364.

13 Ibid., III, 331.

14 Grosart, ed., *Divine Weeks*, marginal gloss at I.v.713.

15 Raleigh, *Historie of the World*, 1.3.8.5.

16 Ibid.

17 Browne, *Pseudodoxia Epidemica* (1646; Menston: Scolar, 1972), 130. (Robbins supplies the wording of the first edition at *PE*, 199n19–20.)

18 See Daston, "Marvelous Facts," and Park and Daston, "Unnatural Conceptions."

19 Shakespeare, *The Tempest*, II.ii.32–33, 88–89.

20 John Guillim, *A Display of Heraldrie*, 3rd edn. (London, 1638), 261.

21 Guillim, *Display of Heraldrie*, 264.

22 Park and Daston, "Unnatural Conceptions," 36. Paré states that the ostrich "ne bouge de terre pour prendre l'air, neantmoins passe un cheval de vistesse" (Ambroise Paré, *Des monstres et prodiges* [1573], ed. Jean Céard [Geneva: Librairie Droz, 1971], 126). Of the crocodile, he comments: "Il a la langue si empeschee qu'il semble n'en avoir point, qui est cause qu'il vit partie en terre, partie en eau: comme estant terrestre, elle luy tient lieu de langue et comme estant aquatiq, il est sans langue. Car les poissons, ou ils n'ont point du tout de langue, ou ils l'ont fort liee et empeschee" (110).

23 Newton notes that "[t]he difficulty of Satan's voyage is very well express'd by so many monosyllables as follow, which cannot be pronounced but slowly, and with frequent pauses" (Thomas Newton, ed., *Paradise Lost: a Poem in Twelve Books* [London, 1749], II.948n).

24 So effective is this exposure, that in *Paradise Regained*, the mere naming of the hippogrif – the product of a griffin and a horse, a creature doubly hybrid – is equivalent to dismissing it as a preposterous fiction unworthy of inclusion in the story:

> So saying, he caught him up, and without wing
> Of hippogrif bore through the air sublime
> Over the wilderness and o'er the plain; (*PR*, IV.541–43)

25 *CPW*, I, 543; Svendsen, *Milton and Science*, 145–46.

26 *CPW*, V.i, 381, 385, 387.

27 William Davenant, *Gondibert* [1651], ed. David Gladish (Oxford: Clarendon Press, 1971), II.v.32,34.

28 Robert T. Gunther, *Early Science in Oxford*, vol. III. (1925; London: Dawsons, 1968), 356. There is a photograph of the scapula facing page 355.

29 Tradescant, *Musæum Tradescantianum*, 9.

30 Evelyn, *Diary*, III, 215. The entry (June 3, 1658) includes the sketch.

31 Newton, ed., *PL*, I.200n.

32 Ibid.

33 For versions of the legend, see Harold Fisch, "Creation in Reverse: the Book

of Job and *Paradise Lost*," *Milton and Scriptural Tradition: the Bible into Poetry*, ed. James Sims and Leland Ryken (Columbia, MO: University of Missouri Press, 1984), 106–07; Frye, *Milton's Imagery*, 92–93; D. M. Hill, "Satan on the Burning Lake," *NQ* 2nd ser. 31 (1956), 157–59; James Hall Pitman, "Milton and the *Physiologus*," *MLN* 40 (1925), 439–40; Svendsen, *Milton and Science*, 33–35; James Whaler, "The Miltonic Simile," *PMLA* 46 (1931), 1050–51; White, *Book of Beasts*, 197–98.

34 Frye, *Milton's Imagery*, 93.

35 White, *Book of Beasts*, 197.

36 Evelyn, *Diary*, III, 215.

37 The orc is a devouring sea-monster, kin to the leviathan. After the Fall, paradise becomes "an island salt and bare, / The haunt of seals and orcs, and sea-mews' clang" (*PL*, XI.834–35).

38 *OED*, trunk, sb., sense 4.a.

39 *OED*, fistula, sb., sense 3; spout, sb., sense I.i.a.

40 Hubert, *Catalogue*, 27, 26.

41 Aristotle, *Historia animalium*, trans. A. L. Peck (vols. I and II) and D. M. Balme (vol. III), Loeb Classical Library, 3 vols. (London: William Heinemann, 1965–91), I, 25 [489b].

42 Pliny, *Natural History*, trans. H. Rackham et al., Loeb Classical Library, 10 vols. (1938–63; Cambridge, MA: Harvard University Press; London: William Heinemann, 1969–84), III, 178–79.

43 *OED*, gill, sb.², sense 2; and trunk, sb., sense I.4.

44 Alexander Gil, *The Sacred Philosophie of the Holy Scriptures* (London, 1635). The work was reissued in 1651 under the title, *The Truth of Christian Religion*.

45 Gil, *Sacred Philosophie*, Art.VI,84.

46 Thomas Hobbes, *Leviathan* [1651], ed. C. B. MacPherson (Harmondsworth: Penguin, 1968), 362.

47 John M. Steadman, "Leviathan and Renaissance Etymology," *JHI* 28 (1967), 576.

48 Thomas Hobbes, "The Answer of Mr. Hobbes to Sir Will. Davenant's Preface Before Gondibert," *Gondibert*, by William Davenant, ed. David Gladish (Oxford: Clarendon Press, 1971), 51.

49 Nigel Smith, *Literature and Revolution in England, 1640–1660* (New Haven: Yale University Press, 1994), 166–67.

6 FROM RARITIES TO REPRESENTATIVES

1 Shakespeare satirizes the practice in *The Tempest*, when he has Trinculo muse on the fortune to be had from displaying Caliban:

> A strange fish! Were I in England now, as once I was, and had but this fish painted, not a holiday fool there but would give a piece of silver. There would this monster make a man: any strange beast there makes a man. When they will not give a doit to relieve a lame beggar, they will lay out ten to see a dead Indian. (II.ii.27–32)

2 *Philosophical Transactions of the Royal Society of London*, vol. I (1665–66), 321.

3 Hubert, *Catalogue*, 4–5. Arthur MacGregor, however, asserts that "Hubert's museum was by no means typical in its exuberant appeal to the masses" ("The Cabinet of Curiosities in Seventeenth-Century Britain," Impey and MacGregor, eds., *The Origins of Museums*, 153).

4 Michael Hunter, "The Cabinet Institutionalized: the Royal Society's 'Repository' and Its Background," Impey and MacGregor, eds., *The Origins of Museums*, 165. Katie Whitaker implies that the term *curious* shifts its meaning at this time and begins to indicate something that is elaborately and delicately constructed. She describes the new culture of curiosity arising after the mid-century as exchanging "speechless astonishment" for "reasoned articulate wonder which sought understanding" ("The Culture of Curiosity," Jardine, Secord, and Spary, eds., *Cultures of Natural History*, 81).

5 Hunter, "Cabinet Institutionalized," 164.

6 Shakespeare, *Antony and Cleopatra*, II.vii.40.

7 See George, "Alive or Dead," 180–81.

8 They are housed at the University Museum, Oxford. See Keith Davies, "Zoological Specimens in the University Museum Attributed to the Tradescant Collection," MacGregor, ed., *Tradescant's Rarities*, 346–49.

9 Ferrante Imperato, *Dell'historia naturale* (Naples, 1599). Robert Gunther notes that the arrangement of early curiosity cabinets imitated that of the familiar apothecary's shop (*Early Science*, 286). Romeo, seeking at the end of *Romeo and Juliet* to buy poison from a poor apothecary, recalls that "in his shop a tortoise hung, / An alligator stuffed, and other skins / Of ill-shaped fishes" (V.i.42–44). (Alligators were not distinguished from crocodiles in the period.)

10 Evelyn, *Diary*, II, 330.

11 While the first volume of the *History of Four-Footed Beasts* is a fairly close translation of the first volume of Gesner's *Historia animalium*, Topsell's second volume, on serpents, takes material from Gesner's volumes on oviparous quadrupeds, fishes, serpents, and insects, as well as from other sources.

12 Torquato Tasso, *Creation of the World*, trans. Joseph Tusiana (Binghamton, NY: Medieval & Early Renaissance Texts & Studies, 1982), V.109.

13 Du Bartas, *Divine Weeks*, I.vi.277.

14 The Latin version was published in 1676, the corrected and expanded English version in 1678. Linnaeus based his classification of birds on Ray's. For the best discussion of Ray's contributions to zoological classification, see Charles Raven, *John Ray, Naturalist: His Life and Works* (Cambridge University Press, 1942), 308–418.

15 Wightman, *The Growth of Scientific Ideas*, 373.

16 Mayr, *The Growth of Biological Thought*, 167.

17 Except, of course, for the salamander, believed to walk through fires and extinguish them. See T. H. White for the bestiaries' report of the salamander (White, ed. and trans., *The Book of Beasts*, 182–84), and Browne, *PE*, 214–16, for a skeptical view.

18 Aristotle, *Historia animalium*, I, 30–33 [490b]. On Aristotle's classification of animals, see Peck's "Introduction" to vol. I of *Historia animalium*, v–xxxii; G. E. R. Lloyd, "The Development of Aristotle's Theory of the Classification of Animals," *Phronesis* 6 (1961), 59–81; and Mayr, *History of Biological Thought*, who provides a convenient summary (149–54). The individual volumes of Gesner's *Historia animalium* are *De quadrupedibus viviparis; De quadrupedibus oviparis; De avium natura; De piscium et aquatilium animantium natura*. Aldrovandi's works, similarly titled, are listed in the bibliography. One might argue à la Foucault that the leaner volume titles of Jonston's *Historia naturalis* (*De quadrupedibus; De avibus; De piscibus et cetis; De insectis, de serpentibus et draconis*) befit a new episteme. One might also argue that they revert to the looser divisions of Genesis. The categories "blooded" and "non-blooded" were changed by Lamarck to "vertebrate" and "invertebrate."

19 The first entry under "*Fourfooted Beasts*" in the Tradescants' museum catalog is "Lions head and teeth" (Tradescant, *Musæum Tradescantianum*, 5).

20 Raven, *John Ray*, 379. Ray's discussion of the classification of mammals and reptiles occurs in *Synopsis animalium quadrupedum et serpentini generis* (London, 1693).

21 Raven, *John Ray*, 373.

22 Ibid., 379.

23 Ray, *Synopsis animalium*, 55 [Raven's translation].

24 Topsell conveniently recounts all the legends (Topsell, *The History of Four-Footed Beasts*), III, 682–92. See also William Ashworth's "Persistent Beast" for a lively account of depictions of the ichneumon (the mongoose). Some authorities suggest that the *trochilus* is actually the Egyptian black-headed plover, *Pluvianus aegyptius*, which feeds on the crocodile's insect parasites.

25 There may be, in the pairing of the crocodile and hippopotamus in Raphael's narrative, an implied allusion to a statue in the Belvedere Gardens in Rome, which represents a hippopotamus gripping in its jaws the tail of a crocodile. Pierre Belon includes a drawing of the statue in *L'histoire naturalle des estranges poissons marins* (Paris, 1551, 50) and *De aquatilibus* (Paris, 1553, 25). For the statue, see Joan Lloyd, *African Animals*, 79–80. See Du Bartas, *Divine Weeks*, I.vi.270 for the term *skalie Crocodile*. One-word epithets are Du Bartas's hallmark, e.g., "the wily Foxe," "the fearfull Hare," "th'wanton Weazell."

26 Williams, *Common Expositor*, 60.

27 Lewalski, *Rhetoric*, 44–45.

28 See Arthur O. Lovejoy, *The Great Chain of Being: a Study of the History of an Idea* (1936: Cambridge, MA: Harvard University Press, 1964), 24–66, for the genesis of the notion of the great chain of being.

29 Lovejoy, *Great Chain*, 52.

30 Topsell, *History of Four-footed Beasts*, III, 693. See *OED*, crocodile, sb., sense 1.b.

31 See chapter 5 for a discussion of the trunk and gills of the whale.
32 Humanity is the "one particularly privileged point" in the system of universal analogies, notes Michel Foucault; "all analogies can find one of their necessary terms there" (*Order of Things*, 22).
33 Thus Foucault (*Order of Things*, 21) summarizes the elaborate system of correspondences worked out by Cesalpino.
34 Browne calls coral "a Lithophyton or stone plant" (*PE*, 134).
35 See *OED*, barometz, which suggests that the vegetable lamb was produced by turning upside down the roots and frond stalks of the woolly fern, *Cibotium barometz*.
36 See Robbins's annotation for sixteenth- and seventeenth-century references to the lamb of Tartary (*PE*, II, 897nn29–35).
37 Svendsen, tracing sources for the image of the golden compasses, notes that "the figure was, after the Aldine press mark, perhaps the best known printer's device in the Renaissance" (*Milton and Science*, 259n). The golden compasses in book VII, by implication the original of the Renaissance device, declare God's responsibility for realizing the book of the world.
38 Ironically, in view of its role in representing kingliness, the lion was a relatively common exotic animal, even in medieval Europe, for "the 'King of Beasts' was a favourite royal gift" (Wilma George and William Brunsdon Yapp, *The Naming of the Beasts: Natural History in the Medieval Bestiary* [London: Duckworth, 1991], 48). It was also a favorite tourist attraction. From the thirteenth century, the lions, lynxes, ounces, and other great cats kept at the Tower of London steadily drew visitors and naturalists. In *De rariorum animalium atque stirpium historia* (1570), John Caius describes trying to draw the Tower's restless lynx ("Mobile animal est"). It became completely still – precisely as a domestic cat might have done – only when it spotted a woodpecker carried in a basket by a tourist (*The Works of John Caius*, ed. E. S. Roberts [Cambridge University Press, 1912], 30–31).
39 The phrase is Fowler's, who lists some of those representations at *PL*, IV.340n. See also Frye, *Milton's Imagery*, 239–55, and McColley, *Gust for Paradise*, 78–84, 94–99. Raphael's account of the lion, lynx, leopard, and tiger springing from the earth has been compared to the Vatican paintings of another Raphael. See Newton's edition of *Paradise Lost*, VII.463n, a note which also contains an interesting discussion of the verb *calved*.
40 London, *Royal Beasts*, 14.
41 Under the author's initials on the title-page of *Eikonoklastes* appear three verses from Proverbs 28, the first of which declares: *"As a roaring Lyon, and a ranging Beare, so is a wicked Ruler over the poor people."* A facsimile of the original title-page is printed in *CPW*, III, 337.

7 REHABILITATING THE POLITICAL ANIMAL

1 Wilson, *Invisible World*, 212.
2 Timothy Raylor, "Samuel Hartlib and the Commonwealth of Bees,"

Culture and Cultivation in Early Modern England: Writing and the Land, ed.
Michael Leslie and Timothy Raylor (Leicester University Press, 1992), 118.
There may be a remnant of analogical thinking, however, in the title of
Hartlib's treatise.

3 Raylor, "Samuel Hartlib," 117–18.
4 See William Meredith Carroll, *Animal Conventions in English Renaissance Non-Religious Prose (1550–1600)* (Westport, CT: Greenwood, 1954), 79 and 154n417, for a list of Renaissance pairings of the bee and ant.
5 Bacon, *Works*, IV, 410.
6 Paul Hammond, "The Language of the Hive: Political Discourse in Seventeenth-Century England," *The Seventeenth Century* 9 (1994), 121.
7 *OED*, commonwealth, sense 2.
8 Topsell, *History of Four-footed Beasts*, III, 892.
9 Timothy Raylor believes Purchas's work to be an argument for "Cromwellian rule, at a time when the possibility of a Cromwellian monarchy was being mooted" ("Samuel Hartlib," 111).
10 Raylor, "Samuel Hartlib," 109.
11 Ibid.
12 Pliny, *The Historie of the World*, trans. Philemon Holland (London, 1601), I, 328. (See Pliny, *Natural History*, III, 498–99.)
13 John Evelyn, *John Evelyn's Manuscript on Bees from Elysium Britannicum*, ed. D. A. Smith (London: Bee Research Association, 1965), 18.
14 Boyle, *Works*, II, 340.
15 The suburbs of London had a reputation for immorality and looseness in the period. In *Measure for Measure*, Elbow accuses Pompey of being a "parcel-bawd; one that serves a bad woman, whose house, sir, was, as they say, plucked down in the suburbs" (*MM*, II.i.61–63). Milton associates the suburbs explicitly with courtiers in *Eikonoklastes*, when he refers to Charles's adherents as "consisting most of dissolute Sword-men and Suburb-roysters" (*CPW*, III, 345).
16 J. B. Broadbent, "Milton's Hell," *ELH* 21 (1954), 190.
17 Swelling is associated, in the language of mid-seventeenth-century journalism, with increasing one's importance by having more space to publish one's opinions. Nigel Smith has observed that the authors of the mid-century newsbooks "were fascinated by the opportunity to 'swell,' to expand from one to two sheets (or even more). They were in fact confessing the low status of newsbooks and expressing a hope for the greater esteem attached to learned folios" (*Literature and Revolution*, 57).
18 Raylor, "Samuel Hartlib," 106.
19 James Whaler's exhaustive study of bee similes in epic poetry misses this point ("Animal Simile in *Paradise Lost*," *PMLA* 47 [1932], 545–52).
20 *CPW*, II, 554.
21 Charles Butler, *The Feminine Monarchie: or, The History of Bees* (1609; London, 1623), A1r.

22 Thomas Browne's most memorable observation on bees in *Pseudodoxia Epidemica* has to do with how they make their characteristic sound, which he usually describes as "humming" (*PE*, 282).

23 Lieb, *Dialectics of Creation*, 179.

24 See, for instance, Virgil's fourth *Georgic*.

25 Samuel Purchas, *A Theatre of Politicall Flying-Insects* (London, 1657), 13.

26 For the burning of naphtha and bitumin, see chapter 11 below.

27 Diodorus Siculus, *The History of Diodorus Siculus*, trans. H[enry] C[ogan] (London, 1653), 78. Renaissance commentators linked Babylon and Babel (see Williams, *Common Expositor*, 160), and London was repeatedly compared to both in the seventeenth century (see Christopher Hill, *The English Bible and the Seventeenth-Century Revolution* [Harmondsworth: Penguin–Allen Lane, 1993], 217–19, and Smith, *Literature and Revolution*, 25–26). John Evelyn's *Fumifugium* connects London with Babylon by way of the former's smoky stench. (See chapter 11 below.)

28 Had Milton *wished* to redefine the beehive as a commonwealth (i.e., a limited monarchy), he had ammunition from a royalist. In the first *Defence of the People of England* (1651), he quotes the Salmasius of *De primatu papae* (1645) against the Salmasius of *Defensio regia* (1649). In the earlier book, Salmasius had argued against the Council of Trent's claim that the government of the beehive supports the rule of the Pope. "The government of the bees is a commonwealth," Milton quotes Salmasius as insisting, "and is so described by scientists; the king they have is harmless, and is more a leader than a tyrant; he does not flog or prod or kill his subject bees" (*CPW*, IV, 348). Milton puns on the triple teeth (Tridentine), calling Salmasius "a toothless drone" (*CPW*, IV, 348), but there is no attempt in *Paradise Lost* to rehabilitate the beehive on the grounds that its king is harmless. This is understandable: what restrains the king bee in Salmasius's reading is apparently not law but the personality of the king.

29 Raylor, "Samuel Hartlib," 104–05.

30 In *Animadversions*, Milton likens the "Apostolick Successors" to a decline from an (idolatrous) age of gold to "*Constantinian* silver, together with the iron, the brasse, and the clay of those muddy and strawy ages that follow" (*CPW*, I, 700–01). In "Lycidas," corrupt clergy "Grate on their scrannel pipes of wretched straw" (124).

31 As Merritt Hughes notes in his edition of *Paradise Lost*, Milton may well have taken the idea of female worker bees spoiling the drones from Charles Butler's *The Feminine Monarchie* (*PL*, VII.485–92n). But Milton's representation of the worker and the drone as a married couple (a representation enhanced by the use of the generic singular) permits him to move into the realm of the political.

32 *CPW*, II, 259.

33 In this analogy, the husband's authority is the "natural" fact upon which the political argument is based. As Johann Sommerville notes in his edition of Robert Filmer's *Patriarcha*, the fact that some seventeenth-century theorists

argued "in favour of an authoritarian and patriarchal family, and against an authoritarian state," reveals that at least a few people realized the analogy was *construed* as "natural" (Johann P. Sommerville, "Introduction," *"Patriarcha" and Other Writings*, by Robert Filmer, Cambridge Texts in the History of Political Thought [Cambridge University Press, 1991], ix).

34 *CPW*, VII, 427.
35 The phrase "magnanimosque duces" appears at *Georgics* 4.4, and "ingentis animos angusto in pectore" at 4.83 (Virgil, *Eclogues, Georgics, Aeneid I–VI*, trans. H. Fairclough, rev. edn., Loeb Classical Library [Cambridge, MA: Harvard University Press; London: William Heinemann, 1935]).
36 *CPW*, VII, 460.
37 Topsell, *History of Four-footed Beasts*, III, 1024.
38 Guillim, *Display of Heraldrie*, 214.
39 I disagree with Fowler's suggestion that *perhaps* may mean that Raphael "is unconvinced about the justice (rightness) of republicanism" (*PL*, VII.490–92n). The alliteration of *Pattern* and *perhaps*, and the fact that *perhaps* hovers at the end of a line before a new line begins with *Hereafter* suggests that the targets of uncertainty are the pattern and the future.
40 Boyle, *Works*, V, 430.
41 Thomas Birch, *The History of the Royal Society of London*, 4 vols. (London, 1756–57), I, 322. Five months earlier Hooke had shown them a drawing of an ant's head (Birch, *History*, I, 243).
42 Hooke, *Micrographia*, 203.

8 NAMING AND NOT NAMING

1 There is one genus of plane tree (*Platanus*). The species Evelyn speaks of is probably *P. orientalis*, the oriental plane. See D. J. Mabberley, *The Plant-Book: a Portable Dictionary of the Vascular Plants*, 2nd edn. (Cambridge University Press, 1997), 565, "Platanus."
2 Henrey, *British Botanical*, I, 108.
3 John Evelyn, *Sylva, or A Discourse of Forest-Trees, and the Propagation of Timber in his Majesties Dominions* (London, 1664), 57–58. Unless otherwise noted, quotations are from the 1664 edition of *Sylva*. See Henrey for a discussion of the history and reception of *Sylva* (*British Botanical*, I, 101–14).
4 In the seventh Prolusion, Milton speaks of the pleasure to be derived from conversations with the learned and eminent, "qualia sub illa platano plurima saepe fertur habuisse divinus *Plato*" (Milton, *Works*, XII, 264).
5 Pliny, *Historie*, I, 357–58. (See Pliny, *Natural History*, IV, 6–7.)
6 Pliny (who, however, undoubtedly got his information from Theophrastus) was in fact correct in this apparently improbable assertion. In his study of Greek plants, Baumann remarks: "In Crete, actually, twenty-nine examples of planes with evergreen leaves were recorded by E. Platakis in 1966 and most of them confirmed by the present writer in 1990. It is a mutation going back to Antiquity of an otherwise deciduous tree" (Hellmut Baumann, *The*

Greek Plant World in Myth, Art and Literature, trans. William Stearn and E. R. Stearn [Portland: Timber Press, 1993], 46). (See Theophrastus, *Enquiry into Plants and Minor Works on Odours and Weather Signs,* trans. Arthur Hort, Loeb Classical Library, 2 vols. [London: Heinemann; New York: G. P. Putnam's Sons, 1916], I, 64–65.)

7   *The Geneva Bible: a Facsimile of the 1560 Edition* (Madison: University of Wisconsin Press, 1969). See Fowler, *PL,* IV.478n.

8   John Parkinson, *Theatrum Botanicum, The Theatre of Plants* (London, 1640), 1428.

9   This is the American plane tree, *P. occidentalis.* See Mabberley, *Plant-Book,* 565, "Platanus."

10 John Gerard, *The Herball or Generall Historie of Plantes,* ed. Thomas Johnson (London, 1636), 1489. Gerard knows only the oriental plane tree, and Johnson does not correct the entry. He evidently does not realize that the Tradescants' young trees are western planes. By the time Evelyn published the revised and expanded 1670 edition of *Sylva,* he was able to report that the western plane "rises to a goodly *Tree*" (*Sylva, or A Discourse of Forest-Trees, and the Propagation of Timber in his Majesties Dominions* [London, 1670], 114).

11 That is, there are otherwise in paradise no species of trees that have only deciduous varieties.

12 See Christopher Fitter, "'Native Soil': the Rhetoric of Exile Lament and Exile Consolation in *Paradise Lost,*" *Milton Studies* 20 (1984), 147–62. Xerxes was said to have become so fond of a plane tree that he called it his mistress and his goddess, hanging upon it gold jewelry and silken scarves. (Evelyn includes this story in later editions of *Sylva.*)

13 Boyle, *Works,* VI, 22.

14 *CPW,* II, 514.

15 Newton, ed., *PL,* IX.585n.

16 The *OED* (apple, sb., sense 4) follows suit.

17 *OED,* apple, sb., sense 2.a.

18 Even if Satan could plead not guilty on the technicality that *apple* may refer to fruit in general, the term is informal and familiar and hence inappropriate to God's high prohibition. It constitutes a lie of stylistic register.

19 Leonard, *Naming in Paradise,* 206–07.

20 Leonard provides a review of critical opinions on this matter (*Naming in Paradise,* 204–06).

21 Leonard, *Naming in Paradise,* 205.

22 Ibid., 206.

23 Svendsen provides a list of references to the Sodom apple in medieval and Renaissance works (*Milton and Science,* 28–29). Moldenke and Moldenke argue that Josephus, one of the chief sources of the story, was in fact describing *Solanum incanum:* "The handsome yellow fruit is a berry, about an inch in diameter . . . It is at first pulpy inside, but as it ripens this pulp dries up and, on being pressed, the ripe fruit bursts and emits a cloud of what appears to be 'dust and ashes' . . . the supposed ashes being its seeds" (Harold Moldenke and Alma Moldenke, *Plants of the Bible* [1952; New York:

Dover, 1986], 221). Mabberley notes that *Citrullus colocynthis* is also called "vine of Sodom" or "gall" (*Plant-Book*, 160, "Citrullus"). Other possibilities for the Sodom apple are *Solanum aculeatissimum* (Mabberley, *Plant-Book*, 669, "Solanum") and *Calotropis procera* (Mabberley, *Plant-Book*, 117, "Calotropis"). See *OED*, apple, sb., sense 3. For John Evelyn's comparison of London's smoke-damaged fruits to the apples of Sodom, see chapter 11.

24 As with the forbidden fruit, Milton calls them "apples" when rhetoric requires. He does so in *Eikonoklastes*, where they occur as a figure for empty prayer: "Thus these pious flourishes and colours examin'd throughly, are like the Apples of *Asphaltis*, appearing goodly to the sudden eye, but look well upon them, or at least but touch them, and they turne into Cinders (*CPW*, III, 552).

25 John M. Steadman, "Tantalus and the Dead Sea Apples (*Paradise Lost*, X, 547–73)," *JEGP* 64 (1965), 39.

26 Gerard, *Herball*, 1513. Fowler and Hughes both cite Gerard; Svendsen summarizes the views of earlier editors and commentators (many of whom cite Gerard as the source) but argues that the elements in the tree's description are largely traditional (*Milton and Science*, 31–32).

27 James Patrick McHenry, "A Milton Herbal," *Milton Quarterly* 30 (1996), 69. Pliny's description is "foliorum latitudo peltae effigiem Amazonicae habet" (*Natural History*, IV, 16–17).

28 Svendsen, *Milton and Science*, 31–32. Svendsen mentions, specifically, Arthur Golding's translation, *The Excellent and Pleasant Worke of Julius Solinus Polyhistor* (1586), and the 1587 English version of Joannes Jonston's natural history, *A History of the Wonderful Things of Nature*.

29 Raleigh, *Historie of the World*, 1.1.4.2.

30 Greene points out that Theophrastus accurately identified as roots what others had described as the banyan's "branches" (*Landmarks*, I, 147). For strangler figs, see Mabberley, *Plant-Book*, 281–82, "Ficus."

31 Milton could not have known this tract, published in 1683 as one of Browne's posthumous *Miscellany Tracts*. Browne's discussion of the fig tree is significant in any case not for its experimentalist outlook but for its conventionality.

32 *The Works of Sir Thomas Browne*, 2nd edn., ed. Geoffrey Keynes, 4 vols. (London: Faber & Faber, 1964), III, 10.

33 The suspicion arises, moreover, that Browne is in pursuit of a pun and this makes him less critical than usual of a "vulgar" opinion. The *OED* records his as the sole use of *contection*, a noun which Browne has formed from the participle of the Latin verb *contegere*, "to cover up." Participial forms of the Latin verb *contexere*, "to weave together," had also been adapted to English usage in the seventeenth century: the adjectives *context* and *contexted* mean "woven together." Browne could easily have formed (or imagined) a substantive, *contextion*, from *context* or *contexted*. *Contection* and *contextion* would be closely identical when pronounced – and would provide a neat linking of Adam and Eve's sewing together of fig leaves in order to cover themselves.

34 David Quint, *Epic and Empire: Politics and Generic Form from Virgil to Milton* (Princeton University Press, 1993), 255.

9 BOTANICAL DISCRETION

1 C. S. Lewis, *A Preface to "Paradise Lost"* (1942; Oxford University Press, 1961), 49.

2 Abraham Ortelius, *Theatrum Orbis Terrarum; or, The Theatre of the Whole World* (London, 1606), iii^v.

3 Parkinson, *Theatrum*, 1545; Gerard, *Herball*, 1517. The palm is, in fact, a woody monocot, which means that it is essentially a non-tree whose stem, covered with bark, looks like a tree trunk. I am indebted to Julie Mulroy for this information.

4 Parkinson, *Theatrum*, 1545.

5 Curtius, *European Literature*, 195.

6 Edmund Spenser, *The Faerie Queene*, ed. A. C. Hamilton (London: Longman, 1977), I.i.8–9.

7 In contrast to the catalog of trees in *Paradise Lost*, the catalog of flowers in "Lycidas" (142–50) is full of epithets: "rathe primrose," "tufted crow-toe," "pale jessamine," and so on. David Daiches comments that each flower "is given an adjective or a descriptive phrase as flowers so often are in the classical pastoral even though the actual description may be original" ("Some Aspects of Milton's Pastoral Imagery," *More Literary Essays* [University of Chicago Press, 1968], 114).

8 *OED*, branching, vbl. sb., sense 2.

9 Modern naturalists agree that the shittah tree is the accacia. See Moldenke and Moldenke, *Plants of the Bible*, 24–26.

10 Browne, *Works*, III, 7.

11 Bacon, *Works*, III, 293.

12 Ibid., II, 335.

13 Ibid., II, 335

14 Ibid., II, 329n1.

15 As Bacon knew, an unruly list, that is, a list which will not submit itself to the exigencies of an orderly scheme, retains its power to disturb. That disturbance ought, ideally, to generate new ideas about the very nature of ordering. Thus for instance a Borgesian list rhetorically generates Foucault's *The Order of Things*.

16 Gerard, *Herball*, 1352 (misnumbered 1452).

17 Parkinson, *Theatrum*, 1532.

18 Browne, *Works*, III, 35.

19 Parkinson even confesses that he does not know whether the cedar's branches grow "upright" or "straight out" (*Theatrum*, 1532).

20 There may have been one, or at the most two, cedar trees in England before 1650, but the evidence is inconclusive. Jacob Strutt, describing the great cedar at Hammersmith House, states that the tree "may probably be

coeval" with the house that was Cromwell's residence during the Protectorate (*Sylva Britannica; or, Portraits of Forest Trees* [London, 1830], 107). In his edition of Evelyn's *Sylva*, Alexander Hunter notes that a huge cedar "on the North side of Hendon Place," blown down in 1779, was "supposed to have been two hundred years old, and planted in the reign of Queen Elizabeth. Tradition says by her Majesty herself" (Alexander Hunter, ed., *Silva: or, a Discourse of Forest-Trees and the Propagation of Timber in his Majesty's Dominions*, by John Evelyn, 2 vols. [York, 1812], II, 3n). On the other hand, Hunter also states: "It is very certain, from what Mr. Evelyn says in the beginning of this chapter, that the Cedar of Lebanon was not, in 1664, cultivated in England" (Hunter, ed., *Silva*, II, 4n). William Aiton, citing Ray's *Philosophical Letters*, gives 1683 for the earliest date of its cultivation in England (*Hortus Kewensis*, 3 vols. [London, 1789], III, 369). (The reference to the cedar appears in a letter of Hans Sloane to Ray in 1684. See John Ray, *Philosophical Letters between the Late Learned Mr. Ray and Several of his Ingenious Correspondents* [London, 1718], 171.)

21 Evelyn reports in *Sylva* that he has "frequently rais'd it of the *seeds*" (*Sylva*, 61).

22 Browne, *Works*, III, 36.

23 Thomas Fuller, *A Pisgah-Sight of Palestine and the Confines Thereof* (London, 1650). *Pisgah-sight* contains twenty-one maps, engraved by several different artists whose styles are quite distinct. The map of Lebanon, which precedes the first page of part two, was engraved for Fuller by William Marshall. See Kenneth Nebenzahl, *Maps of the Holy Land: Images of Terra Sancta through Two Millenia* (New York: Abbeville, 1986), 128–31.

24 Strutt, *Sylva Brittanica*, 103.

25 John Evelyn, *Sylva, or A Discourse of Forest-Trees, and the Propagation of Timber in his Majesties Dominions* (London, 1679), 125.

26 Hunter, ed., *Silva*, II, 5n.

27 Satan arrives in Eden at noon (*PL*, IV.30), when looking up at the treetops would mean looking into the sun.

28 Parkinson, *Theatrum*, 1532.

29 Evelyn, *Sylva*, 61.

30 In the 1679 edition of *Sylva*, Evelyn notes that North American colonists shingle their houses with it (125).

31 José de Acosta, *The Naturall and Morall Historie of the East and West Indies*, trans. E. G. (London, 1604), 291–92.

32 Thomas Greene, *The Descent from Heaven: a Study in Epic Continuity* (New Haven: Yale University Press, 1963), 403.

33 Greene, *Descent from Heaven*, 400.

34 See Simon Schama, *The Embarrassment of Riches: an Interpretation of Dutch Culture in the Golden Age* (Berkeley: University of California Press, 1988), esp. chapter 5.

35 Gunther, *Early British Botanists*, 303–71, includes a number of lists of domestic and exotic plants growing in individual gardens in the sixteenth and

seventeenth centuries. A number of "wish lists" also survive from the period. See, for instance, MacGregor, "Tradescants as Collectors," 19–20.

36 Andrew Cunningham, "The Culture of Gardens," Jardine, Secord, and Spary, eds., *Cultures of Natural History*, 48–49.

37 Cunningham, "Culture of Gardens," 50.

38 Many historians of science question the "scientific" value of the curiosity collection, though not of the botanical garden. The distinction between those kinds of collections would not perhaps have been as apparent to someone living in the seventeenth century, especially given the increasing commercialism of the plant trade in the period.

39 This is not to imply that "kind," or species, was an entirely stable concept. In informal usage, the name "cedar" could refer in the seventeenth century to a fir, or even to a cypress or a juniper. See McHenry, "Milton Herbal," 59.

40 Parkinson, *Theatrum*, 154

41 Gerard, *Herball*, 1352 (misnumbered 1452).

42 Parkinson, *Theatrum*, 1533.

43 In his edition of Browne's works, Wilkin cites the testimony of John Burckhardt, who in 1822 traveled to see the cedars on Mount Libanus: "The trunks of the old trees are covered with the names of travellers and other persons, who have visited them: I saw a date of the seventeenth century. It is an interesting conjunction of time and immortality" (John Lewis Burckhardt, *Travels in Syria and the Holy Land* [London, 1822], 20; cited in Wilkin, ed., *Browne's Works*, IV, 159n6). The seventeenth-century carver was undoubtedly hoping his name would thereby have a share in the cedar's presumed immortality.

44 Browne, *Works*, III, 36.

45 Evelyn, *Sylva*, 61. Donald Worster observes that Henry David Thoreau saw Evelyn as a "pagan animist," finding in *Sylva* the expression of "a natural piety that . . . promised a more restrained use of the woodlands" (*Nature's Economy: a History of Ecological Ideas*, 2nd edn. [Cambridge University Press, 1994], 87–88).

10 FLOURISHING COLORS

1 The "flowery plat" (*PL*, IX.456) where Satan finds Eve gardening alone comes closest, perhaps, to suggesting a flower bed, as the term seems to combine *plot* and *flat*. (*OED*, bed, sense II.8, suggests that flatness is the primary quality of any sort of foundational bed, including a flower bed.) In fact, *plat* means simply "patch of ground."

2 Support for Fowler's claim is provided by *OED*, knot, sense 1.7, and nice, sense 8. For illustrations of knots, see Kenneth Woodbridge, *Princely Gardens: the Origins and Development of the French Formal Style* (New York: Rizzoli, 1986), 99, and Roy Strong, *The Renaissance Garden in England* (London: Thames & Hudson, 1979), 40–41.

3 See Woodbridge, *Princely Gardens*, 110–11, and Strong, *Renaissance Garden*, 186–87, 196.

4 See Strong, *Renaissance Garden*, 16–17, for an example of the symbolic program of knot gardens.

5 *OED*, border, v., sense 1, and border, sb., senses 5.a. and b.

6 Jack Goody, *The Culture of Flowers* (Cambridge University Press, 1993), 206–09, discusses the impact of imported fabrics upon English handwork in the period. In *Paradise Lost*, the ground is embroidered with flowers; in "Lycidas," the flowers themselves are dressed in embroidery: "every flower that sad embroidery wears" (148).

7 Henry Hawkins, *Parthenia Sacra* ([Paris,] 1633), 11.

8 Milton need not have had recourse to etymology; the word could have this sense in English, as Fowler notes. (*OED*, sb., emblem, sense 1, cites *PL*, IV.703 as the second example.) The *OED* records 1656 as the first time *emblem* is used in this sense, but Geoffrey Whitney, the emblematist, writes in 1586 that the word *emblem*, meaning inlaid work, "Is, and hathe bin alwaies in use amongst us" (*A Choice of Emblemes* [Leyden, 1586], quoted in Rosemary Freeman, *English Emblem Books* [1948; New York: Farrar, Straus and Giroux–Octagon, 1966], 37). Whitney then gives the word's Greek root. It seems likely, given Milton's characteristic reforming impulses, that he is stripping the word down to its etymological foundation in order to restore a "purer" meaning.

9 *CPW*, III, 343.

10 In her work on the English emblem book, Rosemary Freeman notes that the "old mentality," the tendency to allegorize the natural world, "ceased to exist" sometime in the second half of the seventeenth century (*English Emblem Books*, 2). This mentality sustained the emblem; its demise meant the demise of the emblem. Freeman cites Bunyan's *Pilgrim's Progress* (the first part of which was published in 1678) as "the last coherent formulation of this way of thinking" (*English Emblem Books*, 2).

11 Horace Walpole, *Horace Walpole's Correspondence with George Montagu*, ed. W. S. Lewis and Ralph Brown, 2 vols. (New Haven: Yale University Press, 1941), vols. IX and X of *Horace Walpole's Correspondence*, 42 vols. (1937–80), I, 215. Letter to George Montague, August 25, 1757.

12 Ricks, *Milton's Grand Style*, 95.

13 *OED*, stalk, sb.^{1}, sense 2.a.

14 Wilson, *Invisible World*, 23–24.

15 *OED*, spring, sb.^{1}, sense III.11.

16 *OED*, fade, v.^{1}, sense 1.

17 *OED*, wilt, v., sense 1.

18 In " 'And Without Thorn the Rose' " George Whiting traces the theological background of Eden's thornless rose, noting that Ambrose and Basil assert that thorns were added to the rose to make it reflect fallen human life, with pain always implicit in happiness (" 'And Without Thorn the Rose,' " *RES* ns 10 [1959], 60–62). We can assume that the Church Fathers arrived at the thornless rose by working backwards from Adam's punishment at Genesis 3.18, when he is told that the ground will henceforth bring forth thorns and thistles.

19 John Parkinson, *Paradisi in Sole Paradisus Terrestris* (London, 1629), 416. Parkinson also mentions the "Rosa Incarnata," which he translates as the "Carnation Rose," which "is of a pale blush colour all the flower thorough-out" (*Paradisi*, 412).

20 As Arnold Williams notes, the fruitfulness of the plants created on the Third Day and the coincidence of fruit and flower are usually of more concern to Renaissance biblical commentators than the color of the flowers in paradise (*Common Expositor*, 58).

21 See Aristotle, *Problemata*, trans. E. S. Forster (Oxford: Clarendon Press, 1927), vol. VII of *The Works of Aristotle*, ed. W. D. Ross, 12 vols. (1908–52). The work was attributed to Aristotle in the Renaissance.

22 Raleigh, *Historie*, D2ᵛ–D3ʳ.

23 John Donne, *The Epithalamions, Anniversaries and Epicedes*, ed. W. Milgate (Oxford: Clarendon Press, 1978), 49.

24 John Carey, *John Donne: Life, Mind and Art* (New York: Oxford University Press, 1981), 246–47.

25 Bacon, *Works*, II, 340.

26 Ibid., II, 340–41.

27 Ibid., II, 473. See Aristotle, *Problemata* 2.258 [38.8].

28 Bacon, *Works*, II, 379.

29 The term *gillyflower* generally denotes the pink (including the carnation), the wall flower, and flowers resembling them. (See *OED*, gillyflower; and Mabberley, *Plant-Book*, 301, "gilliflower.")

30 Bacon, *Works*, II, 504.

31 Ibid., III, 158.

32 *OED*, purple, a. and sb., senses A.1 and 2, and B.1.

33 John Donne, *The Elegies and The Songs and Sonnets*, ed. Helen Gardner (Oxford: Clarendon Press, 1965), 53.

34 For the various colors denoted by carnation, see *OED*, carnation², sb. and a., senses A.1.a and b.; A.2; and B.a and b.

35 Roses do not have a gene for delphinidin, which makes delphiniums and other flowers blue.

36 On the new optics, see G. N. Cantor, "Physical Optics," Olby et al., eds., *Companion*, 630–32.

37 Fulton gives 1663 as the date of publication, although no copies of the first version of the tract, "The History of Colours Begun," are now extant (John F. Fulton, *A Bibliography of the Honourable Robert Boyle, Fellow of the Royal Society*, 2nd edn. [Oxford: Clarendon Press, 1961], 43). Boyle says in the preface that he wrote "this Essay . . . to a private friend," not gathering up the loose sheets for the press "for several years after they were written," and that "divers years ago" he showed some of the experiments contained in the treatise "to a learned company of *Virtuosi*" (*Works*, I, 663).

38 Boyle, *Works*, I, 671.

39 Ibid., I, 695.

40 Ibid., I, 695–96.

41 Ibid., I, 671.

42 As Joseph Glanvill puts it, "*Adam* needed no Spectacles. The acuteness of his natural Opticks . . . shew'd him much of Coelestial magnificence and bravery without a *Galilæo*'s tube" (Joseph Glanvill, *The Vanity of Dogmatizing* [1661], ed. Moody Prior [New York: Columbia University Press for The Facsimile Text Society, 1931], 5).

43 *Eysenhardtia polystachya*, or kidneywood. Its "wood chips placed in water against a black background produce peacock blue phosphorescence" (Mabberley, *Plant-Book*, 277, "Eysenhardtia").

44 Boyle, *Works*, I, 729–30.

45 Fulton, *Bibliography*, 43.

46 Ibid.

47 *Mirabilis jalapa*, also called four-o'clock (Mabberley, *Plant-Book*, 459, "Mirabilis").

48 Boyle, *Works*, I, 669.

49 Ibid.

50 Ibid. *OED*, disposition, sense II.8.

51 Boyle, *Works*, I, 743–44.

52 Ibid., I, 669.

53 See, for instance, Pliny's description of the phoenix, which some editors speculate may be the Asian golden pheasant (*Natural History*, III, 292–95). Azure and gold also appear prominently in the description of Raphael's phoenix-wings in *PL*, V.282–83: "downy gold / And colours dipped in heaven."

54 Strong, *Renaissance Garden*, 46.

II THE BALM OF LIFE

1 Greene, *Descent*, 401.

2 "Balm of Gilead" is the modern term for what is usually called "balm" in English translations of the Bible. (*OED*, balm, sb., sense IV.10.a. and head-note preceding illustrative quotations.) Some Coverdale Bibles and the Bishops' Bible, which translate the Hebrew term as "triacle," are called Treacle Bibles. (See A. S. Herbert, ed., *Historical Catalogue of Printed Editions of the English Bible 1525–1961*, by T. H. Darlow and H. F. Moule [1903], rev. edn. [London: The British and Foreign Bible Society; New York: The American Bible Society, 1968], 18 and 71.) There is still disagreement about the identity of the scriptural balm. The *OED* suggests *Balsamodendron gilead-ense* or *B. opobalsamum*; Moldenke and Moldenke, *Plants of the Bible*, suggest *Commiphora opobalsamum* (84–86); and Mabberley, *Plant-Book*, suggests *Liquidambar orientalis* (414, "Liquidambar"), whose common name is Oriental Sweetgum. Mabberley notes that *Commiphora myrrha* is the myrrh of the Bible and *Commiphora gileadensis* is the source of the modern balm of Gilead (*Plant-Book*, 139, "Commiphora").

3 Parkinson, *Theatrum*, 1529.

4 The problem was an ancient one. Pliny notes that "there is no marchandise and commoditie in the world, wherein there is practised more fraud and deceit, than in the trafficke of Baulme" (Holland, *Historie*, 1.377; Pliny, *Natural History*, IV, 86–87).

5 Gerard, *Herball*, 1529.

6 If Beelzebub himself believed it, or even if he did not but expected to convince his fellows of it, he would have used it to bolster support for his plan. Instead, he mentions it to them *after* they have voted. Beelzebub's hint that balm will cure them is thus a sop, either cynical or pathetic. The fallen angels declare allegiance to a world of lies when they follow Satan into rebellion. Beelzebub's claim for Eden's balm is merely one of the many lies the fallen angels are now bound to uphold.

7 Parkinson, *Theatrum*, 1528.

8 Ibid.

9 Robert Burton, *The Anatomy of Melancholy*, ed. Thomas Faulkner et al., 3 vols. (Oxford: Clarendon Press, 1989–94), II, 216.

10 McHenry, "Milton Herbal," 55.

11 The balm mentioned in connection with hell and heaven is another matter. See McHenry, "Milton Herbal," 55–56.

12 Gerard, *Herball*, 1039.

13 Parkinson, *Paradisi*, 480.

14 One might object that the phrase, "blowing myrrh and balm," is Satan's and therefore inevitably a *mis*representation. But Satan's words, too, must be read in context. To insure Eve's willingness to follow him, he must adhere closely enough to the truth not to alarm her.

15 Parkinson, *Theatrum*, 1528.

16 Ibid., 1593.

17 For myrrh as a common garden herb, see *OED*, myrrh^2, and Gerard, *Herball*, 1039; for myrrh as an exotic gum-resin, see *OED*, myrrh^1, sense 1. (The *OED* cites Milton's "A Masque" [936] as containing the last use of *myrrh* meaning the shrub or tree yielding the resin. *OED*, myrrh^1, sense 2.) For bee or lemon balm, see Parkinson, *Paradisi*, 479–80.

18 Acosta, *Naturall and Morall History*, 285–86.

19 Ibid., 289.

20 Gerard, *Herball*, 1527.

21 John Gerard, *The Herball or Generall Historie of Plantes* (London, 1597), 1344–45.

22 Gerard, *Herball*, 1528; see Prosper Alpini, *De plantis aegypti liber* (Venice, 1592), 24.

23 Gerard, *Herball*, 1528.

24 Parkinson, *Theatrum*, 1570.

25 Ibid.

26 Nicolas Monardes, *Joyfull Newes Out of the Newfound World*, trans. John Frampton (London, 1580), 7^v.

27 See Quint, *Epic and Empire*, 253–67.

28 J. Martin Evans, *Milton's Imperial Epic: "Paradise Lost" and the Discourse of Colonialism* (Ithaca: Cornell University Press, 1996), 44–45.

29 Evans, *Milton's Imperial Epic*, 45.

30 *OED*, spoil, sb., sense 8.a.

31 Milton's indifference to trade was, however, commented on by his opponents. See Nicholas von Maltzahn, "From Pillar to Post: Milton and the Attack on Republican Humanism at the Restoration," *Soldiers, Writers and Statesmen of the English Revolution*, ed. Ian Gentles, John Morrill, and Blair Worden (Cambridge University Press, 1998), 272–83, 280.

32 Gerard, *Herball*, 1527.

33 Aubrey writes that he began his survey of Surrey in 1673.

34 John Aubrey, *The Natural History and Antiquities of the County of Surrey*, 5 vols. (London, 1719), I, 13. The tree may have already disappeared by 1662; it is not named in Elias Ashmole's list of "Trees found in Mrs. Tredescants Ground when it came into my possession" (Gunther, *Early British Botanists*, 346, who reprints the list). Gunther notes that Ashmole "wrote [the list] out at the end of his copy of Parkinson's *Paradise*, now in the Bodleian Library" (*Early British Botanists*, 346).

35 Evans, *Milton's Imperial Epic*, 45.

36 Diodorus, *History*, 142.

37 Evans, *Milton's Imperial Epic*, 49.

38 Lewis, *Preface*, 44.

39 Indeed, sulfur dioxide – produced by the burning of extraneous sulfur-containing compounds in hydrocarbons like bitumen and naphtha – is the chief component of "acid rain." (I am indebted to my colleague Dr. Ken Kite for advice about the chemical effects of burning "naphtha and asphaltus.")

40 John Evelyn, *Fumifugium: or, The Inconveniencie of the Aer and Smoak of London Dissipated* (London, 1661), 6.

41 One of Vitruvius's first principles, Evelyn points out, is that whoever intends to build must "sedulously examine the *Aer* and *Situation* of the places where he designs to build" (*Fumifugium*, 4). London is most fortunate in both regards.

[It] is built upon a sweet and most agreeable Eminency of Ground, at the Northside of a goodly and well-condition'd River . . . The *Fumes* which exhale from the Waters and lower Grounds lying South-ward, by which means they are perpetually attracted, carried off or dissipated by the Sun, as soon as they are born and ascend. (*Fumifugium*, 4)

Milton recommends Vitruvius in *Of Education* (*CPW*, II,390). (See also Helen Darbishire, ed., *The Early Lives of Milton* [London: Constable, 1932], 60.)

42 Evelyn, *Fumifugium*, 5.

43 Ibid., 6.

44 Ibid., 7. Evelyn cites as evidence the fact that "when *New-castle* was besieg'd and blocked up in our late Wars," so that there was a "great Dearth and Scarcity of Coales" and consequently "little Smoake," London gardens and orchards produced plentifully (*Fumifugium*, 7).

45 Evelyn, *Fumifugium*, 10, 12.
46 Ibid., 12–13. Evelyn is quoting here from Kenelm Digby's *A Late Discourse Made in a Solemn Assembly* (1658), usually known as *Discourse on Sympathetic Powder*.
47 Evelyn, *Fumifugium*, 6.
48 Ibid., a1ᵛ.
49 Ibid., 11.
50 Boyle, *Works*, V, 43. The essay was appended to *Languid and Unheeded Motion*, published in 1685.
51 Boyle, *Works*, V, 43.
52 Evelyn, *Fumifugium*, 9.
53 Ibid., 24 (misnumbered 14).
54 Ibid.
55 Ibid., 7.
56 Ibid., 3.
57 Geoffrey Hartman, "Adam on the Grass with Balsamum," *Beyond Formalism: Literary Essays 1958–1970* (New Haven: Yale University Press, 1970), 124.
58 Hartman, "Adam on the Grass," 124n2. Hartman's definition of *reeking* is taken from Laura E. Lockwood, *Lexicon to the English Poetical Works of John Milton* (New York, 1907).
59 Hartman, "Adam on the Grass," 124–25. Fowler demonstrates that the sun's feeding on vapors (and specifically on vapors from the sea) is a commonplace (*PL*, V.423–26n). The passage in book VIII, which limits itself to the vapours from Adam's body, is startling only in its narrow focus, Fowler suggests, ultimately becoming "a magnificent piece of microcosmic grandiloquence" (*PL*, VIII.256n).
60 Hartman, "Adam on the Grass," 146–47.
61 Ibid., 147.
62 *OED*, balsam, sb. (and a.), sense A.1.4.
63 Browne, *"Religio Medici,"* 41.

CONCLUSION

1 See *PL*, X.651–706.
2 Ricks, *Milton's Grand Style*, 109.
3 Hope, at *PL*, V.119; strength, at VIII.633.
4 Von Maltzahn, "From Pillar to Post," 265–66.
5 In "From Pillar to Post," von Maltzahn analyzes the attacks on *The Readie and Easie Way* by Roger L'Estrange, Samuel Butler, and George Starkey.

Bibliography

PRIMARY

Acosta, José de. *The Naturall and Morall Historie of the East and West Indies*. Trans. E. G. London, 1604.

Aldrovandi, Ulisse. *De animalibus insectis*. Bologna, 1602.

Monstrorum historia. Bologna, 1642.

Ornithologiae. 3 vols. Bologna, 1599–1603.

De piscibus . . . et de cetis. Bologna, 1613.

De quadrupedibus solipedibus. Bologna, 1616.

De quadrupedibus digitatis viviparis . . . et de quadrupedibus digitatis oviparis. Bologna, 1637.

Quadrupedum omnium bisulcorum historia. Bologna, 1621.

Serpentum, et draconum historia. Bologna, 1640.

Alpini, Prosper. *De plantis aegypti liber*. Venice, 1592.

Histoire du baulme. Trans. Antoine Colin. Lyon, 1619.

Aristotle. *Historia animalium*. Trans. A. L. Peck (vols. I and II) and D. M. Balme (vol. III). Loeb Classical Library. 3 vols. London: William Heinemann, 1965–91.

Problemata. Trans. E. S. Forster. Oxford: Clarendon Press, 1927. Vol. VII of *The Works of Aristotle*. Ed. W. D. Ross. 12 vols. 1908–52.

Aubrey, John. *The Natural History and Antiquities of the County of Surrey*. 5 vols. London, 1719.

Bacon, Francis. *The Works of Francis Bacon*. Ed. James Spedding, R. L. Ellis, and D. D. Heath. 14 vols. 1857–74. Stuttgart-Bad Cannstatt: Friedrich Frommann Verlag, 1961–63.

Belon, Pierre. *De aquatilibus*. Paris, 1553.

L'histoire naturelle des estranges poissons marins. Paris, 1551.

Portraits d'oyseaux, animaux, serpens, herbes, arbres, homes et femmes d'Arabie & Egypte. Paris, 1557.

Birch, Thomas. *The History of the Royal Society of London*. 4 vols. London, 1756–57.

Bondt, Jacob de. (See Piso.)

Boyle, Robert. *The Usefulness of Experimental Natural Philosophy*. Oxford, 1664.

The Works of the Honourable Robert Boyle. Ed. Thomas Birch. 6 vols. London, 1772. [*Works*]

Browne, Thomas. *Pseudodoxia Epidemica: or, Enquiries into Commonly Presumed Truths.* 1646. Menston: Scolar, 1972.

    Pseudodoxia Epidemica. Ed. Robin Robbins. 2 vols. Oxford: Clarendon Press, 1981.

    "Religio Medici" and Other Works. Ed. L. C. Martin. Oxford: Clarendon Press, 1964.

    The Works of Sir Thomas Browne. 2nd edn. Ed. Geoffrey Keynes. 4 vols. London: Faber & Faber, 1964.

Burton, Robert. *The Anatomy of Melancholy.* Ed. Thomas Faulkner et al. 3 vols. Oxford: Clarendon Press, 1989–94.

Butler, Charles. *The Feminine Monarchie: or, The History of Bees.* 1609. London, 1623.

Caius, John. *De rariorum animalium atque stirpium historia.* 1570. In *The Works of John Caius.* Ed. E. S. Roberts. Cambridge University Press, 1912.

Cogan, Thomas. *Haven of Health.* 1584. London, 1636.

Coryate, Thomas. *Coryats Crudities.* 1611. London: Scolar, 1978.

Coverdale, Roger, trans. *Biblia. The Byble: that is, The Holy Scrypture of the Olde and New Testament.* [Zurich?,] 1535.

Davenant, William. *Gondibert.* 1651. Ed. David Gladish. Oxford: Clarendon Press, 1971.

Della Porta, Giambattista. *Natural Magick.* London, 1658.

Diodorus Siculus. *The History of Diodorus Siculus.* Trans. H[enry] C[ogan]. London, 1653.

Donne, John. *The Elegies and The Songs and Sonnets.* Ed. Helen Gardner. Oxford: Clarendon Press, 1965.

    The Epithalamions, Anniversaries and Epicedes. Ed. W. Milgate. Oxford: Clarendon Press, 1978.

Du Bartas, Guillaume de Saluste, Sieur. *The Divine Weeks and Works.* Trans. Josuah Sylvester. Ed. Susan Snyder. 2 vols. Oxford: Clarendon Press, 1979.

Evelyn, John. *The Diary of John Evelyn.* Ed. E. S. de Beer. 6 vols. Oxford: Clarendon Press, 1955.

    Fumifugium: or, The Inconveniencie of the Aer and Smoak of London Dissipated. London, 1661.

    John Evelyn's Manuscript on Bees from Elysium Britannicum. Ed. D. A. Smith. London: Bee Research Association, 1965.

    Sylva, or A Discourse of Forest-Trees, and the Propagation of Timber in his Majesties Dominions. London, 1664.

    Sylva, or A Discourse of Forest-Trees, and the Propagation of Timber in his Majesties Dominions. London, 1670.

    Sylva, or A Discourse of Forest-Trees, and the Propagation of Timber in his Majesties Dominions. London, 1679.

Fuller, Thomas. *A Pisgah-Sight of Palestine and the Confines Thereof.* London, 1650.

The Geneva Bible: a Facsimile of the 1560 Edition. Madison: University of Wisconsin Press, 1969.

Gerard, John. *The Herball or Generall Historie of Plantes.* London, 1597.

    The Herball or Generall Historie of Plantes. Ed. Thomas Johnson. London, 1636.

Gesner, Conrad. *Historia animalium.* 5 vols. Zurich, 1551–87.

Gil, Alexander. *The Sacred Philosophie of the Holy Scripture.* London, 1635.

Glanvill, Joseph. *The Vanity of Dogmatizing.* 1661. Ed. Moody Prior. New York: Columbia University Press for The Facsimile Text Society, 1931.

Grew, Nehemiah. *Musæum Regalis Societatis.* London, 1681.

Guillim, John. *A Display of Heraldrie.* 3rd edn. London, 1638.

Hartlib, Samuel. *Ephemerides. The Hartlib Papers.* CD-ROM. Ann Arbor, MI: UMI, 1995.

    The Reformed Common-wealth of Bees. London, 1655.

Hawkins, Henry. *Parthenia Sacra.* [Paris,] 1633.

Hobbes, Thomas. "The Answer of Mr. Hobbes to Sir Will. D'Avenant's Preface Before Gondibert." In *Gondibert.* By William Davenant. Ed. David Gladish. Oxford: Clarendon Press, 1971, 45–55.

    Leviathan. 1651. Ed. C. B. MacPherson. Harmondsworth: Penguin, 1968.

Holland, Philemon, trans. *The Historie of the World.* By Pliny. London, 1601.

Hooke, Robert. *Micrographia.* London, 1665.

Hubert, Robert. *A Catalogue of Many Natural Rarities.* London, 1664.

Imperato, Ferrante. *Dell'historia naturale.* Naples, 1599.

James VI and I. *Daemonologie.* Edinburgh, 1597.

Johnson, Thomas. *Cornucopiæ, or Divers Secrets.* London, 1595.

Jonson, Ben. *Volpone or, The Fox.* Ed. R. B. Parker. The Revels Plays. Manchester University Press, 1983.

Jonston, Joannes. *Historia naturalis.* 4 vols. Frankfurt, 1650–53.

    A History of the Wonderful Things of Nature. London, 1657.

L'Ecluse, Charles de. *Exoticorum libri decem.* Leiden, 1605.

L'Estrange, Hamon. "Observations on *Pseudodoxia Epidemica.*" British Museum Sloan MS 1839.

Milton, John. *Complete Prose Works of John Milton.* Gen. ed. Don M. Wolfe. 8 vols. in 10. New Haven: Yale University Press, 1953–82. [*CPW*]

    The Poems of John Milton. Ed. John Carey and Alastair Fowler. London: Longman, 1968.

    The Works of John Milton. Gen. ed. F. A. Patterson. 18 vols. New York: Columbia University Press, 1931–38.

Monardes, Nicolas. *Joyfull Newes Out of the Newfound World.* Trans. John Frampton. London, 1580.

Mouffet, Thomas. *The Theater of Insects.* Vol. III of *The History of Four-footed Beasts and Serpents and Insects.* By Edward Topsell. 3 vols. 1658. New York: Da Capo, 1967.

Mundy, Peter. *The Travels of Peter Mundy in Europe and Asia, 1608–1667.* Ed. Richard Carnac Temple. 5 vols. in 6. Hakluyt Society second series 17, 35, 45–46, 55, 78. London: Hakluyt Society, 1907–36.

Ortelius, Abraham. *Theatrum Orbis Terrarum; or, The Theatre of the Whole World.* London, 1606.

Paré, Ambroise. *Des monstres et prodiges.* 1573. Ed. Jean Céard. Geneva: Librairie Droz, 1971.

Parkinson, John. *Paradisi in Sole Paradisus Terrestris.* London, 1629.

Theatrum Botanicum, The Theatre of Plants. London, 1640.

Philosophical Transactions of the Royal Society of London. Vol. 1. 1665–66.

Piso, Gulielmi. *De Indiae utriusque re naturali et medica*. Amsterdam, 1658.

Pliny. [Plinius Secundus] *The Historie of the World*. Trans. Philemon Holland. London, 1601.

Natural History. Trans. H. Rackham et al. Loeb Classical Library. 10 vols. 1938–63. Cambridge, MA: Harvard University Press; London: William Heinemann, 1969–84.

Power, Henry. *Experimental Philosophy in Three Books: Containing New Experiments Microscopical, Mercurial, Magnetical*. London, 1664.

Purchas, Samuel. *A Theatre of Politicall Flying-Insects*. London, 1657.

Raleigh, Walter. *Historie of the World*. London, 1614.

Ray, John. *Further Correspondence of John Ray*. Ed. Robert W. T. Gunther. London: The Ray Society, 1928.

The Ornithology of Francis Willughby. London, 1678.

Philosophical Letters between the Late Learned Mr. Ray and Several of his Ingenious Correspondents. London, 1718.

Synopsis animalium quadrupedum et serpentini generis. London, 1693.

The Wisdom of God Manifested in the Works of the Creation. London, 1691.

Rondelet, Guillaume. *Libri de piscibus marinis*. Lugduni, 1554–55.

Ross, Alexander. *Arcana Microcosmi: or, the Hid Secrets of Man's Body Discovered*. London, 1652.

Sennert, Daniel. *Thirteen Books of Natural Philosophy*. 1632. [Trans. N. Culpepper and A. Cole.] London, 1661.

Shadwell, Thomas. *The Virtuoso*. 1676. Ed. Marjorie Nicolson and David Rodes. Regents Restoration Drama Series. Lincoln, NB: University of Nebraska Press, 1966.

Shakespeare, William. *The Complete Works*. Rev. edn. Gen. ed. Alfred Harbage. Baltimore, MD: Penguin, 1969.

Smith, John. *Advertisements for the Unexperienced Planters of New England*. London, 1631.

Spenser, Edmund. *The Faerie Queene*. Ed. A. C. Hamilton. London: Longman, 1977.

Sprat, Thomas. *History of the Royal Society*. London, 1667.

Tasso, Torquato. *Creation of the World*. Trans. Joseph Tusiana. Binghamton, NY: Medieval & Early Renaissance Texts & Studies, 1982.

Theophrastus. *Enquiry into Plants and Minor Works on Odours and Weather Signs*. Trans. Arthur Hort. Loeb Classical Library. 2 vols. London: Heinemann; New York: G. P. Putnam's Sons, 1916.

Topsell, Edward. *The History of Four-Footed Beasts and Serpents and Insects*. 3 vols. 1658. New York: Da Capo, 1967.

Tradescant, John. *Musæum Tradescantianum: or, A Collection of Rarities Preserved at South-Lambeth neer London*. London, 1656.

Virgil [Publius Vergilius Maro]. *Eclogues, Georgics, Aeneid I–VI*. Trans. H. Fairclough. Rev. edn. Loeb Classical Library. Cambridge, MA: Harvard University Press; London: William Heinemann, 1935.

Webster, John. *The Saints Guide, or, Christ the Rule, and Ruler of Saints.* London, 1654.

Wilkins, John. *An Essay Towards a Real Character, and a Philosophical Language.* 1668. Menston: Scolar, 1968.

SECONDARY

Ackerman, James S. "Early Renaissance 'Naturalism' and Scientific Illustration." Ellenius, ed., *The Natural Sciences*, 1–17.

Aiton, William. *Hortus Kewensis.* 3 vols. London, 1789.

Alpers, Svetlana. *The Art of Describing: Dutch Art in the Seventeenth Century.* University of Chicago Press, 1983.

Arber, Agnes. *Herbals: their Origin and Evolution. A Chapter in the History of Botany 1470–1670.* [1912; 1938] 3rd edn. Ed. William Stearn. Cambridge University Press, 1986.

Ashworth, William B., Jr. "Emblematic Natural History of the Renaissance." Jardine, Secord, and Spary, eds., *Cultures of Natural History*, 17–37, 461–62.

"Natural History and the Emblematic World View." Lindberg and Westman, eds., *Reappraisals*, 303–32.

"The Persistent Beast: Recurring Images in Early Zoological Illustration." Ellenius, ed., *The Natural Sciences*, 46–66.

Bazin, Germain. *The Museum Age.* Trans. J. Cahill. Brussels: Desoer, 1967.

Baumann, Hellmut. *The Greek Plant World in Myth, Art and Literature.* Trans. William Stearn and E. R. Stearn. Portland: Timber Press, 1993.

Beier, Lucinda. *Sufferers and Healers: the Experience of Illness in Seventeenth-Century England.* London: Routledge & Kegan Paul, 1987.

Bennett, Joan S. *Reviving Liberty: Radical Christian Humanism in Milton's Great Poems.* Cambridge, MA: Harvard University Press, 1989.

Sir Thomas Browne. Cambridge University Press, 1962.

Bentley, Richard, ed. *Paradise Lost.* By John Milton. 1732. New York: AMS, 1974.

Blunt, Wilfrid. *The Art of Botanical Illustration.* 3rd edn. Ed. William Stearn. London: Collins, 1955.

Bourdieu, Pierre. *Distinction: a Social Critique of the Judgement of Taste.* Trans. R. Nice. Cambridge, MA: Harvard University Press, 1984.

Bowler, Peter. *The Fontana History of the Environmental Sciences.* Fontana History of Science. London: HarperCollins–Fontana, 1992.

Broadbent, J. B. "Milton's Hell." *ELH* 21 (1954), 161–92.

Burckhardt, John Lewis. *Travels in Syria and the Holy Land.* London, 1822.

Cantor, G. N. "Physical Optics." Olby et al., eds., *Companion*, 627–38.

Carey, John. *John Donne: Life, Mind and Art.* New York: Oxford University Press, 1981.

Carey, John, and Alastair Fowler, eds. *The Poems of John Milton.* London: Longman, 1968.

Carroll, William Meredith. *Animal Conventions in English Renaissance Non-Religious Prose (1550–1600).* Westport, CT: Greenwood, 1954.

Catalogue of Botanical Books in the Collection of Rachel McMasters Miller Hunt. 3 vols. Pittsburgh: Hunt Botanical Library, 1958–61.

Cawley, Robert. "The Timeliness of *Pseudodoxia Epidemica*." Cawley and Yost, eds., *Studies*, 1–40.

Cawley, Robert, and George Yost, eds. *Studies in Sir Thomas Browne*. Eugene, OR: University of Oregon Press, 1965.

Chalmers, Gordon Keith. "Hieroglyphs and Sir Thomas Browne." *Virginia Quarterly Review* 11 (1935), 547–60.

"Sir Thomas Browne, True Scientist." *Osiris* 2 (1936), 28–79.

Chartier, Roger. *Cultural History: Between Practices and Representations*. Trans. L. Cochrane. London: Polity, 1988.

Christopher, Georgia B. *Milton and the Science of the Saints*. Princeton University Press, 1982.

Clark, Stuart. "The Scientific Status of Demonology." Vickers, ed., *Occult*, 351–74.

Thinking with Demons: the Idea of Witchcraft in Early Modern Europe. Oxford: Clarendon Press, 1997.

Clericuzio, Antonio. "Carneades and the Chemists: a Study of *The Sceptical Chymist* and its Impact on Seventeenth-Century Chemistry." Hunter, ed., *Boyle Reconsidered*, 79–90.

Coffin, David R. *The English Garden: Meditation and Memorial*. Princeton University Press, 1994.

The Villa D'Este at Tivoli. Princeton Monographs in Art and Archaeology 34. Princeton University Press, 1960.

Cole, F. J. "The History of Albrecht Dürer's Rhinoceros in Zoological Literature." Underwood, ed., *Science Medicine and History*, 1, 337–56.

Colie, Rosalie L. "Dean Wren's Marginalia and Early Science at Oxford." *Bodleian Library Record* 6 (1960), 541–51.

The Resources of Kind: Genre-Theory in the Renaissance. Ed. Barbara Lewalski. Berkeley: University of California Press, 1973.

Comito, Terry. *The Idea of the Garden in the Renaissance*. New Brunswick: Rutgers University Press, 1979.

Cook, Harold J. "The New Philosophy and Medicine in Seventeenth-Century England." Lindberg and Westman, eds., *Reappraisals*, 397–436.

Corcoran, Mary Irma. *Milton's Paradise with Reference to the Hexameral Background*. 1945. Washington, DC: Catholic University of America Press, 1967.

Cunningham, Andrew. "The Culture of Gardens." Jardine, Secord, and Spary, eds., *Cultures of Natural History*, 38–56, 462–63.

Curtius, Ernst Robert. *European Literature and the Latin Middle Ages*. Trans. Willard R. Trask. 1953. New York: Harper and Row–Harper Torchbooks, 1963.

Daiches, David. "Some Aspects of Milton's Pastoral Imagery." *More Literary Essays*. University of Chicago Press, 1968, 96–114.

Dance, S. Peter. *The Art of Natural History: Animal Illustrators and their Work*. Woodstock, NY: Overlook, 1978.

Darbishire, Helen, ed. *The Early Lives of Milton*. London: Constable, 1932.

Daston, Lorraine. "Baconian Facts, Academic Civility, and the Prehistory of Objectivity." *Annals of Scholarship* 8 (1992), 337–63.

"Marvelous Facts and Miraculous Evidence in Early Modern Europe." *Critical Inquiry* 18 (1991), 93–124.

Davies, Keith. "Zoological Specimens in the University Museum Attributed to the Tradescant Collection." MacGregor, ed., *Tradescant's Rarities*, 346–49.

Dear, Peter. "Jesuit Mathematical Science and the Reconstitution of Experience in the Early Seventeenth Century." *Studies in the History and Philosophy of Science* 18 (1987), 133–75.

"Narratives, Anecdotes, and Experiments: Turning Experience into Science in the Seventeenth Century." *The Literary Structure of Scientific Argument: Historical Studies*. Ed. Peter Dear. Philadelphia: University of Pennsylvania Press, 1991, 135–63.

Debus, Allen G. *Man and Nature in the Renaissance*. Cambridge History of Science Series. Cambridge University Press, 1978.

Delaunay, Paul. *La zoologie au seizième siècle*. Histoire de la Pensée 7. Paris: Hermann, 1962.

Dijksterhuis, E. J. *The Mechanization of the World Picture: Pythagoras to Newton*. 1950. Trans. C. Dikshoorn. 1961. Princeton University Press, 1986.

Druce, G. C. "The Amphisbaena and its Connexions in Ecclesiastical Art and Architecture." *Archaeological Journal* 67 (1910), 285–317.

Duncan, Joseph E. *Milton's Earthly Paradise: a Historical Study of Eden*. Minneapolis: University of Minnesota Press, 1972.

Eamon, William. *Science and the Secrets of Nature: Books of Secrets in Medieval and Early Modern Culture*. Princeton University Press, 1994.

Eisenstein, Elizabeth L. *The Printing Press as an Agent of Change: Communications and Cultural Transformations in Early-Modern Europe*. 2 vols. Cambridge University Press, 1979.

Eliot, Thomas Stearns. "Milton I." *On Poetry and Poets*. London: Farrar, Straus, Giroux – Noonday, 1957, 156–64.

Ellenius, Allan, ed. *The Natural Sciences and the Arts: Aspects of Interaction from the Renaissance to the 20th Century*. Acta Universitatis Upsaliensis. Figura Nova, no. 22. Stockholm: Almqvist & Wiksell, 1985.

Evans, J. Martin. *Milton's Imperial Epic: "Paradise Lost" and the Discourse of Colonialism*. Ithaca: Cornell University Press, 1996.

Fallon, Stephen. *Milton among the Philosophers: Poetry and Materialism in Seventeenth-Century England*. Ithaca: Cornell University Press, 1991.

Ferry, Anne. *The Art of Naming*. University of Chicago Press, 1988.

Findlen, Paula. *Possessing Nature: Museums, Collecting, and Scientific Culture in Early Modern Italy*. Berkeley: University of California Press, 1994.

Fisch, Harold. "Creation in Reverse: the Book of Job and *Paradise Lost*." *Milton and Scriptural Tradition: the Bible into Poetry*. Ed. James Sims and Leland Ryken. Columbia, MO: University of Missouri Press, 1984, 105–16.

Fish, Stanley. *Surprised by Sin: the Reader in "Paradise Lost."* 1967; Berkeley: University of California, 1971.

Fitter, Christopher. "'Native Soil': The Rhetoric of Exile Lament and Exile Consolation in *Paradise Lost*." *Milton Studies* 20 (1984), 147–62.

Forsyth, Neil. *The Old Enemy: Satan and the Combat Myth*. Princeton University Press, 1987.

Foucault, Michel. *The Order of Things: an Archaeology of the Human Sciences*. Trans. A. Sheridan. London: Tavistock, 1970.

Freeman, Rosemary. *English Emblem Books*. 1948. New York: Farrar, Straus and Giroux–Octagon, 1966.

French, Roger, and Andrew Wear, eds. *The Medical Revolution of the Seventeenth Century*. Cambridge University Press, 1989.

Frye, Roland Mushat. *Milton's Imagery and the Visual Arts: Iconographic Tradition in the Epic Poems*. Princeton University Press, 1978.

Fulton, John F. *A Bibliography of the Honourable Robert Boyle, Fellow of the Royal Society*. 2nd edn. Oxford: Clarendon Press, 1961.

George, Wilma. "Alive or Dead: Zoological Collections in the Seventeenth Century." Impey and MacGregor, eds., *Origins of Museums*, 179–87.

George, Wilma, and William Brunsdon Yapp. *The Naming of the Beasts: Natural History in the Medieval Bestiary*. London: Duckworth, 1991.

Giamatti, A. Bartlett. *The Earthly Paradise and the Renaissance Epic*. Princeton University Press, 1966.

Gilbert, Allan H. *A Geographical Dictionary of Milton*. New Haven: Yale University Press, 1919.

Gillispie, Charles Coulton. *The Edge of Objectivity: an Essay in the History of Scientific Ideas*. Princeton University Press, 1960.

Ginzburg, Carlo. "The High and the Low: the Theme of Forbidden Knowledge in the Sixteenth and Seventeenth Centuries." *Myths, Emblems, Clues*. Trans. John and Anne Tedeschi. London: Hutchinson Radius, 1990, 6–76.

Girouard, Mark. *Life in the English Country House: a Social and Architectural History*. New Haven: Yale University Press, 1978.

Goody, Jack. *The Culture of Flowers*. Cambridge University Press, 1993.

Grafton, Anthony. *Defenders of the Text: the Traditions of Scholarship in an Age of Science, 1450–1800*. Cambridge, MA: Harvard University Press, 1991.

Greene, Edward Lee. *Landmarks of Botanical History*. Ed. Frank Egerton. 2 vols. Stanford University Press, 1983.

Greene, Thomas. *The Descent from Heaven: a Study in Epic Continuity*. New Haven: Yale University Press, 1963.

Greenleaf, W. H. *Order, Empiricism and Politics: Two Traditions of English Political Thought 1500–1700*. London: Oxford University Press for Hull University Press, 1964.

Gregerson, Linda. *The Reformation of the Subject: Spenser, Milton, and the English Protestant Epic*. Cambridge University Press, 1995.

Grosart, Alexander, ed. *The Divine Weeks and Works*. By Guillaume Du Bartas. Trans. Joshuah Sylvester. Vol. 1 of *Joshuah Sylvester: The Complete Works*. 2 vols. 1880. Hildesheim: George Olms, 1969.

Gunther, Robert T. *Early British Botanists and their Gardens: Based on Unpublished Writings of Goodyer, Tradescant, and Others*. Oxford University Press, 1922.

Early Science in Oxford. Vol. III. 1925. London: Dawsons, 1968.

Hall, Marie Boas. *Robert Boyle and Seventeenth-Century Chemistry*. Cambridge University Press, 1958.

"Thomas Browne Naturalist." Patrides, ed., *Approaches to Sir Thomas Browne*, 178–87.

Hammond, Paul. "The Language of the Hive: Political Discourse in Seventeenth-Century England." *The Seventeenth Century* 9 (1994), 119–33.

Harms, Wolfgang. "On Natural History and Emblematics in the 16th Century." Ellenius, ed., *The Natural Sciences*, 67–83.

Harrison, Peter. *The Bible, Protestantism, and the Rise of Natural Science*. Cambridge University Press, 1998.

Hartman, Geoffrey. "Adam on the Grass with Balsamum." *Beyond Formalism: Literary Essays 1958–1970*. New Haven: Yale University Press, 1970, 124–50.

Harwood, John. "Science Writing and Writing Science: Boyle and Rhetorical Theory." Hunter, ed., *Robert Boyle Reconsidered*, 37–56.

Haskin, Dayton. *Milton's Burden of Interpretation*. Philadelphia: University of Pennsylvania Press, 1994.

Henrey, Blanche. *British Botanical and Horticultural Literature before 1800*. 3 vols. London: Oxford University Press, 1975.

Henry, John. "Doctors and Healers: Popular Culture and the Medical Profession." Pumfrey, Rossi, and Slawinski, eds., *Science, Culture and Popular Belief*, 191–221.

"Occult Qualities and the Experimental Philosophy: Active Principles in Pre-Newtonian Matter Theory." *History of Science* 24 (1986), 335–81.

Herbert, A. S., ed. *Historical Catalogue of Printed Editions of the English Bible 1525–1961*. By T. H. Darlow and H. F. Moule. 1903. Rev. edn. London: The British and Foreign Bible Society; New York: The Americn Bible Society, 1968.

Hill, Christopher. *The English Bible and the Seventeenth-Century Revolution*. Harmondsworth: Penguin–Allen Lane, 1993.

Milton and the English Revolution. New York: Viking, 1977.

Hill, D. M. "Satan on the Burning Lake." *NQ* 2nd ser. 31 (1956), 157–59.

Hoeniger, F. D., and J. F. M. Hoeniger. *The Growth of Natural History in Stuart England from Gerard to the Royal Society*. Folger Booklets on Tudor and Stuart Civilization. [Charlottesville, VA:] University Press of Virginia for the Folger Library, 1969.

Hughes, Merritt Y., ed. *John Milton: Complete Poems and Major Prose*. New York: Odyssey, 1957.

Hunter, Alexander, ed. *Silva: or, a Discourse of Forest-Trees and the Propagation of Timber in his Majesty's Dominions*. By John Evelyn. 2 vols. York, 1812.

Hunter, Michael. "Alchemy, Magic and Moralism in the Thought of Robert Boyle." *BJHS* 23 (1990), 387–410.

"The Cabinet Institutionalized: the Royal Society's 'Repository' and its Background." Impey and MacGregor, eds., *Origins of Museums*, 159–68.

"Introduction." Hunter, ed., *Boyle Reconsidered*, 1–18.

Science and the Shape of Orthodoxy: Intellectual Change in Late Seventeenth-Century Britain. Woodbridge: Boydell, 1995.

Hunter, Michael, ed. *Robert Boyle Reconsidered*. Cambridge University Press, 1994.
　Science and Society in Restoration England. Cambridge University Press, 1981.
Huntley, Frank L. *Sir Thomas Browne: a Biographical and Critical Study*. Ann Arbor: University of Michigan Press, 1962.
Hutchison, Keith. "What Happened to Occult Qualities in the Scientific Revolution?" *Isis* 73 (1982), 233–53.
Impey, Oliver, and Arthur MacGregor. "Introduction." Impey and MacGregor, eds., *Origins of Museums*, 1–4.
Impey, Oliver, and Arthur MacGregor, eds. *The Origins of Museums: the Cabinet of Curiosities in Sixteenth- and Seventeenth-Century Europe*. Oxford: Clarendon Press, 1985.
Jacob, J. R. *Robert Boyle and the English Revolution: a Study in Social and Intellectual Change*. New York: Burt Franklin, 1977.
Jardine, Lisa. *Francis Bacon: Discovery and the Art of Discourse*. Cambridge University Press, 1974.
Jardine, Nicholas, J. A. Secord, and E. C. Spary, eds. *Cultures of Natural History*. Cambridge University Press, 1996.
Keynes, Geoffrey. *John Evelyn: a Study in Bibliophily*. Cambridge University Press, 1937.
　John Ray: a Bibliography, 1660–1970. 1951. Amsterdam: Gérard Th. van Heusden, 1976.
Kibbey, Ann. *The Interpretation of Material Shapes in Puritanism: a Study of Rhetoric, Prejudice, and Violence*. Cambridge University Press, 1986.
Koehler, G. Stanley. "Milton and the Art of Landscape." *Milton Studies* 8 (1975), 3–40.
Koyré, Alexandre. *From the Closed World to the Infinite Universe*. Baltimore: Johns Hopkins University Press, 1953.
Leonard, John. *Naming in Paradise: Milton and the Language of Adam and Eve*. Oxford: Clarendon Press, 1990.
Levin, David Michael. *Modernity and the Hegemony of Vision*. Berkeley: University of California Press, 1993.
Levine, Joseph M. "Natural History and the History of the Scientific Revolution." *Clio* 13 (1983), 57–73.
Lewalski, Barbara. "Innocence and Experience in Milton's Eden." *New Essays on "Paradise Lost."* Ed. Thomas Kranidas. Berkeley: University of California Press, 1971, 86–117.
　"Paradise Lost" and the Rhetoric of Literary Forms. Princeton University Press, 1985.
Lewis, C. S. *A Preface to "Paradise Lost."* 1942. Oxford University Press, 1961.
Lieb, Michael. *The Dialectics of Creation: Patterns of Birth and Regeneration in "Paradise Lost."* Boston: University of Massachusetts Press, 1970.
Lindberg, David, and Robert Westman, eds. *Reappraisals of the Scientific Revolution*. Cambridge University Press, 1990.
Lloyd, G. E. R. "The Development of Aristotle's Theory of the Classification of Animals." *Phronesis* 6 (1961), 59–81.

Lloyd, Joan Barclay. *African Animals in Renaissance Literature and Art*. Oxford Studies in the History of Art and Architecture. Oxford: Clarendon Press, 1971.

Loisel, Gustave. *Histoire des ménageries de l'antiquité à nos jours*. 3 vols. Paris: Octave Doin et Fils and Henri Laurens, 1912.

London, H. Stanford. *Royal Beasts*. East Knoyle: The Heraldry Society, 1956.

Lovejoy, Arthur O. *The Great Chain of Being: a Study of the History of an Idea*. 1936. Cambridge, MA: Harvard University Press, 1964.

Mabberley, D. J. *The Plant-Book: a Portable Dictionary of the Vascular Plants*. 2nd edn. Cambridge University Press, 1997.

MacCaffrey, Isabel. *"Paradise Lost" as "Myth."* Cambridge, MA: Harvard University Press, 1959.

MacCallum, Hugh R. "Milton and the Figurative Interpretation of the Bible." *UTQ* 31 (1961–62), 397–415.

McColley, Diane. *A Gust for Paradise: Milton's Eden and the Visual Arts*. Urbana: University of Illinois Press, 1993.

MacDonald Ross, G. "Occultism and Philosophy in the Seventeenth Century." *Philosophy, its History and Historiography*. Royal Institute of Philosophy Conference, 1983. Ed. A. J. Holland. Dordrecht: D. Reidel, 1985, 95–115.

MacGregor, Arthur. "The Cabinet of Curiosities in Seventeenth-Century Britain." Impey and MacGregor, eds., *Origins of Museums*, 147–58.

"Collectors and Collections of Rarities in the Sixteenth and Seventeenth Centuries." MacGregor, ed., *Tradescant's Rarities*, 70–97.

"The Tradescants as Collectors of Rarities." MacGregor, ed., *Tradescant's Rarities*, 17–23.

"The Tradescants Gardeners and Botanists." MacGregor, ed., *Tradescant's Rarities*, 3–16.

MacGregor, Arthur, ed. *Tradescant's Rarities: Essays on the Foundation of the Ashmolean Museum 1683 with a Catalogue of the Surviving Early Collections*. Oxford: Clarendon Press, 1983.

McHenry, James Patrick. "A Milton Herbal." *Milton Quarterly* 30 (1996), 45–115.

Marjara, Harinder S. *Contemplation of Created Things: Science in "Paradise Lost."* University of Toronto Press, 1992.

Mayr, Ernst. *The Growth of Biological Thought: Diversity, Evolution, and Inheritance*. Cambridge, MA: Harvard University Press, 1982.

Merton, Robert. *Science and Imagination in Sir Thomas Browne*. 1949. New York: Octagon, 1969.

Moldenke, Harold, and Alma Moldenke. *Plants of the Bible*. 1952. New York: Dover, 1986.

Murray, David. *Museums: Their History and Their Use*. 3 vols. Glasgow: James MacLehose, 1904.

Nathanson, Leonard. *The Strategy of Truth: a Study of Sir Thomas Browne*. University of Chicago Press, 1967.

Nauert, Charles G. *Agrippa and the Crisis of Renaissance Thought*. Illinois Studies in the Social Sciences, Number 55. Urbana: University of Illinois Press, 1965.

Nebenzahl, Kenneth. *Maps of the Holy Land: Images of Terra Sancta through Two Millenia*. New York: Abbeville, 1986.

Newton, Thomas, ed. *Paradise Lost: a Poem in Twelve Books*. By John Milton. London, 1749.

Nicolson, Marjorie. "Milton and the Telescope." *ELH* 2 (1935), 1–32. Rpt. in *Science and Imagination*. By Marjorie Nicolson. Ithaca: Great Seal–Cornell University Press, 1956, 30–57.

Nissen, Claus. *Die botanische Buchillustration, ihre Geschichte und Bibliographie*. 2 vols. Stuttgart: Hiersemann, 1951.

Olby, R. C., et al., eds. *Companion to the History of Modern Science*. London: Routledge, 1990.

Olmi, Giuseppe. "Science–Honour–Metaphor: Italian Cabinets of the Sixteenth and Seventeenth Centuries." Impey and MacGregor, eds., *Origins of Museums*, 5–16.

Orgel, Stephen. *The Illusion of Power: Political Theater in the English Renaissance*. Berkeley: University of California Press, 1975.

Ornstein, Martha. *The Role of Scientific Societies in the Seventeenth Century*. 1913. London: Archon Books, 1963.

Otten, Charlotte. "'My Native Element': Milton's Paradise and English Gardens." *Milton Studies* 5 (1973), 249–67.

Oxford English Dictionary. 2nd edn. Ed. J. A. Simpson and E. C. S. Weiner. Oxford University Press, 1989.

Park, Katharine, and Lorraine Daston. "Unnatural Conceptions: the Study of Monsters in Sixteenth- and Seventeenth-Century France and England." *Past and Present* 92 (1981), 20–54.

Parker, William Riley. *Milton: a Biography*. 2nd edn. Ed. Gordon Campbell. 2 vols. Oxford: Clarendon Press, 1996.

Patrides, C. A., ed. *Approaches to Sir Thomas Browne: the Ann Arbor Tercentenary Lectures and Essays*. Columbia, MO: University of Missouri Press, 1982.

Patterson, Frank, and French Fogle. *An Index to the Columbia Edition of the Works of John Milton*. 2 vols. New York: Columbia University Press, 1940.

Pebworth, Ted-Larry. "Wandering in the America of Truth: *Pseudodoxia Epidemica* and the Essay Tradition." Patrides, ed., *Approaches to Sir Thomas Browne*, 166–177.

Peck, A. L. "Introduction." *Historia Animalium*. By Aristotle. Trans. A. L. Peck (vols. I and II) and D. M. Balme (vol. III). Loeb Classical Library. 3 vols. London: Heinemann, 1965–91, I, v–xcvii.

Pitman, James Hall. "Milton and the *Physiologus*." *MLN* 40 (1925), 439–40.

Post, Jonathan F. S. *Sir Thomas Browne*. Boston: Twayne-G. K. Hall, 1987.

Prest, John. *The Garden of Eden: the Botanic Garden and the Re-Creation of Paradise*. New Haven: Yale University Press, 1981.

Pumfrey, Stephen, Paolo Rossi, and Maurice Slawinski, eds. *Science, Culture and Popular Belief in Renaissance Europe*. Manchester University Press, 1991.

Quilligan, Maureen. *Milton's Spenser: the Politics of Reading*. Ithaca: Cornell University Press, 1983.

Quint, David. *Epic and Empire: Politics and Generic Form from Virgil to Milton.* Princeton University Press, 1993.

Raven, Charles. *English Naturalists from Neckam to Ray: a Study of the Making of the Modern World.* Cambridge University Press, 1947; New York: Kraus Reprint, 1968.

John Ray, Naturalist: His Life and Works. Cambridge University Press, 1942.

Raylor, Timothy. "Samuel Hartlib and the Commonwealth of Bees." *Culture and Cultivation in Early Modern England: Writing and the Land.* Ed. Michael Leslie and Timothy Raylor. Leicester University Press, 1992, 91–129.

Reeds, Karen Meier. *Botany in Medieval and Renaissance Universities.* New York: Garland, 1991.

"Renaissance Humanism and Botany." *Annals of Science* 33 (1976), 519–42.

Ricks, Christopher. *Milton's Grand Style.* Oxford: Clarendon Press, 1963.

Robbins, Robin. "Browne's Cosmos Imagined: Nature, Man, and God in *Pseudodoxia Epidemica.*" Patrides, ed., *Approaches to Sir Thomas Browne,* 155–65.

"Introduction." *Pseudodoxia Epidemica.* By Thomas Browne. Ed. Robin Robbins. 2 vols. Oxford: Clarendon Press, 1981, I, xxi–lxi.

Robin, P. Ansell. *Animal Lore in English Literature.* London: John Murray, 1932.

Rogers, John. *The Matter of Revolution: Science, Poetry, and Politics in the Age of Milton.* Ithaca: Cornell University Press, 1996.

Rossi, Paolo. *Francis Bacon: From Magic to Science.* Trans. Sacha Rabinovitch. London: Routledge & Kegan Paul, 1968.

Sargent, Rose-Mary. *The Diffident Naturalist: Robert Boyle and the Philosophy of Experiment.* University of Chicago Press, 1995.

Sawday, Jonathan. *The Body Emblazoned: Dissection and the Human Body in Renaissance Culture.* London: Routledge, 1995.

Schama, Simon. *The Embarrassment of Riches: an Interpretation of Dutch Culture in the Golden Age.* Berkeley: University of California Press, 1988.

Schmitt, Charles B. "Experience and Experiment: a Comparison of Zabarella's View with Galileo's in *De Motu.*" *Studies in the Renaissance* 16 (1969), 80–138.

Scoular, Kitty W. *Natural Magic: Studies in the Presentation of Nature in English Poetry from Spenser to Marvell.* Oxford: Clarendon Press, 1965.

Sebald, W. G. *The Rings of Saturn.* 1995. Trans. Michael Hulse. London: Harvill, 1998.

Shapin, Steven. "Pump and Circumstance: Robert Boyle's Literary Technology." *Social Studies in Science* 14 (1984), 481–520.

A Social History of Truth: Civility and Science in Seventeenth-Century England. University of Chicago Press, 1994.

Shapin, Steven, and Simon Schaffer. *Leviathan and the Air-Pump: Hobbes, Boyle, and the Experimental Life.* Princeton University Press, 1985.

Shapiro, Barbara J. *Probability and Certainty in Seventeenth-Century England: a Study of the Relationships between Natural Science, Religion, History, Law, and Literature.* Princeton University Press, 1983.

Sloan, Phillip R. "Natural History, 1670–1802." Olby et al., eds., *Companion,* 295–313.

Smith, Nigel. *Literature and Revolution in England, 1640–1660.* New Haven: Yale University Press, 1994.

Smith, Rebecca. "The Source of Milton's Pandemonium." *MP* 29 (1931), 187–98.

Snyder, Susan. "Introduction." *The Divine Weeks and Works.* By Guillaume de Saluste, Sieur Du Bartas. Trans. Josuah Sylvester. Ed. Susan Snyder. 2 vols. Oxford: Clarendon Press, 1979, I, 1–110.

Sommerville, Johann P. "Introduction." *"Patriarcha" and Other Writings.* By Robert Filmer. Cambridge Texts in the History of Political Thought. Cambridge University Press, 1991, ix–xxiv.

The Spenser Encyclopedia. Ed. A. C. Hamilton et al. University of Toronto Press, 1990.

Stavely, Keith. *The Politics of Milton's Prose Style.* New Haven: Yale University Press, 1975.

Steadman, John M. "Leviathan and Renaissance Etymology." *JHI* 28 (1967), 575–76.

"Tantalus and the Dead Sea Apples (*Paradise Lost*, x, 547–73)." *JEGP* 64 (1965), 35–40.

Stewart, Stanley. *The Enclosed Garden: the Tradition and the Image in Seventeenth-Century Poetry.* Madison: University of Wisconsin Press, 1966.

Strong, Roy. *The Renaissance Garden in England.* London: Thames & Hudson, 1979.

Strutt, Jacob. *Sylva Britannica; or, Portraits of Forest Trees.* London, 1830.

Svendsen, Kester. *Milton and Science.* Cambridge, MA: Harvard University Press, 1956.

Taylor, George Coffin. *Milton's Use of Du Bartas.* Cambridge, MA: Harvard University Press, 1934.

Thomas, Keith. *Man and the Natural World: a History of the Modern Sensibility.* New York: Pantheon, 1983.

Thorndike, Lynn. *A History of Magic and Experimental Science up to the Seventeenth Century.* 8 vols. New York: Columbia University Press, 1923–58.

Turner, Gerard l'E. "The Cabinet of Experimental Philosophy." Impey and MacGregor, eds., *Origins of Museums*, 214–22.

Turner, James Grantham. *One Flesh: Paradisal Marriage and Sexual Relations in the Age of Milton.* Oxford: Clarendon Press, 1987.

The Politics of Landscape: Rural Scenery and Society in English Poetry 1630–1660. Cambridge, MA: Harvard University Press, 1979.

Underwood, E. Ashworth, ed. *Science Medicine and History: Essays on the Evolution of Scientific Thought and Medical Practice Written in Honour of Charles Singer.* 2 vols. London: Oxford University Press, 1953.

Variorum Commentary on the Poems of John Milton. Gen. ed. Merrit Y. Hughes. 3 vols. in 5 to date. New York: Columbia University Press, 1970– .

Vickers, Brian. "The Royal Society and English Prose Style: a Reassessment." *Rhetoric and the Pursuit of Truth: Language Change in the Seventeenth and Eighteenth Centuries.* Ed. Brian Vickers and Nancy S. Struever. Los Angeles: William Andrews Clark Memorial Library, 1985, 3–76.

Vickers, Brian, ed. *Occult and Scientific Mentalities in the Renaissance.* Cambridge University Press, 1984.

von Maltzahn, Nicholas. "From Pillar to Post: Milton and the Attack on Republican Humanism at the Restoration." *Soldiers, Writers and Statesmen of the English Revolution.* Ed. Ian Gentles, John Morrill, and Blair Worden. Cambridge University Press, 1998, 265–85.

Walpole, Horace. *Horace Walpole's Correspondence with George Montagu.* Ed. W. S. Lewis and Ralph Brown. 2 vols. New Haven: Yale University Press, 1941. Vols. IX and X of *Horace Walpole's Correspondence.* 42 vols. 1937–80.

Webster, Charles. "Alchemical and Paracelsian Medicine." *Health, Medicine and Mortality in the Sixteenth Century.* Ed. C. Webster. Cambridge University Press, 1979, 301–34.

From Paracelsus to Newton: Magic and the Making of Modern Science. Cambridge University Press, 1982.

The Great Instauration: Science, Medicine and Reform 1626–1660. London: Duckworth, 1975.

Westfall, Richard S. *The Construction of Modern Science: Mechanisms and Mechanics.* 1971. Cambridge University Press, 1977.

Science and Religion in Seventeenth-Century England. 1958. Ann Arbor: University of Michigan Press, 1973.

Whaler, James. "Animal Simile in *Paradise Lost.*" *PMLA* 47 (1932), 534–53.

"The Miltonic Simile." *PMLA* 46 (1931), 1034–74.

Whitaker, Katie. "The Culture of Curiosity." Jardine, Secord, and Spary, eds., *Cultures of Natural History,* 75–90, 465–67.

White, T. H., ed. and trans. *The Book of Beasts, Being a Translation from a Latin Bestiary of the Twelfth Century.* London: Jonathan Cape, 1954.

Whiting, George. " 'And Without Thorn the Rose.' " *RES* ns 10 (1959), 60–62.

Milton's Literary Milieu. Chapel Hill: University of North Carolina Press, 1939.

Wightman, William P. D. *The Growth of Scientific Ideas.* New Haven: Yale University Press, 1951.

Williams, Arnold. *The Common Expositor: an Account of the Commentaries on Genesis 1527–1633.* Chapel Hill: University of North Carolina Press, 1948.

"Politics and Economics in Renaissance Commentaries on Genesis." *Huntington Library Quarterly* 7 (1943–44), 207–22.

Williams, George Huntston. "Christian Attitudes toward Nature." *Christian Scholar's Review* 2, nos. 1–2 (1979), 3–35, 112–26.

Wilkin, Simon, ed. *Sir Thomas Browne's Works.* 4 vols. London, 1826–35.

Wilson, Catherine. *The Invisible World: Early Modern Philosophy and the Invention of the Microscope.* Princeton University Press, 1995.

Wolfe, Don M. "Introduction." *Complete Prose Works of John Milton.* Gen. ed. Don M. Wolfe. 8 vols. in 10. New Haven: Yale University Press, 1953–82, I, 1–210.

Woodbridge, Kenneth. *Princely Gardens: the Origins and Development of the French Formal Style.* New York: Rizzoli, 1986.

Worster, Donald. *Nature's Economy: a History of Ecological Ideas.* 2nd edn. Cambridge University Press, 1994.

Index